BEETHOVEN &

THE AGE OF REVOLUTION

BEETHOVEN &

THE AGE OF REVOLUTION

FRIDA KNIGHT

INTERNATIONAL PUBLISHERS New York

65111

209

Library of Congress Cataloging in Publication Data

Knight, Frida.
Beethoven and the age of revolution.

Bibliography: p.
1. Beethoven, Ludwig van, 1770-1827.   I.   Title.
[ML410.B4K66 1974]   780'.92'4 [B]   74-8247
ISBN 0-7178-0422-4 (pbk.)

Contents

Acknowledgements

This book was begun in 1970, Beethoven's bicentenary year, in a rash moment of enthusiasm over the discovery of the Conversation Books of 1817 to 1823—those extraordinary but little-known documents which bring the composer and his friends to life as vividly as if one were sitting beside them listening to their talk; where even if Beethoven's voice is often silent he is present all the time, and we share his company and confidences as it were at first hand. So I should like first of all to acknowledge my debt to the late Georg Schünemann who deciphered and edited the *Konversationshefte*, vols. I to III—on which I have freely drawn—and to the East German publishing house, VEB Leipzig, now bringing out the complete *Hefte* which will thus be accessible to the world (although not yet translated into English).

Today, anyone attempting a new study of Beethoven must draw at every stage on the mass of advanced scholarship now available. I am particularly indebted to the 1967 edition of Thayer's *Life of Beethoven*, brought up to date in so masterly a way by Professor Elliot Forbes. Selections of this are reprinted by permission of Princeton University Press.

The *Letters*, translated and edited by Emily Anderson, have been an indispensable standby, and are quoted by permission of Macmillan, London. The *Henschelverlag* (Berlin) volume of selected letters (*Briefe*) has proved useful. I have wherever possible referred to the original German, both in letters and in conversations, and made fresh translations.

I have to thank many scholars for advice: in particular, Professor Dr Georg Knepler of Berlin; Professor Dr Rudolf Klein of Vienna; Mr Martin Cooper, Dr Peter Stern, Mr A. E. F. Dickinson, and Mr Charles Cudworth. I am obliged to Frau Hildegarde Weber, Mrs A. M. Jansen and Mr Christopher Ballantine for helpful suggestions; to Mr John Fauvel and Mrs Katharine Thomson for criticising the typescript; and to B.C.J.G.K., a pillar of strength throughout.

I could not have written the book without access to the libraries of the University of Cambridge, and of Salzburg; the *Stadtbibliothek* and the *Nationalbibliothek* of Vienna, and the Pendlebury Library of Cambridge. I wish to express my gratitude to their Librarians for their generosity in allowing me the necessary facilities, and to their assistants for much kindness and unstinting help.

FRIDA KNIGHT

Cambridge 1972

BEETHOVEN &

THE AGE OF REVOLUTION

Foreword

So many books have been written about Beethoven that it may well seem presumptuous to add to them. My only excuse for launching yet another is that I know of none that sets out to look at Beethoven and his work *specifically* in the context of the social and political events of the very stirring times in which he lived.

When one looks back at the French Revolution, the Napoleonic Wars, the intervals of uneasy peace, the post-war economic crises of that epoch, it is hard not to feel that these must have considerably influenced Beethoven's work. When one studies his life and music with this in mind, the historical and social influences take on an importance which has perhaps not been sufficiently recognised.

A close study of Beethoven's work, letters, notebooks and conversations reveals his feelings about people and about life around him.

It also shows his abiding and lively interest in politics and social and economic questions. This interest sprang from his deeply generous and independent character; it was reflected in his correspondence and his talk, and expressed in his greatest music. How did his concern with the human condition, in an age of Revolution, affect his life and creativity? This is an attempt to find out. And if it deals all too briefly with the technical aspects of the actual music, and skims over much biographical detail, this is because these have been amply covered by many scholars far better qualified than I, to whom the reader should go for further enlightenment. I hope, however, that within its limited scope my contribution may provide some new angles, a fresh approach and even more future pleasure for the listener to Beethoven's music.

I

Youth in Bonn

1770–1792

Ludwig van Beethoven (b. Bonn, 16 December 1770; d. Vienna, 26 March 1827) "German composer of Flemish descent; son and grandson of musicians at the court of the Elector of Cologne at Bonn. Taught by various local musicians and published a pf work at the age of 12. Became cembalist in the orchestra and accompanist at the theatre in 1783, court organist in 1784." Such is the outline of his early life given in *Everyman's Dictionary of Music*,[1] and scores of books have filled in the personal details. But the surroundings in which Beethoven grew up, the atmosphere of contemporary Germany, the historical reasons for society being as it was, his friends being what they were, and he himself doing what he did—these have not so often been discussed, and in a life where the environment (natural, social, political) was so important it seems proper to begin by looking at that.

Eighteenth-century Germany then—that conglomeration of princely states each nominally controlled by distant Vienna, but administered in highly individual style according to its Elector or Landgrave: what was Beethoven's Germany like to look at?

A contemporary visitor arriving in the Rhineland in winter wrote that it contrasted rather bleakly with gay, life-loving France. "The ruins of fortified castles glimpsed high up in the mountains, the houses built of earth, narrow windows, snow covering the plains as far as the eye can see, offer something silent in nature and in men—yet something interesting and poetic. The high roads are planted with fruit trees to refresh the traveller. The landscapes around the Rhine are superb—the river could be described as the tutelary genius of the nation, pure, rapid, majestic as the life of a hero of antiquity." The traveller admired the gardens, the architecture, rich in monuments of past glory, the lovingly decorated, well-kept, hospitable little dwellings—and found one of the

[1] London 1972

most striking features was that "townspeople and country folk, soldiers and labourers *nearly all know music*. . . . I have entered wretched cottages blackened with smoke, and suddenly heard the mistress, and the master of the house too, improvising on the harpsichord, as Italians improvise verses. On market days players of wind instruments perform on the town hall balcony over the public square, so that the local peasants can share in the sweet enjoyment of the first of the arts."[1]

Another visitor, from London, described the itinerant musicians "who go about the country in small bands like wandering troubadours, so clever and eminent in their way as to deserve notice; for a few florins these poor fellows will amuse you with such an exhibition of tone and skill as would set up an English artist of the first water . . . happy and with a gentility of mind, owing to their acquaintance with music, much superior to other people of their *caste*".[2] While, as a contemporary violin-maker, J. A. Otto, wrote: "men who could make no more progress as musicians travelled through most of the towns in Germany mending instruments: there are few towns to be found without either an hautboy player, a fiddler or a town musician who take upon themselves to repair or rather *botch* violins . . ."[3] Apart from the rich musical tradition, the instrumental aptitude of Germans is, it is suggested, due to their powers of serious study, whereas the more easy-going Italians do not bother to master techniques but just enjoy themselves singing.

The earnest studious nature of the Germans was often noted by visitors, along with their stolidity and phlegm.

Thomas Holcroft wrote, in 1799, of the "laborious and slow" ways of the city porters of Hamburg who kept him waiting about: "As Germans they were quick; we had heard much of the inflexible phlegm of this people, but as yet we were novices in its practical effects.[4] "And a young Cambridge academic travelling in the Rhineland in 1789 remarked that "the drivers possess that amiable character of this nation, a degree of Phlegm that thunder, hail, lightning and rain could not induce them to quicken their pace."[5] All reports agreed[6] though that "they have many good qualities, are exceedingly civil to strangers and

[1] Madame de Staël, *De l'Allemagne*, i, p. 124 (London 1813)
[2] A Musical Professor, *A Ramble in Germany*, p. 75
[3] Jacob-August Otto, *Treatise on the Construction of the Violin*, p. 23, trans. London 1833. Otto was one of 30 famous German violin-makers of this time.
[4] Holcroft, *Life* (in Hazlitt, *Works*, ed. P. P. Howe), vol. III, p. 257
[5] Knight, *University Rebel* (London 1971), p. 77
[6] *Ibid.*, p. 80

are very partial to our country". It may be mentioned here that Beethoven's character, so lacking in phlegm, most likely derived from the fact that his forebears were not German but Flemish; and it has been suggested that some interbreeding during the Spanish occupation of the Netherlands might account for the composer's black hair, dark eyes, swarthy complexion and fiery southern nature.[1]

To return to Madame de Staël's impressions of German society: "The country is peaceable, very much against war, owing to its partition into many states: this is reflected in the lack of national politics and social links, laws, interests, literature, public opinion, which do not exist in Germany."

"Each state is independent, science well cultivated", we are told; "but the whole nation is so subdivided that one wonders to which part of the Empire should this name 'nation' belong?" They have no interest in liberty: "Old charters, ancient civic privileges, family history, are the glory and charm of small states, very dear to the Germans but to the neglect of strong national consciousness, so necessary, placed as it is between the European colossuses Russia and Austria."[2]

Of the two, it was the Austrian colossus with its feudal catholicism which overshadowed the north-west, though more modern ideas were struggling into being in a few pockets of independence.

Joseph II, emperor of Austria, was introducing reforms all over his realm and had already in Austria centralised law, education and economics in an enlightened administrative system; but it was difficult to reform the German principalities without complete restructuring. Joseph did the best he could by sending progressive administrators to the outlying provinces; for instance, his brothers Leopold and Maximilian to Lombardy and to Bonn respectively.

Both Archdukes did well. Milan became an outstanding centre in Italy between 1780 and 1790, and Bonn was an example of enlightenment to West Germany. Maximilian paid no heed to the disapproval of the Church in Cologne, but set about bringing in new laws, opening a new university staffed with broad-minded scientists and philosophers; he fostered art and music in his court, which was already distinguished for its choir and orchestra of fine young men in resplendent red and gold livery; he improved his theatre and put on the best drama and

[1] Cf. E. Closson, *The Fleming in Beethoven*. Teodor Wysewa also found Flemish influence in Beethoven's works "which have been compared to Rubens, Rembrandt, and Van Eyck in their healthy grandeur, characteristic of a sanguine race endowed with good solid sense". *Beethoven et Wagner*, Paris 1898.
[2] de Staël, *op. cit.*, i, p. 30

operas of the time. Maximilian encouraged new ideas and young talent. It was he who appointed Beethoven court organist at fourteen years old, and sent him (at sixteen) to Vienna for the first time, following the court musician Neefe's recommendation, "This young genius deserves support to enable him to travel."

*   *   *

On 1 April 1787 the Munich newspaper, *Tageszeitung*, noted among visitors to the city, "Herr Peethofen, Musikus von Bonn", on his way from his home town to Vienna. The young musician, shy, awkward, with dark eyes and a mop of black hair, travelled alone towards his dream of visiting the Imperial city, seeing Emperor Joseph, playing to Mozart. He was only to be away from Bonn for a short time, as his family needed him, and he was bound to go back without delay to them and his job as organist and viola player in the court orchestra.

Like all musicians of the time he longed to settle in Vienna, which was unmatched by any other city in the world for music and drama. London and Paris had fine orchestras, Cologne its church music, Prague and Berlin their opera, Dresden and Leipzig their organs, but Vienna excelled them all. It was the home of Haydn, Gluck, Mozart, Salieri, and any gifted young musician might be excused for imagining that it held a golden future for him too.

Five years were to pass before young Beethoven could become a citizen of Vienna. In the meantime he could only spend a few days looking around and marvelling at the city, which a poetical contemporary described as "like a superb ring—in the centre, a great jewel set among emeralds and surrounded by small variegated stones".[1] He could explore the old town, "no bigger than it was when Richard Cœur de Lion was imprisoned near its gates . . . its narrow streets and its palaces a little like Florence",[2] as Madame de Staël thought. He would not see the quarters of the labouring people beyond the walls, but he could visit Stefansdom and the Hofburg, home of the Habsburgs and nerve centre of the Holy Roman Empire from which vast areas of Europe were controlled. He could wander about the public gardens and stare at the magnificence, hoping to catch a glimpse of the Emperor, unaware that this empire built up by a system of freebooting and intermarriage, and held down by wars and repression, was facing crisis and upheavals along with feudal monarchies everywhere. It all looked so solid that most of the Viennese themselves were unaware of

[1] Pezzl, *Skizze von Wien* (Vienna 1780)   [2] de Staël, *op. cit*, i, p. 65

it; life was cushioned by the spoils of empire, and those who could afford to eat, drink and dance in the beautiful city were remarkably unconcerned. But the storm was coming, and one man at least sensed it and in his limited way he had taken what he hoped were safety measures.

Emperor Joseph knew of the stirring among the subject peoples, and (as already mentioned) had set out in 1780 to redress some of the wrongs imposed by generations of ancestors. Adopting ideas from French philosophers which he had picked up on his travels to Paris, he had entirely changed the policies of his dictatorial mother, the Empress Maria Theresa, and set out a programme of widespread benevolent despotism. In a few years he had restored peasant rights, reduced the privileges of church and nobility, liberalised education, lifted restrictions on Jews and Freemasons,[1] built educational institutions, hospitals, schools. He acted from the highest motives, but his plans were carried out hastily and autocratically, arousing violent opposition from clergy and aristocracy while not winning much support from the conservative small bourgeoisie or backward peasantry. None the less, he had a devoted following among the educated class and the more radical workers, and what he did could not be entirely wasted. His idealism shone out in an obscurantist age and was an inspiration to the young and enthusiastic—such as the "musikus from Bonn".

All we know about Beethoven's stay in Vienna is that it was brief— less than two weeks—and that he caught a glimpse of the Emperor just before Joseph left to join his armies in the eastern provinces on an ill-fated campaign against the Turks; and that he extemporised on the pianoforte to Mozart, who told his friends to "watch that young man, for some day he will give the world something to talk about". We know too that he had a few theory lessons from Mozart and heard the great man play the piano "in a fine but choppy style—no legato".

It is history's loss, and music's too, that the two geniuses did not meet again. Beethoven would dearly have liked to; but news came from Bonn of his mother's serious illness, and the boy caught the first post-chaise back, stopping on 25 April at Munich, where his name was listed this time as "Herr Peethofen, Kurköllnischer Kammervirtuos von Bonn".[2]

When he got back he found to his distress that his mother was in an

[1] Freemasons had been persecuted under Maria Theresa as being a secret society opposed to the Roman Catholic church; their enlightened ideas drew many intellectuals into the movement, including Goethe in Germany, Mozart in Austria.
[2] Thayer, *Life of Beethoven*, pp. 87–8

advanced state of consumption. She lingered on for several weeks, but at the end of July she died, leaving her three boys, Ludwig, Caspar Carl and Johann, and a little girl of eighteen months old, in the precarious care of Johann, the feckless hard-drinking father who already had difficulty in making ends meet on his salary as tenor in the court choir.

Maria Magdalena's death was Ludwig's first great sorrow, and he poured out his feelings to his friend Dr Schaden of Augsburg: "She was such a good loving mother, my best friend; o! who was happier than I when I could still say the dear name *mother* and it was heard, and who can I say it to now?"[1]

He was suffering from asthma, which he feared might develop into consumption, and from melancholia—"almost as great an evil as my malady itself". The little sister died in November, one more grief to bear. In poverty, ill, depressed, weighed down by his father's hopeless irresponsibility (Johann was sacked from his job for drunkenness, and had to be rescued at least once from arrest for alcoholism), Ludwig took on the burden of keeping the family. He worked hard and long hours, teaching and studying, playing the court chapel organ and the viola in the theatre orchestra. With all these responsibilities he grew mature and serious, and aged beyond his seventeen years.

He did, however, manage fairly often to escape from the troubles at home by going on free evenings to the Zehrgarten tavern, the favourite resort of professors of the new Bonn university, and of "young men whose education and position at court made them eligible". Beethoven's social position was a humble one: a report by the court employment office described him as "of good deportment and poor"; but his dynamism, warm personality, and exceptional gifts made him immediately attractive. The chaplain of the neighbouring Hohenlohe court, Carl Ludwig Junker, an amateur composer and editor of a liberal almanack devoted to the arts, who met him for the first time in 1788, wrote of "the dear good Beethoven . . . the greatness of this amiable light-hearted man, his almost astonishing execution as a virtuoso", and added: "He is exceedingly modest and free from all pretension." His manners were on a par with the other members of the band, which Junker described as "very polite and refined" even under difficult conditions of performance: at the public concert "they had a hard time of it . . . the large audience crowded so closely around them that they could scarcely play and the sweat was streaming down their

[1] Beethoven, *Briefe* (Henschelverlag, Berlin 1969) I, p. 5

faces; but they bore it all quietly and composedly without showing the least annoyance . . . at a minor court complaints and abuses would have been freely lavished".[1] Beethoven got on well with everybody and made friends outside the circle of court musicians, among the university people who frequented the Zehrgarten. One of these was "the poor but amiable student Wegeler", later an eminent doctor and professor at Bonn university, who introduced the young musician to the von Breuning family with whom Wegeler was staying. They immediately made him feel at home in their pleasant house overlooking the river. This was the beginning of a lifelong friendship with the young Breunings whose father, a high court official, had recently died and whose mother, an exceptionally kind and cultured woman, greatly helped Ludwig over his bereavement.

Beethoven spent holidays in the country with the Breunings, giving the children music lessons, rambling in their company over the beautiful Rhineland region and developing the passion for nature which was to become so much part of his creative make-up; he came to know it in all its aspects—as Heine's "fair land, full of loveliness and sunshine", and Byron's frowning castle crag of Drachenfels—aspects often recalled later in music terms. He joined in their cultural and social doings, lost his heart hopelessly to various young ladies of their circle, for whom he set love lyrics to music; and he enjoyed the stimulating evenings in the Breuning home where the leading lights of the local intelligentsia met and discussed art, science and the politics of the day.

Here he got to know their uncle and guardian, Canon Lorenz Breuning, described by Thayer as "a fine specimen of the enlightened clergy of Bonn . . . a striking contrast to the priests and monks of Cologne". It was there that he met Count Waldstein, confidant of the Elector and later Chancellor to the Emperor, who had recently arrived in the town and was later to prove so good a friend. These people helped enormously to develop the young musician's intellectual and spiritual personality. They encouraged him in his composing, stimulated his thinking, directed his reading.

It is often suggested that Beethoven was uneducated, or at best inadequately self-taught, but in fact—although to his dying day he could not do simple arithmetic or spell correctly—he was well read in a wide range of subjects; he could speak some French and Italian and was familiar with the literature of many lands, classical and modern, most probably thanks to the influence of the Breunings and their friends.

[1] Nohl, *Beethoven depicted by his contemporaries*, trans. London 1880, Thayer, p. 105

Later conversations and jottings in his note-books show that his mind was stocked with the poetry and philosophy that appealed to earnest young Germans—Goethe, Kant, Schiller, Klopstock—the founders of the new school of writing which established a genuine national literature opposed to the frivolous pre-revolutionary French books then in vogue. Their preoccupation with nature on the one hand and national patriotism on the other, certainly moulded Beethoven's thinking, and their heroic subjects—Schiller's *Don Carlos*, Goethe's *Goetz von Berlichingen*, Lessing's *Nathan der Weise*—aroused his idealism, while *Der Junge Werther* stirred his sensibilities.

Besides German authors, translations of foreign literature were available in enlightened Bonn: Jean Jacques Rousseau was fashionable among the intellectuals, and his poem "Que le temps me dure" was set as a song by Beethoven (WoO 116) at about this time. Shakespeare and Beaumarchais were acted, as well as Schiller and Lessing, at the court theatre, where Beethoven certainly saw them in performances during 1786 and 1787.

Besides literature and philosophy, politics and social questions were freely discussed by the Breunings and their cultured friends, at a *Lesegesellschaft* (Literary Society) to which they all belonged. Although Beethoven as a student was not eligible for membership he sometimes attended meetings as a friend of Count Waldstein. This society was very similar to those so popular in England at that time for debating radical ideas, such as the Manchester Philosophical Society, the Lunar Society, the London and Cambridge Constitutional Clubs.

There were indeed many similarities in the intellectual life of provincial England and northern Germany; people came from England (to name only the young Coleridge, William Frend, and Dr Joseph Priestley's son William, among many) to study in Germany, to absorb the new philosophies of Kant and Fichte, read the exciting literature, or take a look at developments in the universities.

Of the latter, Bonn, along with Frankfurt, Leipzig and Jena, was one of the most advanced, since its inauguration by Maximilian in November 1786. This had been a memorable occasion when Bonn was decorated with flags, church bells rang and processions paraded through the streets to a grand ceremony at which Beethoven played the organ. The university soon became renowned.

The Elector had brought in new teachers whose reputations attracted scholars from far and wide. New departments were set up in medicine, law and philology. Before long Bonn was outshining Munster and

Cologne, which led to a violent feud with the Church authorities of those neighbouring places, but did not deflect the Archduke from his academic reforms.

In 1789 Beethoven registered as a student, along with his friend and fellow musician Anton Reicha, in this fine new university, and it is worth having a look at what he found. Madame de Staël gave her impressions of German academies some years later, but they must have been very much the same as those of Beethoven's time: "The crowds of students assembled there were almost like an official state", we are told; "rich and poor students alike were only distinguished by their personal merit, and foreigners from all over the world came and happily submitted to this equality, subject only to natural superiority. There was independence and even a military spirit among the students. The teaching was very different from that in the rest of Europe; in each university several professors competed in each branch of teaching; and this made for considerable emulation." Students of medicine or law "were called on to learn other subjects, hence the universal nature of learning that one notices in almost all educated Germans. . . . The study of both ancient and modern languages was the base of instruction in the universities and contributed to their high repute. Education in German universities begins where it ends in those of most other European nations. Not only are the professors men of surprising erudition, but they are distinguished by very scrupulous methods of instruction. In Germany, to be conscientious is everything, and very properly so."[1]

In some cases Madame de Staël thought that the flourishing of philosophic genius was due to "the absence of political and social activity among the academics", which left more liberty to thinkers. "In Germany he who is not concerned with the Universe has nothing to do."[2] This was true perhaps before and after 1789, but during the short period that Beethoven spent in Bonn university things were different. There was plenty of political and social activity among both teachers and students; the French Revolution and its ideas stirred even the most highminded of professors to an interest in the outside world, and many of Maximilian's recruits to the staff were already confirmed "enlightenment men". Among those whose lectures Beethoven attended was the professor of philology, Eulogius Schneider, an eminent scholar and writer of strong radical views. He had been a Franciscan monk, but had left the Order so as to teach and preach, write and publish in support of the revolution which had just burst on the world.

[1] de Staël, *op. cit.*, i, pp. 162 *et seq.*   [2] *Ibid.*, iii, p. 122

Schneider was fiercely anti-clerical and incurred the wrath of the Cologne ecclesiastics for his sermons denouncing the bigotry, riches and misused power of the Roman Catholic Church, explaining his ideas of Christ's aims and the meaning of Christianity, deploring "Fanaticismus" and "Pfarrerische Zeug" (priestly nonsense). Schneider was undeterred by the storm and threats of disciplinary action that rumbled forth from Cologne, and he continued to defend the Revolution: "One year of freedom is more use to mankind than a century of despotism", he proclaimed, "for despotism stifles thought in the mind and virtue in the heart."

Schneider was, according to Wegeler, a cantankerous individual, and there are stories of his quarrels with the academics at the Zehrgarten, who did not all hold his extreme views. But the more radical young admired and supported him. A book of his poems was published in Frankfurt in 1790, and among the names of subscribers to the volume we find that of L. van Beethoven, *hofmusiker*, Bonn—a clear proof that the young composer admired and shared Schneider's views to the extent of giving from his meagre funds to propagate them in print. One can see the appeal for him, in those days of revolutionary enthusiam, of such lines as those on the taking of the Bastille:

> Think not this a mere stroke of the pen—
> This is more, this is our will,
> The fate of each French citizen.
> Shattered, in fragments, the Bastille—
> Now France is free, and free her men!

Or on feudal oppression in general:

> No longer can they bury him alive,
> The wise man who once dared to write the truth,
> Who stayed untainted by the prince's gifts,
> Undaunted by the oppressor's murd'rous threats.[1]

There are passages too from Schneider's lectures which might have been written by Beethoven twenty years later: "The real worth of mankind is higher than the advantage of birth, and true nobility can only be attained by greatness of spirit and goodness of heart" (Schneider, 1790), is echoed by Beethoven's words "Only art and science exalt men to the point of divinity", and "I know of no other

[1] Kneppler, Georg, *Musikgeschichte des 19 Jahrhunderts*, ii, pp. 538–9

advantages than those which place human beings in the ranks of the higher and the good" (17 July 1812).[1] The professor's influence was deep and long lasting: he struck a chord in the student's heart which would reverberate throughout Beethoven's life.

It was quite natural for the young composer to fall under Schneider's spell and absorb his ideas; they did not drop on stony ground but on rich and fertile soil. All Beethoven's experience of life, though short, had been poverty, hard work, his home's wretchedness compared with the affluence of the Court, long hours labouring to earn a little extra money ever since the age of eleven. All these factors engrained in his passionate nature, mulled over by his keen intelligence, made him immensely receptive to radical ideas; and what he read and heard about the French Revolution inspired visions of justice and freedom, of equality and decent conditions for the under-privileged, and offered guiding lines for behaviour from which he would never swerve.

*   *   *

Up to 1789 it cannot be claimed that there was anything revolutionary in Beethoven's musical output. One would hardly expect to find political outbursts from a young court employee, necessarily well behaved and decorous, busy with his duties and in turning out pieces for the cognoscenti of the court. In the years between 1783 and 1789 his output of sonatas, variations, rondos for pianoforte, organ preludes (proceeding through all the keys of the scale and back again) quartets for piano and strings, showed remarkable mastery of technique, but was conventional bright-schoolboy stuff. And yet there were surprises: clashing discords (harmless enough to twentieth-century ears, but decidedly daring at that time), and unexpected rhythms, and passages of "sanglots entrecoupés" (broken sobs) introducing a naïve romanticism into the classical pattern. The songs that he chose to set also gave a clue to the way the boy's mind was working. For an adolescent he evidently had very decided views on the sort of verse that was worth setting. Admittedly there were a couple of drinking songs, light-hearted and insignificant; otherwise he selected poems for their literary or moral worth. His love songs were by the best poets he knew— Goethe ("Mailied"), Bürger ("Molly's Abschied"), Lessing ("Die Liebe")—which suggests an unusually serious approach for a youngster of under eighteen. And there were two or three songs by minor poets,

---

[1] *The Letters of Beethoven* (trans. E. Anderson) London 1961, Letter 376, p. 381

all with a "message" foreshadowing the later Beethoven's idealistic approach to song-writing. "Feuerfarbe", "Das Blümchen wunderhold", and "Das Liedchen von der Ruhe", all written at about this time, show the young musician's leaning towards philosophical romanticism, a searching for truth. Bürger's "Gegenliebe" was a declaration of faith in human love, and Pfeffel's "Der freie Mann" an assertion of Man's equality.

> Wer ist ein freier Mann?
> Dem nicht Geburt noch Titel
> Nicht Samtrock oder Kittel
> Den Bruder bergen kann.
>
> Der in sich selbst verschlossen
> Der feilen Gunst der Grossen
> Und Kleinen trotzen kann—
> Der ist ein freier Mann.

(Who is a free man? He from whom neither birth nor title,
Peasant smock, nor uniform, hides his brother man;
Who, enclosed within himself, can set at nought
The venal favour of great and small alike—he is a free man.)

An indication that Beethoven did not reject his youthful earnestness when he might have grown blasé or cynical is that he used the tunes of several of these songs in important mature works: the theme of "Gegenliebe" is that of the Choral Fantasia (Op. 80) and the first few bars of "Der Freie Mann", as originally sketched, are identical with the opening of the finale (in the same key, C major) of the Fifth Symphony, and very similar to the beginning of the E flat Piano Concerto (Op. 53). Beethoven must have liked his youthful songs, for he often worked over them later and published them afresh long after he had outgrown their eighteenth-century naïve forms.

His youthful compositions, taken as a whole, show that he was not an infant prodigy in the same sense as Mozart, who poured out operas and symphonies at an early age with immense facility. Beethoven's gifts needed, for their fruition, time and patient work, the right stimuli and conditions; fortunately for posterity these were historically present.

If Beethoven had been restricted to a less enlightened court circle, had not known the Breunings, had not been exposed to the repercussions of the French Revolution, he might have remained a talented and serious musician but not much more. As it was, in 1789 unexpected horizons opened for him, and his sky was lit up by the bright new dawn. His work was illuminated by it from then on. The immediate effect of that dawn is seen in his most important Bonn composition, which was inspired by a contemporary event and expresses all the feelings of a young ardent revolutionary for humanity, progress and justice in an entirely new and imaginative approach, throwing aside convention and astonishing the hearer by its daring. This composition was the Cantata for the funeral of the Emperor Joseph. The great reformer had died on 20 February 1790 to the sorrow of all his liberal-minded supporters. As soon as the news of his death reached Bonn the *Lesegesellschaft* met to plan a memorial celebration. Professor Schneider, who later gave the commemoration address, suggested that a musical feature should be included in the programme; he had already been offered a poem which only needed a setting by one of the excellent local musicians. Beethoven's name was put forward (probably by Count Waldstein, a regular member of the society) and he at once set to work on the cantata. His devotion to the royal reformer, and his well-developed liberal sentiments made the young composer an ideal choice for the task, but unfortunately he was a slow worker and did not manage to complete the music in the short time available. The minutes of the Literary Society's last meeting to prepare the memorial function state that "for various reasons the proposed cantata cannot be performed".

Beethoven did eventually finish it, and it was shown to Joseph Haydn during one of his visits to Bonn on his way to or from England, probably in the summer of 1792. The older composer was evidently impressed, for he strongly urged Beethoven to continue his studies, and promised to give him tuition if he came to Vienna.[1]

Haydn judged the music from the score: there was no performance, as the orchestral players said it was too difficult for them and that certain passages were unplayable. In fact, the cantata was not performed in public till November 1884, nearly a century later; nor was that written in mid-1790 for the coronation of Joseph's brother Leopold, although both works are extremely interesting. Brahms, after hearing the Funeral Cantata, wrote, "It is Beethoven through and through! The beautiful and noble pathos, sublime in its feeling and imagination, the intensity, perhaps violence, in its expression . . . all the

[1] Thayer, pp. 119–20

characteristics which we may observe and associate with his later works."[1]

Beethoven had indeed put his whole heart into this music. The death of Joseph moved him deeply, and the political tenor of the words (which referred to the crushing of reactionary "fanaticism" and the dawn of the Enlightenment) was a new kind of inspiration, one which he found again and again through his life. In fact, for a moment of high drama in the opera *Fidelio*, he came back to one of the motifs of the Joseph cantata: "Then all mankind rose up into daylight", adapting the melody to the librettist Sonnleithner's words. He did not discard this in the 1814 or even in the 1822 versions of the opera, ample proof that it still meant much to him.

The contents of the "Leopold Cantata" were equally radical: Leopold would carry on Joseph's good work, said the poet. The words: "Peoples, weep no more—He will do as Joseph did", are followed by a passage: "Sinkt ihr nieder, Millionen!" foreshadowing almost identical phrases in the "Ode to Joy" which Beethoven set thirty years later. It seems that the young poet, Severin Anton Averdonk, who wrote the text for this as well as the Funeral Cantata, was as great an admirer as Beethoven of Schiller, who was generally revered by the young radicals of Bonn, equally for his poetry and for his political opinions. Schiller and Klopstock had both declared their support for the French Revolution in 1789 and had been made honorary citizens of the Republic of France. Like Wordsworth, Coleridge and many other writers they hailed the coming of a reign of happiness on earth. Schiller, as Heine said, "was possessed by the spirit of his age, he wrestled with it, was overpowered by it, followed it to battle, bore its banner—Schiller fought with his pen for the great ideas of the Revolution".[2]

Two years later the Revolution became unfashionable, and it was no longer safe to proclaim its glories. Schiller, like the English poets, recanted. With the Austrian regime's support of the French emigrés, and the resulting terror in Paris, the climate of opinion changed in Germany, and cooled even in Bonn university. Eulogius Schneider, after writing a poem which attacked Leopold for betraying Joseph's ideals and restoring the privileges of the priests, was threatened with a trial "for seditious and unpriestly writings" by the Cologne authorities. He resigned from the university and took a post as vicar to the Bishop

---

[1] *Neue Freie Presse*, Vienna, 27.6.1897
[2] Heinrich Heine, *The Romantic School*

of Strasburg, a city dominated by the French, and hence more congenial. The events of Schneider's last years are worth mentioning here as an illustration of the tempestuous conditions of the time: settled, as he thought, among sympathetic spirits, including Rouget de Lisle, author of *La Marseillaise* (which he translated into German) Schneider threw himself into activity for the republican cause. He wrote revolutionary verse and prose, became vice-president of republican clubs and member of the Friends of the Constitution and the Jacobin Club, was appointed Public Prosecutor, made a member of the *Comité de sureté général* and Commissar of the revolutionary army. When Robespierre came to power the tide turned; Schneider was arrested by order of Saint-Just. He sent an appeal from prison to the Paris Jacobins, which was intercepted and destroyed by Robespierre. Schneider paid the penalty for his nationality—because Germans and French were by then at each others' throats, and all foreigners were suspect, even the most loyal. He was executed on 10 April 1794.

It is doubtful whether Beethoven ever heard the sad story, or if he had, whether his basic faith would have been shaken. All we know is that he continued to believe in democracy and freedom, looked towards the future and never lost the idealism implanted during those years of awakening.

Up to 1792, however, one could still openly proclaim republican sympathies. Archduke Maximilian kept on good terms with the French (with whom he was geographically too close to risk friction) even after they had executed his sister Marie Antoinette, and after the new Emperor, Francis II, had decided to send the Austrian army to war in support of the emigré French. Maximilian had a tricky time, and suffered a good deal from the high-handed behaviour of the foreigners sent by his brother into his electorate. But he was determined to behave as a neutral towards the French, closer neighbours than the Viennese, for as long as possible. At last, in October 1792, as the French armies, provoked by the counter-revolutionaries on the border, advanced into Germany the Elector packed up his archives and valuables and left Bonn; but he came back again when Prussian forces arrived in Coblentz and temporarily held up the republican armies. Then, however, the French occupied the Netherlands, where they were welcomed by the independence-hungry Flemings; Austrian armies invaded Westphalia, and Maximilian re-packed and moved out once again—this time for good—to Munster. The great days of music making, of gay journeys with the court orchestra down the Rhine, of cultural bonanzas, intellectual debates, stimulating social gatherings were over, for at least a generation.

Beethoven had some time earlier decided to take Haydn's advice and go to study in Vienna. Count Waldstein had urged him to go: "There you will be stimulated by the variety of folklore—Hungarian, Bohemian, Polish, Italian, and so on—if these people cannot address each other in words, music they all of them know."[1]

By 1792, nearly twenty-two years old, it was time for Beethoven to break out of the provincial rut and try his wings; in the cosmopolitan atmosphere of the great city he knew he would learn and grow. It would have been hard, in the ordinary way, to get permission for his journey just at the start of the theatrical and orchestral season. But as the future looked more and more unsettled he managed to obtain leave of absence. He was still engaged by the court, and was allowed journey money with the promise of more to follow. He made arrangements for payments of his father's pension and his brothers' upkeep, packed his bags for a stay of unspecified duration, and said goodbye to Bonn. His friends bade him farewell regretfully but hopefully, and inscribed touching messages and verses from Herder in his album. Eleonore Breuning, the eldest of the Breuning children, who later married Franz Wegeler, wrote prophetically, "Friendship, with whatever is good, grows like the evening shadow till the sun of life sets." Count Waldstein's lines, written on 29 October 1792, were equally prophetic: "With the help of assiduous labour you shall receive Mozart's spirit from Haydn's hands."[2]

Beethoven left Bonn at the beginning of November 1792. It took twenty-five hours to reach Frankfurt by post coach, stopping en route for dinner at Coblentz. And this was only the beginning of the journey to Vienna. An Englishman travelling the same route in June 1789 wrote that "Germany claims the pre-eminence for badness of roads & the most tormenting construction of vehicles."[3] That was in summer, and peace-time; poor Beethoven travelled in winter and through the war zone, and one can hardly imagine the discomfort of the nine-day journey. The French army was advancing fast into Germany and the Hessian troops were rushing to intercept them.

Beethoven's coach arrived in Limburg just forty-eight hours before the town was taken by the French, and an entry in his notebook reads,

[1] Schnabel, Artur, *My Life and Music* (trans. London 1961), p. 22
[2] Thayer, pp. 114–17
[3] Knight, *University Rebel*, p. 77

"Tip to the driver, because he went like the devil right through the Hessian armies, one small thaler." Miraculously they got safely to Frankfurt, and thence in the public conveyance via Nuremberg, Regensburg and Passau to Linz. On or just before 10 November 1792 they arrived in Vienna at last.

2

Vienna

1793–1800

In the autumn mists of 1792 Vienna appeared unscathed, even un-affected by war, in contrast to Bonn where anxious nobles and digni-taries were poised to leave at a moment's notice, should the French march in. The Hofburg stood foursquare, a symbol of solid, sempiternal imperial domination; its occupiers pursued their way of life, their domestic, Catholic, conservative routine, quite unperturbed by the currents of unrest lapping its foundations.

"The great lords parade with magnificent horses and carriages in the Prater, for the sole pleasure of recognising there the friends they have just parted from in a drawing-room", wrote Madame de Staël.[1] "These seigneurs, the richest and most illustrious in Europe do not abuse their privileges, they even allow miserable fiacres to hold up their splendid conveyances. The Emperor and his brothers take their place in the queue and like to be considered as simple individuals. . . ."

The general public seemed perfectly happy, even the immigrants from distant provinces ("one often sees oriental and Polish and Hun-garian costumes in the crowd"), in the holiday atmosphere of the park. Not surprising perhaps in view of Vienna's prosperity and "its reputa-tion of eating more food than any other town. Their picnics are as substantial as other people's full dinners", the French visitor noted, echoing the earlier tourist Pezzl's remark, "People eat breakfast till the midday meal, then go on eating till the evening."[2] Henry Reeve, a doctor from London, summed them up thus: "the Viennois are a very sensual people; they take snuff, and smoke, and delight in music, and go continually to sights, and game and intrigue, and eat and drink and go cloaked up in cold weather, and sit in hot rooms and are never at home and alone . . ."[3] This way of life made for an easy good-

---

[1] Madame de Staël, *op. cit.*, i, p. 71   [2] Pezzl, *Skizze*, p. 90
[3] H. Reeve, *Journal of a Visit to Vienna in 1805* (ed. J. Reeve, London 1885), p. 27

humoured atmosphere: "Everybody is content with himself, nobody complains about his neighbour. There are no beggars in Vienna; charity is liberally administered, private and public benevolence are directed in a spirit of justice. One hears of very few examples of crimes requiring the death penalty, and everything bears the stamp of a paternal, wise, religious society";[1] this was one way of describing the general laxity of morals and clerical domination for which Vienna was famous; another way was the severe judgment of the German de Galanta: "a crowd of priests harboured in Vienna lead a comfortable existence. Aided by the monks they do all they can to maintain the people in a state of mind which serves their cupidity"; "there is more bigotry than piety there, and the monks work to keep the Viennese in ignorance", said Pezzl. Nicolai, an Italian observer, commented that "a host of priests say a Mass daily and receive a florin for it: the rest of the time they seek distractions, particularly with the fair sex. . . . Libertinage is enormous in Vienna and women are very coquettish."[2]

One thing that all visitors agreed on was the kindness and good humour of the Viennese, which outweighed their weaknesses, and made for an agreeable life and a gay city. Madame de Staël's only complaint was that "there is a lack of pinnacles and pillars which are needed for a temple of glory and genius". Literature, philosophy and abstract discussion were sadly lacking.

Admittedly there was a flourishing theatre and a fine opera house, but music was the only art which the Viennese fully appreciated. In this, all concurred, they excelled. There was music everywhere: "No place of refreshment, from the highest to the lowest, is without music, bassoons and clarionets are as plenty as blackberries, and in the suburbs at every turn one alights upon fresh carousings, fresh fiddlings, fresh illuminations."[3] There was music for the people in the Prater, music for the well-to-do in their drawing-rooms, music in the churches. Even the critical Madame de Staël was impressed: "The music of Vienna's Chapel is praiseworthy", she wrote after hearing Haydn's *Creation* there. "Four hundred musicians, a worthy festival of the work", though Haydn, she thought, "spoilt his effects by introducing too literal a picture of crawling serpents and singing birds, too loud a burst of sound at 'Let there be light', so that a wit remarked, 'When the light came on we had to block our ears.'"[4]

[1] de Staël, *op. cit.*, i, p. 72
[2] Robert, André, *L'Idée nationale autrichienne*, Paris 1933, p. 32, pp. 172–4
[3] *Musical Ramble*, p. 137   [4] de Staël, *op. cit.*, i, p. 374

From Dr Charles Burney to August Kotzebue, from Stendhal to Sir George Grove, testimony abounds to the extraordinary richness of musical life in Vienna at the turn of the eighteenth century. But in 1793, when Beethoven settled there, "quality" music was still chamber music privately performed for the nobility and their friends, as it had been for decades, by the private orchestra or ensemble of each great house. Every aspiring player or composer had to have one or more patrons and be prepared to perform or write according to their taste. As the required standard was usually high, this condition did not adversely affect the quality of the music, though if the patrons were unappreciative or uncultured the musician might suffer personally from a sense of servitude, as Mozart and Schubert certainly did.

Beethoven was fortunate in having introductions from Count Waldstein to two extremely musical princes (Lichnowsky and Lobkowitz) and this ensured him appreciation and—more important— security for the immediate future. Very soon after his arrival in Vienna he moved into a room in the house of Prince Karl Lichnowsky which saved him many gulden in rent. None the less he found life expensive and was hard put to it to eat adequately as well as to pay for his lessons and his piano, and dress smartly enough for the elegant company of his patrons. The immediate necessaries of life soon ate up his small reserves. He had to get an overcoat, boots, a writing-desk. Every item of expenditure went down in his note-book: Black silk stockings, I ducat; I pr. winter silk stockings 2 d.; shoes, I florin. "House-rent, 14 florins, eating—each time—12 kreutzers, pianoforte, 6 florins,"[1] he wrote, adding the pathetic comment, "in Bonn I counted on receiving 10 ducats here, but in vain, I have got to equip myself completely anew . . ."

One feels thankful to Lichnowsky who, as well as giving Beethoven a lodging (where he lived for over two years) helped him financially over the most difficult first few weeks in the city.

He was just beginning to settle down when news came from Bonn of his father's death. This was to cause him a great deal of worry on behalf of his brothers and about his own precarious financial position, apart from regrets for the old drunkard—whose habits, incidentally, were caustically referred to by the Elector in a letter to a friend: "The revenues from the liquor excise have suffered a loss in the deaths of Beethoven and Eichhoff."[2]

---

[1] Austrian currency (rough equivalent): I Kreutzer (x)=½d.; I Groschen=1½d.; I Gulden (or florin)=2s.; I Reichsthaler=3s.; I Ducat=9s.

[2] Thayer, *Life of Beethoven*, pp. 135-6

From so far away there was not much that Ludwig could do for his brothers, poor as he himself was. His friend, and former violin teacher, Franz Ries who was still in Bonn as Hofkapellmeister, exerted himself on their behalf, and managed to extract from the court treasury the quarter's salary due to Beethoven and also 100 reichsthaler from the salary owed to his father at his death. The official endorsement of this adds that their employee "is further to receive the three measures of grain graciously bestowed upon him for the education of his brothers". There is something unexpectedly feudal about this, but the three lads were no doubt glad of any addition, in whatever form, to their miserable income.[1]

Beethoven was thus, after a short period of acute anxiety, able to manage. He could even afford to treat his teacher Haydn to an occasional hot drink. Notes in his book read: "Chocolate for Haidn and me 22 x. Coffee 6 x for Haidn and me." This conjures up a charming picture—and Beethoven did, indeed, admire and like the old man. But he was in fact far from satisfied with his teaching. Haydn gave him very few lessons and did not trouble to correct the exercises set. The impatient Beethoven complained to a friend that he "did not find in Haydn's teaching that excellence which he had a right to expect". And when asked by the older man to inscribe the words "Pupil of Haydn" on the title page of his first works, Beethoven was most unwilling to do so; he said that though he had had some instruction from Haydn he had never learned anything from him. It was doubtful, in fact, whether Haydn, himself a daring and successful innovator, as Thayer says, "was the man to guide the studies of a headstrong, self-willed and still more daring musical revolutionist".[2]

Beethoven evidently found he was not. Though Haydn's influence was enormous, and his works were models from which Beethoven was to go forward, the pupil rapidly outpaced the master, and became restive and discontented. Things came to a head when Haydn advised him not to publish his Pianoforte Trio in C minor (Op. 1 no. 3) because it was too daring. The advice was not taken, and when Haydn left Vienna in 1793 for a journey Beethoven found another teacher, the composer Johann Schenk, who agreed to give him lessons provided he kept this dark and did not upset Haydn by leaving him altogether. Later Beethoven studied the violin with Schuppanzigh, the fat and jovial leader of Lichnowsky's quartet, and theory with the famous teacher and Kapellmeister of Stefansdom, Albrechtberger; and for ten

[1] Thayer, p. 137   [2] Ibid., pp. 138–46

years he went for tuition in vocal writing to the imperial Kapellmeister Anton Salieri, who was "willing to give gratuitous instruction
to musicians of small means".

Beethoven was a conscientious pupil, appreciated his teachers and
generally obeyed their rules, but was not for a moment deflected from
his original ideas. Speaking of the influences on him, particularly of
Mozart and Haydn, Nottebohm wrote, "Beethoven built on his
acquired and inherited possessions. He assimilated the traditional forms
and means of expression, gradually eliminated foreign influences and,
following the pressure of his subjective nature with its inclination
towards the ideal, he created his own individual style."[1]

*   *   *

Besides studying and composing Beethoven had many engagements
as a pianist. When his extraordinary gifts became known he was in
demand at all the great houses, to entertain the nobility with his
improvising. This meant fitting in with the habits of the aristocracy,
which did not appeal to him. He enjoyed the company of very few
nobles, and was loth to burden himself with the tedium of polite
society. As Madame de Staël observed, "politeness has introduced the
most boring customs possible into Vienna. All the best people go *en
masse* from one salon to another, three or four times a week. Time is
wasted on getting dressed for these parties, it's wasted on the journey,
on the staircases waiting for one's carriage, on spending three hours at
table; and in these innumerable assemblies one hears nothing beyond
the circle of accepted conventional phrases. This daily exhibition of
individuals to each other is a clever invention by mediocrity to annul
spiritual faculties. A kind of distraction both stupefying and insipid,
forbidding any ideas and turning language into a twittering which men
can learn like the birds." These parties are thought up "so that everyone
does the same thing at the same time; boredom shared with one's
fellows is preferable to the amusement one would have to create for
oneself. Society does not serve, as in France, to develop and animate the
mind, it leaves only emptiness in the head."[2]

One can well imagine Beethoven's boredom at the prospect of being
enmeshed in this scene! Wegeler, in his account of the composer's
refusal to dine at Prince Lichnowsky's every day, puts down his unwillingness to the young man's lack of money sense; but the reason
was just as much that the social occasion seemed to him sheer waste of

[1] Thayer, p. 149   [2] de Staël, *op. cit.*, i, p. 78

time and an imposition on his freedom: "They desire me to be home every day at 3.30, put on better clothes, shave my face, etc.—I can't stand that!" He loathed dressing up. One grand lady recalled, rather disapprovingly, that "while Haydn and Salieri used to sit on the sofa at one side of the little music-room, both most carefully attired in the former mode with wigs, shoes and silk stockings, Beethoven came negligently dressed in the freer fashion of the upper Rhine".[1]

Once when he did dine at the house of a certain old countess and convention required that he should take a lower seat than the aristocratic guests he was furious and stumped out. Politeness seemed to him a needless and unnatural oppression, and he spoke out whatever was in his mind, regardless of people's feelings.

The host or hostess must have been extremely embarrassed when, considering himself slighted, he played rude tricks on their other guests, or when he roared with laughter at the emotion displayed by the court people after he had improvised on the piano at King Frederick of Prussia's palace in 1797. "Who can live among such spoiled children", he cried, and refused to accept the King's offer of a post at the court, in spite of the honour and security it would have given him.[2]

Beethoven became celebrated and reasonably well-off during these years, and could probably have subsisted comfortably on his semi-private performances as a virtuoso, and by giving lessons to the daughters of noble families. Composition was much less well paid, but far more important to him, and every day after he had finished his stint of regular study and said *Lebewohl*, or *Aufwiedersehen* to the young ladies who were privileged to learn from him, he sat down to cover sheets of music paper with compositions, scratching away with quill pens hour after hour.

Between 1793 and '96 he wrote more than seventy works, including three trios, a sextet, several piano sonatas (Op. 2, 7 and 49), a Concerto for Piano in B flat (Op. 81b), many orchestral pieces (twelve German dances, and three sets of six minuets), six sets of variations for piano, songs, and a number of small instrumental works. None of these—not even the concerto or the C minor trio—can be called strikingly daring, but they are stamped with his strong individual personality; two of the songs, "Adelaide" and "Opferlied", written in 1796, are beautiful and unusual, and reflect Beethoven's special interest in the words.

The "message" of "Opferlied", the relation of the Beautiful to the

[1] Nohl, *Beethoven Depicted by His Contemporaries*, p. 25
[2] Thayer, pp. 172–85

Good, appealed to him so strongly that he set it at least four times during his life. Both words and music have a Masonic flavour and suggest that Beethoven felt an affinity with the brotherhood, persecuted and banned as it was.[1] (In 1795 he re-set his song *Der Freie Mann* for a Masonic Lodge to words by Wegeler, himself a Freemason.)

Melodies that satisfied him were rarely wasted: he revised several early songs and had them published years after they were first written, and, as we have seen, sometimes used the themes note for note in later work. Particularly interesting is the setting of *Gegenliebe*, by Bürger, the tune of which reappears in the Choral Fantasia (Op. 80) and which is strikingly similar in form and spirit to the *Alle Menschen* theme of the "Ode to Joy" in the Ninth Symphony. Beethoven was indeed thinking about the Schiller words as early as 1793, as we know from a letter from the Bonn official Fischenisch that January: "He proposes to compose Schiller's 'Freude' and indeed strophe by strophe. I expect something perfect, for as far as I know he is wholly devoted to the great and the sublime."[2] The simple, calm but swift moving melody of "Gegenliebe" probably appeared to him as befitting the idea behind the words of the song (mutual love), of Kuffner's poem (peace and joy), and the "Ode to Joy" (human brotherhood). Here it is enough to note that the same musical idea recurred and was used at intervals of ten or twelve years for the purpose of illustrating a deeply held attitude to humanity. For, although there is not much evidence of Beethoven's sense of social responsibility during the 1790s there is enough to show that he never abandoned his beliefs. Although he was almost wholly absorbed in music, and had hardly enough time even for that, there are letters that prove he was well aware of the events taking place around him and in the world outside Vienna. Politics did not impinge directly on him, the war seemed a long way off, and life in the city went on as before; but Beethoven knew about the unrest below the surface, and the radical activity which still persisted. In view of this we should take a brief look at the political scene, in Austria, now ruled by Leopold's successor, the devout and reactionary Franz II.

*   *   *

The Austrian Jacobins were few in number and they held meetings in the closest secrecy. Up to 1793 Emperor Franz had not felt it necessary

---

[1] Eighteenth-century Freemasonry alongside secret rites and observances had developed a musical symbolism; this was used by Mozart in music written for Masonic ceremonies, and in *The Magic Flute* (typical were progressions of "parallel thirds", massive chords, the keys of E flat major, F and E major). This "Humanitätstil" can also be found in Beethoven.

[2] Thayer, p. 121

to take special measures against them; he was sure that supporters of the French Revolution in his territories were just a few hot-heads whose enthusiasm would soon burn itself out. But on top of the execution of Louis XVI in January, and of Marie-Antoinette (Franz's sister) in October, with the advance of the republican armies came word from the Netherlands, Hungary and Italy of widespread subversion. A "plot" was discovered in Vienna—possibly imaginary, but enough to rouse fear and suspicion, and to impel Franz to order draconian measures. Suspicion fell on liberals, and particularly on intellectuals: "it was enough to have sidewhiskers to be suspected of jacobinism". Salons, even of such good conservatives as Caroline Pichler, were broken up, and all writings which had remote relation to politics seized.[1]

In September 1794 the Austrian police reported two Jacobin conspiracies, one in Vienna and another in Budapest. Nobody knew how serious they were, but even the planting of "liberty trees" in the suburbs of the city was suspicious. In fact the Emperor's tutor, Freiherr von Riedel, and Count Hohenwart, both members of the banned Masonic order, were found to be involved and severe measures were taken to suppress all such goings-on. Several of the Viennese leaders were put in the pillory for three days, then executed; others were condemned to many years' hard labour. The Hungarian Jacobins were equally harshly suppressed.

From then on, Franz's dread of "democracy" became pathological, and so did his animosity to change of any sort. He initiated a system "to secure the most absolute stability which ingenuity could devise". In his view, thought was in general, and except where directed to purely technical matters, the enemy of stability.[2]

The Emperor's police chief was Sarau, a thoroughgoing obscurantist who directed his energies from then on to persecuting the emigrés and members of "secret societies". A few years later all state employees at home and abroad, including archdukes, were required to sign a declaration that they did not belong to a secret society; this term included learned non-political and even religious associations—only groups for the promotion of agriculture being exempt. Mildly liberal Austrians were dismayed, among them the old Minister Joseph von

---

[1] This state of things continued well into the next century; Dr Reeve wrote in 1805, "politics are very seldom made the subject of conversation, they are never mentioned in what is called the best company". *Journal*, p. 30. J. Gott Seume (*Journey to Syracuse*, 1802), hummed "a few bars of the Marseillaise in a café" and "acted as a damper" on the whole company.

[2] Emerson, *Metternich and the Political Police*, p. 158

Sonnenfels, formerly a leading Freemason and adviser to Joseph II, to whom Beethoven later dedicated his Sonata in D, Op. 28, as a mark of respect. But human freedom counted for nothing when imperial safety was thought to be at risk.

Beethoven did not belong to any society, liberal, secret or otherwise, but he might justifiably have been picked on for dangerous thoughts; his opinion of the "upper classes" was distinctly subversive. "I promised to send you something of mine," he wrote to Simrock, his Bonn publisher, in August 1794, "and you interpreted it as empty courtier's talk. How have I come to deserve such a judgment?—pfui! shame on you—who would indulge in such expressions in our democratic times!" He evidently took a lively interest in what was going on—and not only in the weather, though he mentions the extreme heat of summer and the shortage of ice-cream. "Here, various people of importance have been arrested, they say a revolution was going to break out—but I believe that as long as an Austrian has his brown beer and sausages he won't revolt. It is said that the gates on to the suburbs are to be locked at 10 at night. The soldiers are heavily armed. You must not speak too loud here or the Police will give you lodgings for the night."[1]

Beethoven was perfectly aware of the suppression; he felt deeply for the political prisoners—both the countless unknown republicans, and the individual sufferers such as Lafayette, immured since 1792 in the fortress of Olmutz. His sympathies were to be publicly expressed ten years later in the opera *Fidelio*, but there is little doubt that the prisoners' chorus, the portrait of the noble captive and of the reactionary governor were inspired by the oppression of the 1790s.

It is not surprising that there are few references in Beethoven's letters to current events. He could not afford at that time to handle such dynamite or express open sympathy with revolutionary ideas, for his position was far from secure; as a recent arrival and little known free-lance musician it would have been suicidal, and he was not ready to risk his freedom pointlessly; he had not only to earn his living but also to send money to his brothers.

He was determined to fulfil his mission as a composer, and politics, though they interested him deeply, were not his main concern. He had to master counterpoint, harmony, form, and nothing was allowed to deflect him. His hard apprenticeship included ceaseless creative activity, applying theory to practice. The work of the mid-1790s gives the

[1] *Briefe*, 4, p. 9

impression that he still considered himself on probation, and that if he was not actually playing safe, he was at least not risking his teachers' wrath: it is not strikingly rebellious music, and one looks down the list of serenades, variations, songs, small pieces for the piano, without finding any composition as exciting and prophetic as the much earlier Funeral Cantata.

One must, however, be fair: there are in the Piano Sonatas, Op. 49 and Op. 7, the Cello Sonata, Op. 5, the "Rage over a lost penny", and the Op. 1 trios, beauty, freshness and originality; although this music owes a lot to Haydn and Mozart, and is basically eighteenth century in form, its nature is not stable and classical, but evokes an unrealised spirit of adventure. Some of it is frankly in the nature of a musical exercise; in the pieces for wind instruments Beethoven was exploring their possibilities, and this exploration was very useful to him when he came to use them in symphonies and full-scale works. The Sextet for Two Clarinets, Horns and Bassoons, the Variations on *La ci darem*, for Oboes and Horn, WoO 28, are honourable and melodious examples.

These could be called years of preparation for the great future which lay ahead. Parallel with the technical development, the daily grind, the study, the practice, the piano lessons, the social round, there was a mental and spiritual development, due to the fact of his living in the heart of Europe at this particular historical period. And this even more than the mastery of form and counterpoint was to contribute to the making of the great compositions of the second period. The seeds of Beethoven's political awareness were implanted in Bonn, but it was in Vienna that he got his understanding of the human scene, of the revolution, of war in both its tragic and glorious aspects, with the heroic qualities which it threw up; it was the view from Vienna which made it possible for him to create revolutionary works of universal appeal; and above all it was his knowledge of the Italian campaigns of Napoleon Bonaparte and his French republican army. The most direct result was the "Eroica" symphony, but all his important music stemmed from the experience of his time.

3

The Genesis of the Eroica

On May 15th 1796, General Bonaparte entered Milan at the head of that young army which had just crossed the bridge at Lodi and showed the world that after so many centuries Caesar and Alexander had a successor. The miracles of bravery and genius which Italy witnessed during those months awoke a sleeping people.

Stendhal, *La Chartreuse de Parme*, p. 1

The view from Vienna during that last decade of the eighteenth century either warmed the hearts of its citizens or filled them with terror. The ruling class was dominated mind and soul by the fear of change; although the advocates of the feudal *status quo* professed to the world that it was immutable, they saw the threat and dreaded the inevitably approaching upheaval. The more open minds in this society on the other hand watched the future which was taking shape in Europe with hope and fascination; it coloured their thinking and profoundly influenced their creative efforts. To understand the work they produced we have to know what they saw, writers, artists, musicians—Beethoven among them—looking out from their confines in the old-fashioned fastness of Vienna.

From 1792 onwards they saw the revolution spread like a flood through France, lapping the borders of some lands and encroaching into others, carried forward by its armies across frontiers, welcomed by the populace here, repulsed by counter-revolution there. Even where the people's divisions had not penetrated, their ideas entered. Great social changes, upheavals and eruptions were taking place all over the continent, welcomed, feared, or awaited in many frames of mind but never with indifference.

As the French Republic was seen to be threatened by its enemies and to be reacting by internal terror, attitudes changed; many formerly friendly German intellectuals—Schiller, for one, and Klopstock, like the English Lake poets—cooled or grew hostile, while other basically revolutionary spirits like Beethoven remained sympathetic. But all alike watched developments in France with intense interest and anxiously followed the reports of their effects on neighbouring countries, and of the military activities which ensued.

It was clear after 1793, when England joined the counter-revolutionary side, that Europe had said goodbye to peace for a long time to come, and the continuous hostilities, raging now in one area, now in another—the Rhineland, Savoy, the Netherlands, Italy—became, if not the dominant factor, at least part of the background to everyday life. As 1794 and 1795 passed, the war gathered momentum, surging back and forth across the boundaries of the Holy Roman Empire, and in Holland, Belgium, Switzerland, governments and governing classes collapsed before revolutionary republicanism.[1] In Austria, fear of revolt grew; attempts to stem the tide by repressive measures against "Jacobins" (such as those already mentioned)[2] were useless. The "Liberty lads" forged ahead, enthusiastically carrying their message of equality and fraternity to their neighbours.

There were occasional reversals, as in 1795, when the French were halted in north-west Germany by Austrian armies under Prince Charles Habsburg. But royal satisfaction was soon dissipated by the news that in Italy a certain young French general was rapidly overrunning the imperial provinces, taking town after town—Rivoli, Modena, Milan—declaring republics, besieging Mantua, where General Wurmser had a large garrison of Austrian forces, even alarming the Pope by rousing the oppressed people of southern Italy.

It was clear that young Napoleon was a military genius who had through personal dynamism, courage and idealism inspired a hungry, ill-equipped rabble of soldiers to achieve fantastic feats. He had fired them in Nice early in 1796 with words which became famous: "Soldiers, you are naked and ill-fed. The Government owes you much and can give you nothing . . . I intend to lead you into the most fertile plains in the world. Rich provinces and great cities will be in your power, there you will find honour, glory, wealth."[3] This ragged, demoralised band of men, faced with an army twice as numerous—Sardinians, Austrians, Neapolitans—inspired surprise and admiration even from their opponents: "Nakedness, privations and patience", exclaimed Melzi, the Italian historian: "to sleep on the bare earth, to forget all needs, do without tents and baggage, be content with bread

---

[1] Merryn Williams (ed.), *Revolutions*, p. 28 (London 1971 Penguin)
[2] Cf Chap. 2, pp. 9–10   [3] Heriot, *The French in Italy*, p. 87

and bran—like this one could fight for a hundred years. . . . Why has this truth escaped those who direct military operations from their studies and chancelleries?"

It was apparent too, to those not politically blind, that the French were greeted as liberators in many parts of Italy; "in that strange welter of democracy and tyranny which Napoleon's grenadiers brought in, the foundations of Italian national consciousness were laid".[1] It became common knowledge that the equalitarians brought with them the breath of a new age that swept away the abuses of centuries and made it impossible for men so freed to be treated in the same way again.

When the French entered Milan there was a wave of enthusiasm caused by the hypnotic personality of Bonaparte himself, by the parades, trees of liberty, republican fêtes, speeches, jubilation; "the contrast between the young ardent French soldiers and the cold creaking formality of Austria seemed like the metamorphosis of winter into spring, of stuffy middle age into the pristine confidence of youth".[2]

Stendhal best of all describes "the profound emotions aroused by the unexpected arrival of the French army", "the new and passionate way of life that sprang up": "A whole people discovered on 15 May 1796 that everything which until then it had respected was supremely ridiculous, if not actually hateful. The departure of the last Austrian regiment marked the collapse of the old ideas: to risk one's life became the fashion. . . . People saw that in order to be really happy after centuries of cloying sensations, it was necessary to love one's country with real love and to seek heroic actions. They had been plunged in the darkest night by the despotism of the Habsburgs; they overturned it and found themselves flooded with daylight."[3]

Wherever the French took over, the leaven of liberty worked. Bologna, Ferrara, Modena, Reggio, took up arms, planted *arboli de libertà*, proclaimed independence. Later on some resentment was caused by the high-handed way in which the French took toll of the rich palaces, helping themselves to art treasures at the instigation of the Directory, but the "Jacobin" patriots persisted in their enthusiasm, spreading plans for revolution in all Italy, proposing the abolition of the Pope, lighting bonfires of feudal emblems, insulting priests and burning Archduke Ferdinand in effigy.[4] Milan became a great labora-

---

[1] Trevelyan, J., *History of Italy*, p. 297   [2] Heriot, *op. cit.*, p. 97
[3] Stendhal, *La Chartreuse de Parme*, Chap. 1.
[4] Giuseppe Rossini, father of the composer and town trumpeter of Pesaro, led an orchestra for "tree of liberty" celebrations in 1797 and 1800, his son (aged six) acting as "a small mascot". Weinstock, *Rossini*, pp. 6–7.

tory of political doctrines, a school of liberty for the whole peninsula; the red-green-white tricolour which flew over its buildings (and is today the national flag) was a mark of republicanism.

It was some time before the Austrian government grasped how real was the French conquest of hearts and minds. They basked in the successes of Archduke Charles who had driven back the French in the north where only two Rhineland forts remained in enemy hands. But the imperial euphoria was rudely dispelled in the summer of 1796: "All the couriers who reached Vienna with news of Prince Charles' successes were followed by couriers from Wurmser bringing accounts of disasters," wrote William Hazlitt, in his *Life of Napoleon*. "The Court passed September in alternations of joy and sorrow; the satisfaction derived from its triumphs did not compensate for the consternation caused by its defeats. Germany was saved, but Italy looked like being lost." Moreover, "the French soldiers were in excellent condition and spirits. Public opinion (in Italy) was also decidedly in their favour", as it was in most of the oppressed dominions.[1]

French achievements culminated in the victory on 14 November 1796 at Arcole, a hard-fought battle during which Napoleon made a dramatically heroic gesture: "He seized a flag, rushed on the bridge and there planted it: . . . the grenadiers persisted in keeping possession of their general. They seized him by his arms and clothes and dragged him along with them amidst the dead, the dying and the smoke; he was precipitated into a morass in which he sunk up to the middle, surrounded by the enemy. The cry was raised, 'Forward, soldiers, to save the General!' They immediately turned back, rushed upon the enemy, drove him beyond the bridge, and Napoleon was rescued."[2] There were many such stories of incredible devotion, aides dying while protecting their officers, Napoleon receiving three wounds as he covered the body of General Lannes, proclaiming republican victory as he struggled back filthy but glorious to his men. These heroic exploits must have been widely recounted, even back in Vienna.

As the French swept from one success to the next during the autumn, Austrian alarm grew. A call went out for volunteers to fight in Italy and the whole ramshackle monarchy in its hour of need was cemented by a strong impulse of loyalty and nationalism. Beethoven, oddly divided between pro-republicanism and local patriotism, put a battle-song to music—the "Farewell of Vienna's citizens". In this instance

neither the poem nor the sentiments can greatly have appealed to the
composer, but for once he chose to be fashionable; neither the music
nor Friedelberg's verses can be described as divinely inspired, but they
reflected the general mood:

> Friends! Wish our noble journey all success,
> Follow us, beauties, not with looks of distress
> But confident of victory and fame
> Which we will boldly win and when returning claim.
> Welcomed by our Vienna we will be,
> With flags aloft, the proofs of bravery.

These somewhat brash words, ironically dated 15 November, the day
after Arcole, were belied by events. Most of the volunteers failed to
return; many were left dead on the north Italian hills, along with the
soldiers of the regular army. At Arcole, Hazlitt says, "numerous
columns of prisoners and a great number of trophies filed through the
French camp"—those trophies so recently and proudly borne out of
Vienna. At Verona the Austrian general Davidowitch lost 3,000 Croats,
and Alvinzi 18,000 men, 6,000 of them prisoners. The French army
re-entered Verona, and "it would be difficult to describe the astonish-
ment and enthusiasm of the inhabitants".[1]

As news of the slaughter and of the French victories filtered back, the
name Napoleon began to be a word of terror to the Austrian anti-
Jacobins; to those like Beethoven and his friends sympathetic to the
French Republic it symbolised heroic idealism. It must have seemed
stupid and callous to send brave Austrian boys against this apparently
invincible man in an effort to deny the Italians the independence that
they craved.

Whatever the feelings of individuals, there was general apprehension
about the future. Taking advantage of a few weeks' lull in the fighting,
civilian Germans in Italy packed up and hastened homeward, bringing
accounts of what they had witnessed.

Beethoven's former Bonn friends, the violinist Andreas Romberg
and his 'cellist cousin Bernard, arrived in Vienna destitute from Rome;
a benefit concert was arranged for them in January 1797, but, although
they later became famous, they were then hardly known, and it was
only thanks to Beethoven who performed at the concert that it did not
fall flat. It was not noticed in any newspaper, and cannot have been
much help to the penurious artists. The truth was that the thoughts of

the Viennese were on more important things than the indulgence of their musical taste at benefit concerts.[1]

The lull in hostilities after the battle of Arcole only lasted two months, during which the Emperor raised new forces, and Napoleon made peace with the Pope who was terrified of the French encroachment into Italy and willingly signed the treaty of Tolentino on 18 February 1797. Having secured that flank, Napoleon offered terms to Franz, who rejected them without ceremony and continued to mobilise. On 19 March the French general addressed his troops in Bassano in tones which must have sounded ominous indeed to the Austrians. "Soldiers," he reminded them, "You have been victorious in 14 pitched battles, 70 actions; you have taken 100,000 prisoners, 500 fieldpieces, 2,000 cannon . . ." Italy was conquered; overtures to Vienna had been rejected. "Of all the foes who conspired to stifle the Republic in its birth, the Emperor alone remains before you. He and his perfidious cabinet smile with satisfaction at the woes of the Continent." The French proposals had been ignored by Vienna. There was no hope of getting peace except by invading the Hereditary States, not only Austria, but Hungary, Bohemia and other dominions. "It is liberty that you carry to the brave Hungarian nation—you will find there a brave people," Napoleon told his men, ordering them "to respect their religion and manners and protect their property".[2]

In spite of the warning, the Emperor would not talk. In March 1797 Napoleon led his men north into the mountains, forcing the passage of the Tagliamento and Isonzo; they advanced in three prongs, one of these taking Trieste and Fiume, followed up with the conquest of much of Carinthia and the Tyrol, and headed rapidly towards Vienna.

On 7 April, conscious at last of reality, Franz called out the Landsturm. His appeal won an enthusiastic response from the Austrian people, who did not know what they were up against, how inferior their generals were to Napoleon and his adjutants Massena and Bernadotte, or how high was the morale of the French army. All over Austria "large towns offered battalions of volunteers . . . Vienna raised four battalions who received their colours from the Empress, embroidered with her own hands", says Hazlitt.[3] These banners did not survive the battles, but they survive in the songs which Beethoven set; the first, roughly translated, begins

---

[1] Thayer, p. 190
[2] Hazlitt, *op. cit.*, vol. 13, p. 266
[3] Ibid., vol. 13, p. 252

Let us follow these our banners
By Theresa's art enriched;
Their gold trimmings tell us truly
Virtue makes us all like kings

the second:

Mann, Weib und Kind in Oesterreich
Fühlt tief den eignen Wert:
Nie Franken! werden wir von euch besiegt
Besieget, nie betört.

(Man, woman and child in Austria know your own worth:
Never, Frenchmen, shall we be conquered or duped by you.)

In neither case were words or music in the least inspired; the composer's
instinct must have told him how empty were the boasts. In less than
twenty days the Austrians had been defeated in two pitched battles
and several mêlées and driven back beyond the Brenner. The French
H.Q. was not more than 60 leagues (160 miles) from Vienna; Austria's
forces were reduced to less than 80,000 compared to the French
armies' 130,000 which were still advancing.

Hazlitt wrote that "the news of these events . . . struck the inhabitants of Vienna with dismay. The capital was menaced and was destitute of all means of effectual resistance". The most valuable effects and
important papers were packed up. The Danube was covered with boats
which were transporting goods into Hungary "whither also the young
Archdukes and Archduchesses were sent" (there were five daughters
and three sons in Franz's exemplary family). "The people complained
that the ministry did not think of making peace, though they had no
means of stopping the advance of the French arms."[1]

Naturally, people were angry and alarmed. They had been led to
believe that the French were savages if not cannibals, and they now saw
themselves being left to a fate worse than death at their hands. A 16-
page pamphlet was put out to reassure them, with "Answers to the
question: Will the French come to Vienna? To calm a timid inhabi-
tant". The arguments were that (a) the Austrian army would bar the
way, (b) the French could not come by Hungary as they did not know
the language; (c) if they did arrive they would break their heads on the
ramparts of Vienna. None the less, all able-bodied citizens were
called on to enroll, the walls were fortified, and an Austrian general

[1] Hazlitt, *op. cit.*, vol. 13, p. 271

announced that he would teach the Viennese to eat horsemeat—not a very alluring prospect for the food-loving citizens.[1] There is no record of how Beethoven reacted, but with his pro-French sympathies he was probably not unduly panicky.

In fact, Napoleon was not able to reach Vienna that year; owing to either incompetence in Paris or to jealousy of the young general, the Directory did not send him enough reinforcements. He halted at Leoben some 90 miles off, and offered a truce which was accepted by the Emperor; a ceasefire followed, and peace was restored in August 1797 by the Treaty of Campoformio. This gave France the left bank of the Rhine and confirmed Napoleon's political organisation of Italy, except for Venice.

It was all very humiliating for Austria, but her people gave a sigh of relief. Napoleon made some magnanimous gestures, and became almost popular through his kind treatment of the Archbishop of Leoben, and his riposte to the Emperor's acknowledgement of the French Republic, given in writing in the treaty: "Strike that out," said Napoleon. "The Republic is like the sun which shines by its own light; none but the blind can fail to see it."[2]

One can imagine Beethoven's delight at this remark, and his pleasure too at one of Napoleon's conditions in the treaty—the release of Lafayette from the dungeon of Olmütz where he had been incarcerated for four years. (This article cost Napoleon more trouble than all the rest, says Hazlitt; Emperor Franz was no doubt averse to letting any of his prisoners go free.)

Certain other conditions, such as the French demand for a national palace in Vienna, and a French theatre for their ministers, were rejected as excessive by the Austrians, who refused to consider themselves as a conquered people. In the end, though, the treaty was signed, and it was announced that an Ambassador of France would be taking up his post in Vienna. The choice of envoy was the subject of much speculation and of surprise when he turned out to be Jean Baptiste Bernadotte, the young general who had been Napoleon's aide-de-camp in the recent campaigns. Bernadotte was an extremely able man, of humble origin and a distinguished soldier. In 1796 he had been sent with reinforcements from the Rhine to Napoleon in Italy, and he had led many actions on that front "with the utmost coolness and intrepidity"; he was mentioned in a dispatch as "one of the

[1] Robert, A, L'Idée nationale autrichienne, p. 188
[2] Hazlitt, op. cit., vol. 13, p. 273

staunchest friends of the Republic—whose principles would as little allow him to capitulate with the enemies of freedom as with honour itself". (A tribute which rings a little hollow with hindsight, as we learn from his later career.)

There was, despite all these testimonials, little love lost between Bernadotte and Napoleon who did not altogether trust him and after the treaty of Campoformio withdrew from his control half the forces he had brought from the Rhineland. Bernadotte was so offended that he asked the Directory to give him another command or allow him to resign. Instead of either they made him Ambassador to Austria, to the annoyance of Napoleon who objected that "a soldier is a bad envoy to an enemy who has often been beaten", and on account "of the violence of his temper".

According to Hazlitt, "Bernadotte suffered his temper to get the better of his judgment and committed several imprudences. One day (13 April 1798) he thought fit to hoist the tri-coloured flag at the top of his Hotel without apparent reason for doing so. The populace rose, tore down the flag and insulted Bernadotte," and in the excitement of popular feeling, strong cavalry protection alone saved his life. Bernadotte was recalled to Paris a few days later. The Directory sent a message to the Councils proposing war against Austria; this was abortive, owing to Napoleon's objection: "If you intended war, you should have prepared for it independently of Bernadotte who has been materially to blame."[1] It would indeed have been a pity if the bloodshed had started all over again just because of an undiplomatic gesture by an over-enthusiastic diplomat. At a party in Paris, Talleyrand (then only forty-eight, but already highly respected) commented on the incident that "wars would be too frequent if every time an ambassador was insulted arms had to be taken up to avenge him".[2] He thought that Bernadotte should not have left his post in Vienna but should have demanded apologies and "réparation éclatante"—a large-scale compensation—as amende honorable.

During most of his short stay in Vienna, however, the ambassador was respected and popular. He arrived in February 1798 and was presented on 8 April to the Emperor, "who held more conversation with him than any other". He was praised as being well behaved, sedate and modest. Cultured and musical, he had in his retinue Rodolphe Kreutzer, the great French violinist.

Distinguished local musicians were welcomed at the Embassy, and

[1] Hazlitt, op. cit., vol. 13, p. 324   [2] Orieux, Talleyrand, p. 294

Count Moritz Lichnowsky (the Prince's brother) took Beethoven along and introduced him to the ambassador. The two men, politically and culturally sympathetic, got on well and Beethoven often visited Bernadotte during his short residence, and made and talked music with the French diplomats. Through this friendship he must have learned a great deal about the Republic, its plans and achievements, and heard stories about the campaign from which his French friends had so recently returned. The sounds of battle and heroic deeds which ring through so much of his work were inspired by what the young general described; and the festive republican music written for great popular gatherings in Paris by Gossec and Méhul was certainly brought to his notice by Kreutzer, himself a composer of "people's music" at this time.

Beethoven used many of their effects in his later choral work, and even the Ninth Symphony owes musical ideas to the "Choral du Peuple" of Méhul.[1]

But the most direct result of his contact with the French was the Third Symphony, if we are to believe Schindler, who says in his biography that "the first idea for the Heroic Symphony emanated from General Bernadotte, who esteemed Beethoven very highly". It seems unlikely that the general suggested that the symphony should glorify Napoleon, with whom he was not at all on good terms, but most probable that he urged Beethoven to write something in honour of the Republic, its victories and its heroes; and the composer would naturally have been very receptive to the idea.

There can be no doubt that the "Eroica" Symphony grew from a seed planted at that time. The soil in which it germinated was the mass of impressions made by those previous four years of war. And though it would be an insult to consider it for a moment as "programme music" every movement owes its essence to the happenings abroad and to Beethoven's view of them—the great armies poised for battle or joined in action, brave Austrian volunteers against enthusiastic republicans, the cavalry galloping in their thousands over the Italian plains, the infantry struggling up the mountainside, individual soldiers forging ahead with their banners in heroic self-sacrifice, all this is in the first movement; the sorrow of death and the dignity of the funeral in the second; the exhilaration of victory is in the Scherzo and the joy of triumphant human will-power in the finale. And beneath it all,

[1] Beethoven was also much interested in the development in the French Republic of the "magasin de la musique", a kind of co-operative for distributing work by new composers.

expressed in the dialectic of the symphonic form, is the conflict between the old and the new—the struggle for the future—a reflection of the changing world beyond Vienna. This music, having been conceived in these events, had to be written in quite new terms, to break out of the old forms, taking shapes and sounds that had never been heard in past or present but belonging to the future. The symphony was to proclaim with new rhythms, combinations of instruments, harmonies, phrases, a musical revolution born of social revolution.

When writing the symphony in the following years, Beethoven was to build on this revolutionary structure a great masterpiece of personal faith. He embodied in it his own individual experience of struggle against misfortune, sickness and despair, his own particular response to challenge, identifying his personal conquest over fate with Napoleon's legendary conquests. So every aspect of heroism—personal, historic, mythical—can be heard in the musical ideas worked out in the symphony; but the hidden source of these is Beethoven's experience of the changing world of the 1790s, with its hopes of a bright future to be won by the heroic will of mankind. Rooted deep in the consciousness of the composer, this was to influence not only the "Eroica", but all the work to come.

4

Fears, Faith and Friendship
1800–1806

The presence of war and social unrest which had brooded over the latter years of the eighteenth century receded from Vienna after 1799. Although there were several outbreaks of hostilities, halted by as many truces, in neighbouring lands, the Austrian scene was dominated by other preoccupations. Cultural life resumed, salons were restored (including Caroline Pichler's) and music flourished. Beethoven was extremely busy. By the turn of the century he had won success and recognition unusual for a man of under thirty. He had worked through his apprenticeship and was now writing copiously, using his many teachers' contributions to his proficiency, and drawing on all the sources of classical mastery which he had absorbed: the best in Handel, Haydn, Bach, and what was not too elusive of the genius of Mozart. In the works of 1800 he used, perfected and expanded the basic classical forms. He summed up the classical sonata in the Piano Sonata in B flat (Op. 22), the String Quartet in his Op. 18, 1 to 6, the symphony and concerto forms in the First (C major) Symphony and the Piano Concerto in C minor (Op. 37); these can all be called "classical" in spite of the original features in them which startled some of the critics.

From now on Beethoven was to break new ground and advance to the unexplored country where romantic freedom was to be born, leaving the music of the "first period" behind him, though often retaining its melodic and rhythmic ideas for later use.

He lost interest in much of his early work, and when friends and critics later praised the Septet for wind and strings (completed in April 1800) he "could not endure it and grew angry because of the universal applause with which it was received".

When a pupil played some early piano variations, he refused to believe he had written "such nonsense"; and in 1801 he wrote to his friend the violinist Amenda (to whom he had given a copy of Op. 18 no. 1 two years earlier), "Don't lend your Quartet to anybody, because I have greatly changed it, having just learned how to write quartets properly."[1]

Praise or criticism left him equally cool, and he was not deflected from his course by the unfriendly reviewers. His inner certainty protected him from attacks such as that on the Violin Sonatas, Op. 12, in the *Allgemeine Musikalische Zeitung* (*A.M.Z.*) of June 1799: "Herr von Beethoven goes his own gait; but what a bizarre and singular gait it is! . . a heaping up of difficulties on difficulties till one loses all patience and enjoyment"; and on the Piano Variations, WoO 73: "What awkward passages are in them, where harsh tirades in continuous semitones create an ugly relationship and the reverse! . . . He may be able to improvise but he does not know how to write variations."[2]

To be fair to the *A.M.Z.* there were also more percipient critics, by whom his eccentricities were allowed: We read in late 1799, "Beethoven is a man of genius possessed of originality and who goes his own way"; and later still, "It confirms my long-held opinion that Beethoven in time can effect a revolution in music, like Mozart's. He is hastening towards it with great strides."

The composer knew his powers, and now that he was more or less financially secure he could live his life as he chose, free from the need to attend society functions, able to compose as and what he liked. Writing to Wegeler on 29 June 1801 he tells him, "My situation is not at all bad. Lichnowsky who, believe it or not, has always been my warmest friend here, last year set aside a fixed sum of 600 florins which I can draw upon as long as I have no suitable post. My compositions bring me in a lot, and I can say I have more commissions than I can carry out. I have six or seven publishers after each piece and might have more if I chose; people don't bargain with me now, I ask and they pay."

He wants to assist any needy friend ("if I have no money in my purse, I only have to get to work and in a short time he has been helped") and his social conscience moves him to add that "if conditions are improved in our land, my art will be used for the good of the poor". He would like to help young Ferdinand Ries, the son of his friend and former teacher, he says, but "I think that to make his fortune he would do better in Paris than Vienna. Vienna is bursting with people and so even the most able find it difficult to support themselves. In the autumn or winter, when everything starts up again in the town, I will see what I can do for him. . . ."¹

On 1 July he wrote to the violinist Karl Amenda ("no Viennese friend—but one who springs from the soil of my own land"), that "I could sell everything I compose five times over and at a good price".² But the bright prospects were overcast by a shadow. In both the above letters he confessed that in spite of material security he was terribly anxious and unhappy: "That evil demon, my bad health, has put a spoke in my wheel." Since 1799 he had suffered from almost chronic stomach trouble, colic, and diarrhoea, and now, worst of all, he was threatened with deafness. "My ears hum and buzz all the time, day and night. I can truly say my life is miserable, for two years I have avoided almost all social gatherings because I can't possibly say to people 'I am deaf'. To give you an idea of this wonderful deafness . . . in the theatre, if I am a little way off I don't hear the high notes of the instruments or singers. . . . Often I can scarcely hear someone speaking softly, the sounds, yes, but not the words. But as soon as anyone shouts it is unbearable. Heaven knows what will become of me. . . . Already I have often cursed my Creator and my existence. If possible I will defy my fate, though there will be moments in my life when I shall be the unhappiest of God's creatures."³

Wegeler evidently replied sympathetically, and Beethoven wrote again on 16 November giving details of his trouble, in a most pathetic outburst: "You would hardly believe how lonely and sad my life has been for the last two years. My bad hearing haunted me like a ghost and I fled from mankind, must have seemed a misanthropist and yet am so far from being one." He declared that he was determined to be happy, not unhappy: "No, I could not endure that. I will seize fate by the throat, it shall not overcome me. O it would be so beautiful to live a thousand times!"⁴

His determination, and a brief period of cheerfulness were due to his interest in "a dear fascinating girl", the Countess Guicciardi, one of his pupils. But she was an aristocrat, destined by convention to be the wife of somebody of her own station. Marriage with her was out of the question for Beethoven; a few months later he was again in the depths of depression.

In the summer of 1802 he took refuge in the little village of Heiligenstadt, about four miles from the city centre, trying to escape from his

¹ *Briefe*, 14, pp. 18–22   ² *Letters*, L. 53, p. 63
³ *Briefe*, 15, pp. 19–22   ⁴ *Ibid.*, 16, pp. 23–4

miseries in long walks over the pleasant countryside. But consciousness that his hearing was deteriorating drove him to moments of despair. In one of these he wrote a "testament", addressed to his brothers, pouring out his troubles: "O you people who declare me to be malignant, stubborn or misanthropic, what wrong you do me, you do not know the secret reason for my seeming so to you. . . . Though born with a fiery lively temperament, and inclined to enjoy the distractions of society, I have had to cut myself off, to live my life alone. . . . If I go near company I am overwhelmed by feverish anxiety because I am afraid of the danger that my condition may be noticed. . . . How humiliating for me when somebody standing next me heard a flute in the distance and I heard nothing, or someone heard a shepherd singing and again I heard nothing." He struggled between despair and revolt: "Such things almost drove me to desperation, little more was needed for me to end my life—it was only my art, that alone, that held me back, ah it seemed impossible to me to leave the world before I had brought forth everything I felt within me. . . . As my guide it seems I must choose patience—and this I have. I hope unceasingly that my determination will last until it pleases the pitiless Parcae to break the thread. . . ."

In the testament he leaves his "small fortune (if so it can be called)", including Prince Lichnowsky's instruments, to his brothers, begging them to divide it fairly and amicably. "How happy I shall be if I can still be useful to you in my grave—so be it—" His words "with joy I hasten to meet death" are belied by his longing to create: "If death comes before I have had the opportunity to develop all my creative capacities, it will still come too soon in spite of my hard fate. . . ."[1]

He added a short postscript to the lengthy document; in this, his desperation is touchingly revealed not only in its words, but in the distraught dashes which punctuate it like gasps of misery. "10 October 1802—so I take my leave of you—sadly—the dearest hope—which I brought here, to be cured at least to a certain degree—this must now be quite abandoned, like the autumn leaves fallen and faded, my hope has withered too, almost as I came here—I am leaving—even the high courage—which often inspired me during beautiful summer days— has disappeared—O Providence—let me have one pure day of joy—it is so long since I heard the inner resonance of true joy—O when, when, O God—can I feel it again in Nature's temple, or in Man's?—Never?— no—it would be too hard."[2]

It was evidently in the rare moments of "high courage" that Beethoven composed his Second Symphony in D major, which is predominantly cheerful and serene; and he must have overcome his depression for longish periods in order to produce the other works of this year: the Three Sonatas for Piano, Op. 31, the Sonatas for Violin and Piano, Op. 30, Two Romances for Violin and Orchestra, the Bagatelles (Op. 33) and two sets of Variations for Piano, besides settings and various arrangements of Italian songs.

From all the evidence of friends, of letters and of the music, Beethoven had indeed "seized fate by the throat", and only very occasionally allowed himself to relapse into despair. When he did express himself as in the passages quoted, it was to release the tension of the inner struggle. That struggle, which was continuous, nearly always ended in Beethoven's winning by sheer strength of will.

After 1802 he rarely expressed pessimism, though his spasmodic outbursts of anger due to ill-health, irritation or frustration were as proverbial as were his good-humour and gruff laughter. He got on with people because nearly everyone recognised that temperament and genius were inseparable, and accepted his rudeness as the form of honesty which it was.

Deafness and illness did not prevent his getting an important post in 1801, as composer to Schikaneder's new Theater-an-der-Wien, which had moved into the centre of Vienna from the suburb where *The Magic Flute* had been produced, and was one of the focal points for opera and concerts. Beethoven was given living-quarters there and engaged to produce one work a year. He thus had a platform from which he could conduct his new works, and he met the leading people in the musical world on their own ground.

Among others he got to know the writer August Kotzebue, editor of a controversial journal in Berlin and leader of a faction against Goethe, and who later wrote the libretto for *König Stefan*; although he was a somewhat unsympathetic character (and came to an untimely end by political assassination) we have him to thank for an account of Vienna which vividly shows the richness of the semi-private musical life there in 1802. Amateur concerts in salons, he said, almost always included works by Beethoven—"clever, serious, full of deep significance and character, but occasionally a little too glaring".[1]

Besides his duties at the theatre Beethoven managed between 1802 and 1804 to produce an astonishing number of compositions. As well as

[1] Thayer, p. 324

those mentioned above, he completed (in 1803) his oratorio *Christus am Oelberg*, the Kreutzer Sonata, a Trio for Piano, 'Cello and Clarinet, Piano Variations on "God Save the King" and "Rule Britannia",[1] several vocal ensembles and at least ten songs. As before, his choice of words was significant. Among them were six religious poems by Gellert, a contemporary Protestant minister, and a semi-religious lyric, "Der Wachtelschlag" (The Quail).

The settings to these songs are perhaps the nearest we can get to a direct expression of Beethoven's religious ideas at this time. No churchgoer, he had an eighteenth-century faith in a God who had created the universe, cared for his creatures and established moral laws. The Spiritual Songs express this faith simply and directly: "The Heavens declare the glory of God", proclaims one; another, "Love of my neighbour" is a call for toleration and brotherly love; "About Death" is a solemn intonation, over the note of a tolling bell, and "Contrition", rather more conventional, echoes an idea which recurs in Beethoven's private note-books. The connection between God and nature which was so often in his mind is expressed in musical form in *The Quail*: the bird's call is interpreted by the words (in the same rhythm) "Praise your God!—Love your God!—Trust in God!" Later, Beethoven was to introduce the quail's note into the Sixth Symphony. One is tempted to wonder whether that motif is a repetition of the message in the 1803 song; and whether a similar phrase in the Piano Sonata, Op. 28 (The Pastoral) also represents the God-fearing quail?

Beethoven was too deeply imbued with the ideas of the Enlightenment to be affected by Church dogma or superstition. His God was an intensely personal one, and needed no clerical intermediary. But he copied out many passages from mystics and divines, such as the scattered sentences of Sturm's *Betrachtungen*, which he kept by him and which express his own religious attitude:

"To the praise of Thy goodness I confess that Thou hast tried all means to draw me to Thee. Now it hath pleased Thee to let me feel the heavy hand of Thy wrath. . . . Sickness and misfortune hast Thou sent to bring me to a contemplation of my digressions. . . . O God, cease not to labour for my improvement. Only let me in whatsoever manner pleases Thee, turn to Thee and be fruitful of good works."[2]

---

[1] In spite of his admiration for Napoleon at this time, Beethoven had a high opinion of the British constitutional monarchy.
[2] Thayer, pp. 391-2

Nothing, either then or later, suggests that Beethoven was ever inclined to join a church—he was, on the contrary, strongly anti-clerical, for he saw the clergy as supporters of the *ancien régime*, and he was bitterly satirical about the hypocrisy of those who proclaimed themselves God-fearing but in fact flouted the basic laws of Christianity every day. He would have agreed with the visitor who wrote, after attending service at St Stephen's Cathedral, "I have more than once been disgusted at the contrast between the real earnestness of the poor people at their prayers . . . and the open unconcealed laughter of the priests at the altar. . . . What a shameless fraud are they practising upon the credulity of others!"[1]

Beethoven's strong feelings about the Roman Catholic Church were one reason for his waning enthusiasm for France. He was still a republican, but his faith in the French government had recently been badly shaken. Events had proved the Directory to be far from perfect; it had instituted hateful laws and unjust banishments, and had handed over complete authority to Bonaparte at the 18th Brumaire. As a democrat, Beethoven could not approve of this assumption of complete power. Though Napoleon made people address him as Citizen Consul, and surrounded himself with statues of Roman heroes such as Brutus and Scipio, he was flirting with royalists and collaborating with the Church.

When the Treaty of Amiens was signed in 1802 Napoleon had a solemn *Te Deum* sung in Notre Dame Cathedral to celebrate the re-establishment of peace and the restoration of religion. One of his generals said of the occasion that "there lacked only the hundred thousand men who got themselves killed to do away with all that". Thibaudeau, a staunch Jacobin, wrote to Bonaparte that "the men of the Revolution, no longer able to oppose the counter-revolution, will help you carry it out because you are now their only guarantee".[2]

In 1801 Napoleon had signed a Concordat with Pope Pius VII, restoring Church property and authority to the papacy. Beethoven expressed ironical disapproval of his hero in a letter (18 April 1802) to a Leipzig publisher, Franz Hofmeister, who had suggested at some lady's behest that he might write a "revolutionary sonata". "Are you quite mad, gentlemen?—to suggest I should write a sonata of that sort?—At the time of the revolutionary fever, well, yes, something of the sort might have been possible, but now, when everything is back in the old

---

[1] *Musical Ramble*, p. 143
[2] Maurois, *A History of France* (Methuen 1964), p. 324

rut, Bonaparte concluding a concordat with the Pope, such a sonata?
—if you were asking for a 3 voice mass for Sancta Maria or a Vesper,
etc.—then I'd take up my pen right away and write off a Credo in
unum . . . but Good God, a sonata of that sort in these new Christian
times—ho ho, leave me out . . ."[1]

None the less, he was not put off the idea of a heroic republican
symphony which had been at the back of his mind since Bernadotte's
encouragement in 1798. Between May and November 1803 he worked
on it and completed it in April 1804, still intending to dedicate it to
Napoleon. Ferdinand Ries, son of his Bonn friend, who was now
studying music in Vienna, wrote that "he had Bonaparte in his mind,
as he was when he was First Consul. Beethoven esteemed him greatly
at the time and likened him to the greatest Roman Consuls. I saw a
copy of the score lying on his table, with the word 'Buonaparte' at the
extreme top of the title page, and at the very bottom 'Luigi van
Beethoven', but not another word. . . ." A fair copy had been made in
the spring of 1804, to be forwarded to Paris through the French
Embassy, but it is not known whether it was ever sent. (Probably not,
as it surely would have subsequently come to light in France.)[2]

During May 1804, acts were passed by the French Tribunate and
Senate elevating the First Consul to Emperor. He assumed the crown
on 18 May, and a solemn proclamation was issued on the 20th. When
a few days later Ries brought Beethoven the news that Bonaparte had
proclaimed himself Emperor, the composer "flew into a rage and cried
out: 'Is he then too nothing more than an ordinary human being? Now
he too will trample on the rights of man and indulge only his ambition.
He will exalt himself above all others and become a tyrant!' Beethoven
then went to the table, took hold of the title page by the top, tore it in
two and threw it on the floor. The first page was rewritten and only
then did the symphony receive the title 'sinfonia eroica'." On the final
copy's first page Beethoven wrote "composed on Bonaparte", and the
published first edition bears the title "to the memory of a great man"
—words with distinct overtones of nostalgia for the greatness which
had meant so much to Beethoven and was now a lost illusion.

This Third Symphony in E flat (Op. 55) was performed for the first
time in February 1805, at one of the semi-public concerts organised by
two of the bankers who were beginning to take over the functions of
the old aristocracy. The players found the music extremely hard, and
so did the critics. One wrote that "the new symphony, so difficult,

new, original, strange in its effects and of such unusual lengths, did not please"; another considered it "extremely difficult of performance . . . a tremendously expanded, daring and wild fantasia . . . often loses itself in lawlessness".—"There is too much that is glaring and bizarre," said a third critic, ". . . a sense of unity is almost completely lost."

On 7 April the symphony was performed publicly in the Theater-an-der-Wien, and equally misfired. One listener shouted out, "I'll give another kreutzer if the thing will only stop!" But when it was played shortly after this humiliating failure to Prince Louis Ferdinand of Prussia, at Lobkowitz's country seat, "its lofty contents were recognised".[1] Whether the hearers recognised its full meaning, the whole revolutionary import of the work, is doubtful; it is much easier for modern listeners than it was for contemporaries to hear the wind of change blowing through it and to assess its value to music in rushing the barriers and breaking through to the future. It may be because of its citadel-storming quality that this great revolutionary work was Beethoven's favourite among his symphonies, as he told his biographer Schindler many years later.

Beethoven's personal life during the years 1802 to 1806 was not unhappy, and seems to have been reasonably settled (apart from the fact that he changed his residence five times in five years, besides moving into different lodgings in the country every summer). He fell in love several times, the first time with his pupil Countess Guicciardi (this helped him through the misery of 1801-2) the second time with Josephine Brunsvik, also a pupil, sister of his dear friends Count Franz and Teresa Brunsvik.

This affair was deeply serious but hopeless. Josephine was married to a Count Deym, but had separated from him and lived at the family house with her three children. All the factors endemic in the social system which at various times prevented Beethoven from marrying a woman he loved, combined to forbid a union with Josephine: she was a girl of the aristocratic class; she was married, and would not consider a "sensuous" affair outside her wedding contract; being a Roman Catholic, she could not divorce, and even after Deym's death in 1804 she would not "break holy vows". So although loving Beethoven deeply, and encouraging him by accepting and answering his passionate letters, there was no future in the affair. Beethoven longed for marriage: he pleaded, stormed, poured out his heart in correspondence, all in vain. In the end he admitted that it was perhaps better that way. "If I

[1] Thayer, pp. 350-1

had spent my time on women and love", he said, "what would have become of my art?"

This did not prevent him subsequently often falling in and out of love, but never so passionately or for so long as with Josephine.

He also had many platonic friendships with women, gifted pianists to whom he dedicated sonatas, and kind-hearted ladies who helped and advised him in his domestic troubles. And he had a great number of men friends, owing to his expansive personality and enormous interest in human beings.

He remained devoted to his old friends in Bonn and kept in touch with them, often helping their sons (as in the case of Franz Ries) and befriending other young Rhinelanders who had come to Vienna; many of these were fugitives who would have been conscripted into the French army if they had stayed up north. Beethoven was particularly attached at this time to young Stefan von Breuning, Ries and Gleichenstein; another friend from the north was Wilhelm Mähler, a court secretary, who painted at least two portraits of the composer—one in 1804 or 1805 (where the "master" is somewhat romanticised, holding a lyre with the temple of Apollo in the background), and another in 1815 which seems a good deal truer to life.

Beethoven saw these young men often and helped them whenever he could. His loyalty was sometimes shaken owing to his impatience and touchiness (and, later, suspicion caused largely by his deafness). Basically his love for his friends was constant and deep.

The suggestion, which has on occasion been made, that he was a homosexual is manifestly ridiculous and baseless, even though his expressions of devotion sound exaggerated to twentieth-century ears (for instance, to Breuning: "How dear to my heart you are! surely you will come to my arms again as in the past!")[1]

He loved walking with a companion in the country, and Ferdinand Ries has given a vivid description of one typical expedition: "We went so far astray that we did not get back to Döbling till nearly 8 o'clock ... he had all the time been humming, and sometimes howling, always up and down without singing any definite notes; when asked what it was he said 'a theme for the last movement of the sonata [Op. 57 in F minor] has just occurred to me'."[2]

With his pupils he could be firm, even harsh. The young Förster cried sometimes at his severity; but this could be kindly meant, as when Beethoven scolded him for rushing up four flights of stairs to

[1] Thayer, p. 358   [2] *Ibid.*, p. 356

the room in the Mölkerbastei: "Boy, you'll ruin your lungs if you aren't more careful!"

The value Beethoven set on friendship is shown in the lines he wrote in Johannes Buel's album: "Friendship is shade in sunlight and shelter from the storm." Buel who was tutor to Count Browne-Camus (to whom several sonatas are dedicated) described the composer as "full of enthusiasm for his art, original, somewhat of a hypochondriac", so devoted to his friends that he wept with emotion when he received a letter from one.

*   *   *

Any biographical study of Beethoven must attempt to give an impression of him as a person, physically and socially. A few extracts from the many reminiscences of his friends may help to make a fairly faithful sketch, if not a finished portrait.

First, his appearance. From pictures and descriptions we know that he was short, squat, pockmarked, with a shock of dark hair, a great brow, determined mouth, snub nose and brooding, expressive eyes. The romantic view of a lady pupil at this time was that "he was very ugly but noble, refined in feeling and cultured; as a rule shabbily dressed". Carl Czerny on the other hand said that "he cared for his outward appearance", though as a child Czerny's first impression of him had been of a Robinson Crusoe, with bristling coal black hair, unshaven chin and grey shaggy coat.[1] The truth was that Beethoven dressed as he pleased, sometimes untidily to the point of neglect, often (according to the poet Grillparzer) carefully, even elegantly.

His character has been often described, best perhaps by Czerny and by Ries, who writes of him as "thoroughly good and kind man on whom his moods and impetuousness played shabby tricks. He would have forgiven anybody, no matter how grievously he had injured him if he had found him in an unfortunate position." His outbursts of rage were outward and visible signs of his volcanic temperament. This was reflected in his music: there are very few works where stormy passages do not suddenly erupt from a cheerful or serene context, subside, reappear, calm down . . . it was the same in his everyday life.

One of many anecdotes about his violent temper is told by Ries and is certainly typical: "When a waiter brought him the wrong dish and was insolent about it Beethoven threw the whole mess of lungs with plenty of gravy at the waiter's head in a fury—but quickly calmed down

[1] Thayer, p. 227

and roared with laughter." Ries also reliably describes his personal
behaviour: he was awkward and helpless, dropped and broke things,
knocked his inkwell into the piano: no piece of furniture was safe with
him, everything was overturned, soiled or destroyed; when he shaved,
his cheeks were covered with cuts.

There is no need to quote the many other pictures given by visitors
who found Beethoven struggling with elementary physical and domestic tasks, but it is worth giving a few impressions of the personal
characteristics which made him enemies as well as friends in his musical
career. He was completely honest, and never restrained himself in blame
or praise. In the case of musicians, those who played under his baton
often resented the blunt criticism he handed out; but they loved him
because when they did well he so thoroughly appreciated it. "At
rehearsal", Czerny says, "he was very particular about expression, the
delicate nuances as well as an effective rubato . . . and would discuss
them with the individual players. . . . When he then observed that the
players would enter into his intentions and play together with increasing ardour, inspired by the magic power of his creations, his face
would be transfigured by joy, all his features would beam pleasure and
satisfaction . . . and a thundering 'Bravi tutti' would reward the
successful achievement."

One of the most perceptive accounts of Beethoven as a person is that
given by Ignaz Xaver, Ritter von Seyfried, who was Kapellmeister in
the Theater-an-der-Wien from 1797 to 1828. He wrote that "Beethoven was much too straightforward, open and tolerant to give offence
to another by disapprobation or contradiction: he was wont to laugh
heartily at what did not please him. . . . If Beethoven sometimes carried
things to an extreme in his rude honesty in the case of many, mostly
those who had imposed themselves upon him as protectors, the fault
lay only in this, that the honest German always carried his heart on his
tongue and did not know how to flatter; also because . . . he would
never allow himself to be made the plaything of the vain whims of the
Maecenases who were eager to boast of their association with . . . the
celebrated master. And so he was misunderstood only by those who
had not the patience to get acquainted with the apparent eccentric."[1]

On occasions he could be excessively touchy, and upset and hurt
even his best friends—but afterwards always deeply regretted it, as we
know from notes dashed off after some tiff, passionately declaring his
grief, remorse and devoted love.

[1] Thayer, pp. 369-71

Seyfried tells us that at the time Beethoven composed the Third Symphony, the G major Piano Concertos and the Violin Concerto and was working at *Fidelio* (the period 1803-6), "We chatted away many an unforgettable hour . . . for he was then merry, ready for any jest, happy, full of life, witty and not seldom satirical." So much for those who have given the impression that he was consistently bad-tempered, unsociable and disagreeable. Later, deafness and social causes had their effect on him, but at this time his hearing was not too bad.

Czerny wrote that "although he had pains in his ears and the like ever since 1800 he still heard speech and music perfectly well until 1812".[1] He was certainly hearing a great deal of music about this time, and we know that he was fascinated by the works of Cherubini and Méhul when he heard them performed in the Theater-an-der-Wien. These were written for French republican audiences, but were much played in Vienna during the time of truce with France. In spite of his admiration for Cherubini's music, however, Beethoven gave the composer a cool reception when they met in Vienna in 1805. This may have been due to his enthusiasm for the French being on the wane—the Revolution's promise was unfulfilled; Napoleon had greatly disappointed him; Austria had been humiliated by the treaties of Campoformio and Luneville; and the country was again threatened with invasion from France.

5

From Francophile to Austrian Patriot
1805–1806

Early in 1805 the "Third Coalition" against France was formed between England, Russia and Austria. The Coalition made heavy demands on the Austrian budget; in the process of supplying the army, prices of consumer goods rose, and there was a serious shortage of food for civilians. Discontent ensued and there were riots in Vienna. An Austrian businessman, Joseph Carl Rosenbaum, recorded the unrest of July 1805 in his diary. On 7 July he saw a bakery attacked: "The whole shop and all the rooms were robbed clean . . . the mob had broken the fence, the iron gate, the house door. . . . The riot was started by a baker's wife refusing to sell a groschen worth of bread to a young apprentice."

"The tumult began at 5 o'clock and lasted the whole night through," wrote Rosenbaum, adding, "the court is in Baden; the news won't be exactly pleasant to them." The military were called in to control the rioters, and on 8 July Rosenbaum recorded that "a bunch of demonstrators came along, boys carrying bags full of bread; others carried clubs and bedslats. As soon as we arrived the grenadiers began to shoot. . . . Some rowdies took a baker's stick with a rag of linen and used it as a flag. Another an old drum. They proceeded furiously to pelt the soldiers with a hail of stones." Cavalrymen and grenadiers used their bayonets and swords freely on the protesters, and then had to take refuge from the crowd in the cadet school. "The mob threw stones and threatened to force the doors," says Rosenbaum. "The grenadiers fired on the people from the windows. More than a hundred were injured or killed." On 9 July, "Soldiers are quartered in all the suburbs. War preparations. Hordes of demonstrators are rounded up. The order is that at 9 o'clock all houses in the suburbs are to be locked and all inns cleared out."[1]

[1] Quoted by Marek, *Beethoven*, p. 357

Beethoven was in his summer retreat at Hexendorf at the time, and suffered less from food shortages than people in the city; he was deep in the composition of his opera *Fidelio* (or *Leonore* as he first called it), which had been commissioned by Baron Braun, now director of the court theatres, for performance in the autumn. Beethoven worked away, sitting in the shade of an old oak tree in Schönbrunn gardens, and was hardly affected by the rioting. Other aspects of the war preparations did concern him, the uncertainty of the immediate future, and the fate of some of his young Rhineland friends. Young Ries was called up in early September for military service under the terms of French rule in West Germany, and Beethoven wrote to Princess von Liechtenstein asking for help for the youth: "Poor Ries a pupil of mine must shoulder his musket in this unfortunate war and as he is a foreigner must also leave Vienna in a few days. He has nothing, absolutely nothing—and he has to undertake a long journey ... I am sending the poor fellow to you so that you may alleviate to some extent his difficult circumstances."[1]

During the summer Napoleon decided to abandon his plans for an assault on England and to make himself master of the European continent once for all. The Grand Army, which had been massed on the Channel coast ready for invasion, left Boulogne and marched into Germany. On its way it passed through Düsseldorf, where the five-year-old Heinrich Heine saw it and was greatly impressed.

The entry of the French was typical of the take-over in many northern towns: "The drumming in the streets continued, and I stood before the house door and looked at the French troops marching, those joyous and famous people who swept over the world singing and playing, the merry serious faces of the grenadiers, the bearskin shakoes, the tricolour cockades, the glittering bayonets. . . ."[2] The trumpets and drums sounded and the flags waved and the people cried Hurrah, little Heine as lustily as any.

But the picture was very different farther south, where the French were confronted by the Austrian army of 150,000 at Ulm, and from 7 to 20 October fought and finally defeated General Mack, taking 33,000 prisoners.

Vienna was anxious and fearful as Bernadotte's French regiment advanced into Austria, took Salzburg on 30 October and marched down the Danube valley towards the defenceless capital. Nobles, bankers and merchants fled. On 9 November the Empress left with her

---

[1] *Letters*, L. 121, p. 140   [2] Heine, *Reisebilder* (Prose and Poetry), p. 19

retinue. Rosenbaum wrote in his diary, "The court is sending every-thing away, even bedwarmers and shoe-trees. It looks as if they have no intention of ever coming back. . . ."

Baron Braun summoned the singers and employees of his theatres to the Redoutensaal on the morning of Friday 8 November, and told them that "his situation was extremely awkward; by the command of His Majesty he had to remain . . . but he might be taken into custody by the enemy who is expected to arrive in a few days . . . performances were to continue; only in case of a bombardment would he have passes for all." A big questionmark hung over the future of *Fidelio*, and the prospect did not seem promising.

"On the Josephsplatz 100 horses were standing ready to be hitched to transport carriages . . . loaded with gold, Treasury possessions, silver, linen, etc." Many people gathered, resentful of this removal to safety of the private property of the wealthy. Finally ships were provided for people's valuables "against a receipt", His Majesty guaranteeing the safety of these goods, barring acts of God. A group of deputies went off to meet the enemy in order to negotiate the fate of Vienna. Rosenbaum wrote on 11 November ". . . Bank notes of 12 and 24 Kr. denomina-tion were put into circulation. . . Offenheimer stopped payment three days ago and has disappeared. Neupauer and Wertheimer (bankers) have closed their establishments."[1]

On 13 November the vanguard of the French army, 15,000 strong, entered the city with flags flying and martial music sounding. In spite of previous fears there was an almost holiday atmosphere, and "in suburbs and town a curious crowd assembled", according to Caroline Pichler, and "windows of houses and shops stayed open". Dr Reeve wrote in his journal for 13 November, "The French troops . . . marched through Vienna all today and during the night. Many thousands passed through and proceeded without halting over the Danube into Moravia and Bohemia towards Brünn" [Brno]. Reeve saw "the flower of the army, under the command of general Suchet, very fine troops, especially the grenadiers *à cheval* with their high caps and metallic breastplates . . . the men well clothed and armed . . . several women on horseback riding alongside their husbands. Some of the infantry badly clothed, but marching with glee to victory."[2]

Rosenbaum in his diary described the French infantry as "very sloppy, not uniformed alike . . . everything topsy turvy" and as "laden down in the most singular fashion, carrying strips of lard, hams, or

---

chunks of meat dangling from their belts";[1] they passed in their thousands through the city for several days, in search of the Austrian army or to surround the Russian troops further down the Danube.

All reports agreed that "the French behave most considerately, even gallantly", but "take everything—nothing is to be found in the market". "The burden of billetting is unbelievable," said Rosenbaum. For several weeks there was an acute food shortage; Dr Reeve wrote, "famine begins to stare us in the face"; butchers shut up shop, bread was almost unobtainable; an egg cost 4 kreutzers, and a pound of butter 3 florins. However, before long beef and pork were allowed in from Hungary and the Viennese resumed almost normal life and eating habits. But as news from the war zone filtered back they could hardly be cheerful: the French were winning victories all along the line, and the devastation of the Austrian countryside was appalling; on 11 December came the official report of Napoleon's victory at Austerlitz, with Austrian and Russian losses of 20,000 men. Nobody would believe it, nor the announcement of an armistice, till the Viennese saw their wounded being brought back in hundreds, and "many thousands of Russian prisoners marched into Vienna, poor miserable ragged wretched objects", as Reeve reported, to fill the hospitals, convents and schools.[2]

Vienna's troubles were not ended with the armistice; the French demanded 13 million francs from the city, whose economy was already on the brink of bankruptcy. Napoleon was told that payment was impossible, and he let the town off with a fine of two million francs and the task of providing for the French garrison, several thousand strong.

Beethoven suffered along with everyone else from the ordeals of the time, but he resented the occupation chiefly for the disruption it caused in his life. He did not object to meeting individual Frenchmen. Anton Reicha, his former fellow student, introduced him to a violinist from Paris "at a by no means elegant inn"; and Czerny described a visit of several French officers and generals to the composer "for whom he played *Iphigenia in Tauris* from the score, to which they sang the choruses and songs not at all ill".[3] Beethoven's main complaint was that the French invasion had driven away most of his usual supporters —the better-off and aristocratic Viennese—and led to the failure of his new opera which opened at the Theater-an-der-Wien on 20 November.

[1] Rosenbaum, Marek, *op. cit.*, pp. 359–60
[2] Thayer, p. 391   [3] Reeve, *Journal*, p. 79

The production had been due to open on 15 October, but had been banned by the censor, and only allowed after a personal plea from the librettist Sonnleithner explaining that the Empress herself was interested in the opera (she "had found the original very beautiful and affirmed that no opera subject had given her so much pleasure"), that Beethoven had spent over a year and a half working on it and that he had already rehearsed it for performance on the Empress' name-day. The ban was lifted, but by the time the opera was ready, after all the vicissitudes, the invasion had taken place and the usual clientèle were in flight. Among the very few of Beethoven's friends who attended the first night were Lichnowsky and his wife, the poet Collin and Sonnleithner; the rest of the audience was composed largely of French soldiers and officers, who no doubt appreciated the political content of *Fidelio* but did not compensate for the absent Viennese. Henry Reeve, who was there, commented in his journal, "Few people present, though the house would have been crowded in every part but for the present state of public affairs." Reeve thought the story "a miserable mixture of low manners and romantic situations; the airs, duets and choruses equal to any praise . . . Beethoven presided at the pianoforte and directed the performance himself. He is a small dark young-looking man, wears spectacles, and is like Mr Koenig."[1]

The music critics' reviews of the opera did not help its success. Kotzebue's journal *Freymüthige* said that "a new Beethoven opera . . . has not pleased. It was performed only a few times and after the first performance (the theatre) remained completely empty. Also the music was really below the expectations of amateurs and professionals alike. . . ." The *A.M.Z.* reported on 8 January 1806 that "the choruses are ineffectual and one, which indicates the joy of prisoners over the sensation of fresh air, miscarries completely". Without condoning their inexcusable judgment on the prisoners' chorus it should be admitted that the critics had some reason for their discontent; most people agreed that the opera was dramatically ineffective owing to overloading with arias in the first and third acts. At a post mortem by various friends of Beethoven in December he agreed (after much pressure) to cut out two arias and to revise the opera for future presentation.

In spite of cuts and changes, and a new overture, the opera was given again only twice in early 1806. Beethoven was as difficult as only he could be, imagining a cabal against him, showing annoyance at the small takings and lack of popular enthusiasm, and quarrelling with Baron Braun. Notwithstanding its great beauty *Fidelio* was not an economic proposition, and it was dropped from the repertoire for the next eight years.

*   *   *

By 12 January 1806, we learn from Dr Reeve, "the French troops have almost all quitted Vienna. . . . The streets have an odd appearance. But the German nobility now begin to come out of their hiding places and the running footmen and equipages rattle about once more; the theatres are crowded too, after an abstention of two months." Playgoing and parties again became the order of the day. In spite of all the critical events, and the war which raged on in Germany, "politics are seldom talked of", says Reeve. "The people are indifferent upon every topic but mere idle objects of amusement, and the new ballet or play, the dress of the bourgeois, the parade of their emperor's return, etc., is more eagerly talked about than the miserable treaty of peace, the loss of an army, or the overthrow of an empire. The subject is 'traurig' they say, and in this world we ought to amuse ourselves."[1]

Whether or not the Viennese in general wanted to forget about the war and its aftermath, these had a profound effect on Beethoven. During 1806 an important change in his thinking was brought about by external political developments, especially by the military events succeeding the French occupation of Vienna and the treaty of Pressburg. As we have seen, he had several times been disappointed in Napoleon but had none the less continued to support the French Republic and its liberating policy in the occupied territories. He knew of course about the healthy measures taken wherever the French had deposed the feudal governments—as in Milan, where the kingdom of Italy made strides in material prosperity, education and public works, and where the expenses of the government spy service had been cut from 700,000 francs to 200,000 francs a year.[2]

It was common knowledge too that Napoleon's brother Joseph had attempted to clean the Augean political stables at Naples, introducing the Code Napoléon and sweeping decrees against feudalism. When the French were driven out again by the British or the Austrians, terrible repression followed (as in Naples, thanks largely to Nelson) and the clock was put back a century or more.

---

[1] Reeve, *Journal*, pp. 103–19
[2] J. Trevelyan, *A Short History of the Italian People*, p. 313

Those who detested obscurantism and clerical rule could not fail to applaud the daylight let in on the darkness of feudal Europe; none the less they felt there was a limit to what invaders should do. Austrians resented the harsh conditions laid down in the treaty of Pressburg (signed in August 1806) by which Franz II abdicated from the throne of the Holy Roman Empire and declared himself to be merely Emperor of Austria. To those of his subjects who thought and cared about the future of the country it seemed an intolerable humiliation which brought no recompense to Austria in the way of progress.

Beethoven certainly reacted against it, and from then on regarded Napoleon as an imperialist marauder who had betrayed the ideals of the Revolution.

Although still firmly republican, Beethoven came to consider himself a patriot of his adopted country. An incident in the summer of 1806 vividly illustrates this: Beethoven was staying with Prince Lichnowsky on his estate in Silesia. "When the prince had a number of Frenchmen as his guests, he tried to coerce Beethoven into playing for them on the pianoforte, who had stoutly refused. A threat of arrest, surely not made seriously, was taken so by him, and resulted in Beethoven's walking by night to Troppau whence he hurried on the wings of the wind by extra post to Vienna."

The incident made him so angry with Lichnowsky that as soon as he got home he grabbed the bust of his patron out of a cabinet and smashed it on the floor.[1]

He wrote to Camille Pleyel in Paris, "Dear Camillus—that was the name of the Roman who chased the wicked Gauls out of Rome: I too should like to have that name if I could chase them away from all the places to which they don't belong!"[2]

The French advance into Germany seemed to him to prove Napoleon's expansionist aims, and at the time of the battle of Jena (14 October 1806) he followed events anxiously. Meeting his friend Krumpholz in the street, he "as usual, asked him 'What's the news?' Krumpholz answered that the latest report received was that the great hero Napoleon had won another decisive victory over the Prussians. Greatly angered, Beethoven replied, 'It's a pity I don't understand the art of war as well as I do the art of music, I would conquer him!'"[3]

However, these events did not affect the forward surge of Beethoven's creative powers. In 1806 his mastery of all forms he undertook was more assured than ever. Some of his most beautiful, rich and

[1] Thayer, p. 403   [2] *Letters*, L. 165, p. 140   [3] Thayer, p. 403

confident works were written during this year: the G major Piano
Concerto, the Concerto for Violin and Orchestra in D, the Fourth
Symphony, the three String Quartets, Op. 59. The quartets were commissioned by the Russian Ambassador, Razoumovsky, and Beethoven
in a pro-Russian mood (perhaps due to the alliance of the Tsar with the
opponents of the fallen idol Napoleon), seems to have enjoyed writing
them. "He pledged himself to weave a Russian melody into every
quartet," Czerny said, and the result was the third movement of No. 2,
and the finale of No. 1 Czerny also mentioned that the Adagio in E
major, of the second Razoumovsky Quartet, occurred to him "when
contemplating the starry sky and thinking of the music of the spheres".
It is easy to believe, as one listens to this soaring, ethereal movement.
But in 1806, apart from one friendly critic (of the *A.M.Z.*), the quartets
were not appreciated. They were, indeed, strange and difficult to play,
and the virtuoso Bernard Romberg is reported to have trampled his
'cello part underfoot; an English quartet gave up the F major after one
attempt, agreeing that it was "a patchwork by a madman"; and the
Italian violinist Felix Radicati remarked about them: "Ha! Beethoven,
as the world says and as I believe, is music-mad—for these are not
music ... I said to him that he surely did not consider these works to be
music?—to which he replied, 'Oh, they are not for you, but for a later
age!'"[1]

6

Napoleonic Peace and War
1807–1811

During the next few years Beethoven's output was astonishing, even by his standards and those of his admirers. In Austria, for the time being, peace prevailed and conditions were favourable for composition; Beethoven always had access to a first-class orchestra and virtuoso solo players for the performance of his work (and they were glad to play for him); since 1800 the technical possibilities of instruments had greatly increased; pianos too were fuller in tone and had a bigger range than the Mozartian cembalo; audiences were less exclusively aristocratic than before, and more receptive than those entirely brought up on Haydn and the eighteenth century school to new and daring compositions.

From a personal angle things were favourable too; Beethoven's health was reasonably good and his deafness had not worsened. His ideas poured forth and took shape in a constant stream of compositions, ever richer and deeper in content and more confident in expression. Between 1806 and 1810 he wrote the Fourth, Fifth and Sixth Symphonies, the 'Cello Sonata, Op. 69, the Trios for Piano, Violin and 'Cello, Op. 70, the "Harp" Quartet, Op. 74, the Piano Concerto in E flat major, the Choral Fantasia, the Mass in C, three Sonatas for Piano (the Waldstein, Op. 57, the F sharp major, Op. 78, and "Das Lebewohl", Op. 81a), the thirty-two Piano Variations, WoO 80, and the overture Coriolan, to mention only the most important. There were many lesser works too, marches for military band, ariettas, songs. The compositions of this period on the whole pleased the musical public; it was not ultra-modern, and although one work after another was striking and new, each had a general appeal through its wealth of melody, its warmth and humanity.

But the basic quality of Beethoven's music of the "second period" is one which endeared him to his serious contemporaries and to the earnest late Victorians, though not so much to the frivolous public of his own day, nor to the "moderns" of our century: the quality of responsibility which underlay all the fantasy, brilliance and wit. Joseph Joachim named this quality "penitence", but perhaps humility would be a better word. As Tovey remarked, "It was a quality that was, if possible, more out of fashion in Beethoven's time than it is now [1936]. But it will always be inseparable from responsibility so long as human beings have ideals and fail to reach them."

Today, social and cultural issues are clearer to people in general, and the young particularly have a very strong sense of responsibility and are not afraid of Beethoven's "sense of duty, which was to preach". Perhaps unconsciously, they welcome "the supremely masterful and hopeful criticism of life", which, as Tovey says, is contained in his music and is so evident in the works of his early middle age.[1] These— the symphonies, the piano concertos, and the 'cello sonata especially— are straightforward declarations of faith in human goodness and progress, based on the principles of the French Revolution. They are uncomplicated by the mystery or tragic questioning of later compositions or by any urge to puzzle or shock.

One reason for Beethoven's confidence and the sense of security that the music of this period imparts is his cast-iron social and political morality; another reason is that his life during these years was, if not very eventful, happy and spiritually rich. He was sure of himself, established, ideologically and morally at peace, and surrounded by loyal friends whose admiration he returned with affection and respect. All his letters to these friends testify to this, and so do many anecdotes. One, told by Mendelssohn about Beethoven and the pianist Baroness Ertmann, is typical: "When she lost her last child, Beethoven . . . invited her to visit him, and when she came he sat himself down at the pianoforte and said simply, 'We will talk to each other in music,' and for over an hour he played without stopping; and, as she remarked, 'He told me everything and at last brought me comfort.'" Among other friends was the pianist Baroness Erdödy; and a special favourite was Madame Marie Bigot, who played one of his sonatas so well that he said, "That isn't exactly the character I meant to give this piece; but go ahead—*si ce n'est pas tout à fait moi, c'est mieux que moi.*" ("if it isn't quite me, it's better than me.")[2] These ladies were all married to well-to-do aristocrats, and Beethoven's relations with them purely platonic.

---

[1] Donald Tovey, *Beethoven*, pp. 1–2
[2] Thayer, p. 413

For several months he was heart whole, except for his lingering love for Josephine Deym. That affair had revived temporarily in 1805 but apparently came to an end in 1807 with a farewell letter expressing Beethoven's aching sorrow. He signed it "as always, your Beethoven who is eternally devoted to you". In view of this, one wonders whether it was not Josephine to whom the "eternal beloved" letters of 1812 were written—whether in spite of the break, the fire smouldered and flared up five years later? But that enigma, it seems, is as eternal as "the Beloved" herself.

*   *   *

To return to 1807: Beethoven's only anxiety at this time was about financial security, and as indicated earlier it was a baseless one. But frequent letters to publishers reflect it, with their insistence on fair prices and prompt payment for his work. The anxiety perhaps sprang from his early poverty and a feeling of insecurity about the future—in one sense irrational, in another, reasonable, for in the era of Napoleonic wars who could know what tomorrow might bring?

For the moment the fighting seemed far off. Napoleon had overcome Prussians and Russians and had firmly established himself as master of Germany; the Austrians had agreed to live under the humiliating conditions of the Treaty of Luneville. But they could not be unaware of the war: for one thing, England was still fighting France on the high seas and there were shortages due to the blockade of Europe by English ships. This made profiteering possible; and some Austrians did well out of the situation, including Beethoven's brother Johann. He had settled in Linz as a chemist and now made good money selling English tins which were then hard to obtain and fetched a high price in Austria. Later Johann got an important contract to supply medicine to the French army and he became a rich man.[1] Beethoven must have felt the irony of his younger brother doing so well from the fortunes of war; many years later, when Johann signed a letter to him "Johann Beethoven, Property Owner", Ludwig (then in real financial difficulties) replied with one signed, "L. van Beethoven, Brain Owner". But during the first decade of the century he need not have worried; he was well established and his work in constant demand. There were few concerts where a work of his was not performed, either at the semi-public Liebhaber-Concert Institute (run by banker Häring and other affluent amateurs of the *nouveau riche* class) or in aristocratic houses.

[1] Thayer, p. 402

The contemporary newspapers testify to this: The *Allgemeine Musikalische Zeitung* (*A.M.Z.*) wrote on 27 February 1807, "Beethoven's big symphony in E flat . . . will be performed along with the two other symphonies by this composer (in C and D) and also with a fourth still unknown symphony by him, in a very select circle that contributed a very considerable sum for the benefit of the composer."[1] Another journal reports, "two concerts at the house of Prince L(obkowitz)" in April; and in May 1807 the *Wiener Vaterländische Blatt* (*W.V.B.*) reports the first of the Liebhaber concerts held in the University Hall, at which works including the Coriolan and Prometheus overtures were played. These were received with reservations by the critics: "Richness of ideas, bold originality and fullness of power . . . were very much in evidence", said one, but added that they gave "the effect of rough diamonds". Whatever the critics said, the fact that his works were so much in demand should have set Beethoven's mind at rest.

The truth was that he wanted to write another opera, and for this, required time and peace and an assured income. He addressed a petition to the directors of the Royal Theatre, explaining that he needed a fixed salary to enable him to stay in Vienna rather than travel to foreign lands where he knew he could find a well-paid post. "The favour and approval which he has enjoyed from high and low (in Vienna) . . . and the patriotism of a German have made this place more estimable and desirable than any other."

He asked them to ensure his further stay there by offering him "*the means of a comfortable livelihood* favourable to the exercise of his talents". In return he promised to compose "every year at least one grand opera" and "a small opera or a divertissement, choruses or occasional pieces according to the wishes of the Worshipful Direction". He stressed that "if one reflects what an expenditure of time and effort is required for the making of an opera to the absolute exclusion of every other intellectual occupation", his conditions should not be thought unreasonable. None the less, the request was rejected, and so was one for a Benefit Concert. Beethoven wrote to Count Brunsvik on 11 May 1807 that he wanted to go to Hungary to give concerts: "I shall never come to an arrangement with the princely rabble connected with the theatres here", he said, acidly referring to Lobkowitz, Esterhazy and the other grandees directing the court theatre.[2]

He did not give up the idea of writing an opera, but constantly mulled over the problem of a subject; he thought of Prometheus, and

[1] Thayer, p. 416   [2] *Ibid.*, p. 427

of Coriolanus, following up his ballet (Op. 43) and his overture (Op. 52); of an Indian drama, and of one on Jerusalem.

Very much in earnest, he approached the poet Heinrich Collin to ask for his co-operation in writing an opera based on *Macbeth*: A letter to Collin in February 1808 expresses delight "that you are willing to fulfill my greatest wish and your own intentions". Unfortunately, Collin died before Beethoven had time to work on *Macbeth* with him. What a loss to music! The two "brothers in Apollo" (as Beethoven put it) would have been a great partnership, and the Shakespeare tragedy an ideal subject for them.

Beethoven's letters to Collin during 1808 were full of enthusiasm for the project. They also contained frequent complaints of the scurvy behaviour of the Viennese: "I have become accustomed to the basest and vilest treatment in Vienna"—"Away with all consideration for those vandals of art!"[1] Again, in the summer, of the same year: "We shall probably have to wait a bit; for that is what those high and mighty theatre directors have decreed—I have so little reason to expect anything favourable from them that the thought that I shall have to leave Vienna and become a wanderer haunts me persistently."

As a matter of fact, all through 1808 Beethoven was esteemed and fêted by the Vienna public; although he was disgruntled and, as Czerny put it, "had to fight cabals", the people were innocent. "He was always marvelled at and respected as an extraordinary being, and his greatness was suspected even by those who did not understand him."[2] His name was top of the list of Court Councillor Joseph Hartl, the banker, who was a theatre director and supervisor of public charities and who got Beethoven to perform and conduct at charity concerts in the Theater-an-der-Wien. In return for his contributions to such concerts in November 1807 and in April and November 1808, he was granted the use of the theatre for an *Akademie* of his own in December.

The programme of this concert consisted of the Fifth and Sixth Symphonies, the G major Piano Concerto, some songs—and the Choral Fantasia for good measure. Unfortunately, the performance went so badly that the marvels of the new C minor Symphony were not noticed in the local press, which dwelt at great length on the calamities.[3] However, there must have been some there who felt as

---

[1] *Letters*, L. 164, vol. i, pp. 185–6.   [2] Thayer, p. 444.
[3] Cf. Moscheles' comments on the concert (quoted in Thayer, p. 449): "During the last movement of the fantasia I perceived that, like a runaway carriage going downhill, an overturn was inevitable." The players all lost their places and Beethoven had to stop them and start again from the beginning.

Berlioz did when he first heard the Fifth Symphony: "In an artist's life one thunderclap follows swiftly on another, as in those outsize storms in which the clouds, charged to bursting with electric energy seem to be hurling the lightning back and forth and blowing the whirl-wind. . . ." Others must have reacted like the French musician Lesueur who hurried out at the end of the symphony saying "Ouf! I must have some air—it's amazing—wonderful! I was so moved and disturbed that when I . . . attempted to put on my hat I could not find my head!"[1]

Whatever their reactions, those who heard the C minor Symphony must have realised the increasing stature of Beethoven and the disaster to Vienna if he were to leave. Something had quickly to be done to prevent this, for he had been invited by Jerome Bonaparte, Napoleon's youngest brother, then King of Westphalia, to be Kapellmeister at his court. Beethoven seriously considered accepting, and when this was known he was requested by "persons of the highest rank that he state the conditions under which he would remain in Vienna".[2]

He was firmly resolved to go, according to a letter to Breitkopf dated 7 January 1809: ". . . I am forced by intrigues and cabals and low tricks of all kinds to leave the only remaining German fatherland . . . I am only waiting for my decree, to make arrangements for my journey."[3] It seems that Countess Erdödy realised the seriousness of the matter and took the lead in drawing up a contract so favourable to Beethoven that he would abandon the idea of leaving. A document was produced, headed "Conditions", in which the composer set out what he had been offered by the King of Westphalia and what he would expect from Vienna if he rejected the King's offer. He asked for a salary for life of not less than 4,000 florins a year; freedom to make artistic tours; the use of the Theater-an-der-Wien once a year for a concert for his own benefit, in exchange conducting a charity concert, or composing a new work for such a concert; if offered a post in the Imperial Service he would take it, relinquishing the stipulated 4,000 florins. (This was a most unlikely eventuality, as the Emperor was no doubt far too well aware of Beethoven's republican opinions.)

An agreement to these conditions was drawn up by Beethoven, his pupil the Archduke Rudolph, Prince Lobkowitz and Prince Ferdinand Kinsky—all still young, but at this time well enough off to enter into

[1] Berlioz, *Memoirs*, p. 122 (Panther Books)
[2] Thayer, p. 453   [3] *Briefe*, 40, p. 48

these substantial commitments. Later, it will be seen, things changed, but in the meantime Beethoven was very happy. His financial position settled, he had no immediate worries.

His only cause for concern was his brother, Caspar Carl who had married an unsatisfactory wife, Johanna, of whom Beethoven strongly disapproved. Apart from that, and from quarrels, soon made up, with his friends, life was reasonably bright. Beethoven planned to travel, first to various German cities, then to England, and finally to Spain. To Breitkopf in Leipzig he wrote cheerfully: "I am remaining in Vienna ... though indeed I still intend to undertake perhaps a short journey, if the present threatening storm-clouds do not gather."[1]

The storm clouds were those, once again, of approaching war.

*   *   *

Napoleon was once more advancing on Austria. Since his victory over the Russians in June 1807 and the Treaty of Tilsit, comparative peace had prevailed in Germany; but in Spain where he had placed his brother Joseph on the throne he was faced with a hostile rising by the nationalist and Catholic population which was aided by the British. Seeing Napoleon's difficulties Emperor Franz thought it a good moment to try and recover some of his own former realm, and in April 1809 sent Austrian troops into Bavaria for this purpose. To secure Heaven's blessing for these troops, the population of Vienna was called upon to assemble in the churches during the week 17 to 24 April, and prayers were offered up for the success of Austria's army. On the 24th, a long procession headed by the Empress and all the archdukes, followed by the court, town council and the entire clergy, went through the city to a ceremony at the cathedral.[2]

All this had no effect on God or on Napoleon who had left his forces in the Peninsula and arrived at Eckmuhl on the Danube where, on 22 April, he won a resounding victory. Within a fortnight he was on the heights of Schönbrunn, and the exodus of Austrian nobles and princes had begun. The Empress left on 4 May with the royal children; Archduke Rudolph accompanied them, and Beethoven mourned his departure in a sonata inscribed "The Farewell, Vienna, 4th May 1809". The beginning, adagio, expressed the composer's sorrow at losing his friend, and continued with the lively rhythm of travel; the second movement depicted, very literally, the pains of absence; the cheerful

---

[1] *Letters*, L. 199, p. 217   [2] Robert, *L'Idée nationale*, p. 193

galloping finale was evidently written later, just before the Archduke's return.[1]

Most of Beethoven's close friends went, with the court or with the administration. He was left on his own, except for his brother Caspar, in the anxious atmosphere of a beleaguered city.

With a garrison of 16,000 troops, some thousand students and artists, and the civil militia, Archduke Maximilian prepared to defend Vienna. Marshall Berthier called for his capitulation, saying that "the Emperor had always tried to save the defenceless crowd from harm and would regret the necessity of destroying a great city". When this exhortation was ignored, the French prepared to bombard the city from the Spittelberg, facing the Kärntnerthor. Every shot and shell from the battery was liable to plunge into Beethoven's windows on the Mölkerbastei.

At 9 o'clock at night, on 11 May, the battery of twenty howitzers opened fire. Rich and poor, young and old alike at once crowded indiscriminately into cellars and fireproof vaults. Beethoven took refuge in the Rauhensteingasse and spent the greater part of the six hours' shelling in a cellar in his brother Caspar's house, where he covered his head with pillows "so as not to hear the cannons", Ries said. More probably he took the precaution to save his poor ears from the effects of the bursting shells. At 2.30 a.m. on 12 May the white flag was sent up as notice of capitulation to the enemy outposts. All that the resistance had achieved was considerable damage to the roof of the cathedral by French shells and an equal amount to houses in the suburbs by the Austrian returning fire.[2] Napoleon entered the city and occupied Schönbrunn during a few weeks while the armies regrouped. There was a rumour on 21 May that Archduke Charles was about to deliver Vienna, but nothing happened; the bitter truth that the French were the masters was finally brought home to the Austrians at Wagram on 5 and 6 July, when they were completely routed and lost 50,000 men, killed and wounded.

In the meantime Vienna suffered the miseries of occupation. The food shortage was even worse than in 1805; bakeries were requisitioned for the French, and in the absence of flour the Viennese ate bread made of barley from the breweries. There were riots outside shops and

[1] "Das Lebewohl" (Op. 81a) recalls Bach's early harpsichord suite, "Alla lontanza del suo dilettissimo fratello", also "programme" music with postilion's horn and galloping hooves. It would be interesting to know if this is a coincidence, or whether Beethoven knew this work.

[2] Robert, *op. cit.*, pp. 194–6; Thayer, 465; Ries, *Notizen*, p. 121

protests to the local Council against having to lodge and feed large numbers of soldiers (sometimes 100 or more in one house) who were allowed white bread, cheese and meat. However, the French behaved well, were forbidden to steal or otherwise transgress, and were on reasonably cordial terms with their unwilling hosts.

The worst effect on Austria was financial: shortages of goods led to a steep rise in the rate of interest; the French requisitioned vast supplies, which made matters worse, and in two months they withdrew from the city the sum of 10 million florins. A forced loan was imposed on the houses of the city and suburbs, amounting to a quarter of the owners' rentals.[1]

All these consequences of war and defeat weighed especially heavily on the poor, but even Beethoven who was not so badly off at that time felt the pressure severely. Except for Stefan von Breuning, none of his friends were there to help or encourage him—Kinsky was in Prague, Lichnowsky and Waldstein, Marie Bigot and her husband, had all left, the Brunsviks were in Hungary, Zmeskall and other court employees had followed the Emperor to Brunn. Posts were disrupted and communication difficult, but Beethoven did manage in July to reach his publisher with a letter bewailing his position: "We have been suffering misery in a most concentrated form. . . . Since 4 May I have produced very little coherent work, at most a fragment here and there. The whole course of events has affected me body and soul. . . . I haven't yet had a farthing from Count Kinsky—and that when money is most needed—Heaven knows what will happen next—I should normally be having a change of scene and air—the levies are beginning this very day —what a destructive disorderly life is all around me, nothing but drums, cannons, human misery in every form."[2]

One sad event was the death, on 31 May, of Joseph Haydn; in his 78th year the shock and stress of war was too much, and so loyal a patriot must have felt the occupation unbearable. Ironically, his funeral was attended by many of the occupying forces and as Haydn had been a member of their national Institute for Art and Science a great number of French followed his coffin.

They were there too at the memorial service some days later, among them Henri Beyle (Stendhal) who wrote to his sister: "all the musicians of the town gathered at Schottenkirche to render Mozart's Requiem in [Haydn's] honour. I was there, in uniform, in the second row. The first row was filled with the great man's family—two or three little poor

[1] Robert, op. cit., p. 200   [2] Briefe, 44, p. 52

women in black. . . ."[1] Beyle may also have rubbed shoulders with Beethoven who, unless prevented, would certainly have been there to pay a last tribute to Haydn, his master.

Although he resented the French presence Beethoven did not mind meeting individuals, and in fact made good friends with young Baron de Trémont who came with a letter of introduction from Anton Reicha, then teaching in Paris. They talked for hours in a mixture of bad German and atrocious French, "philosophy, religion, politics, and especially of Shakespeare, his idol". They also discussed Napoleon, and Beethoven expressed admiration "for his rise from such obscure beginnings; his democratic ideas were flattered by it". This led Trémont to think that he would really rather have liked to go to Paris and be commanded by Napoleon to an audience.[2]

The French Emperor's worst offence in the composer's eyes was that Napoleon's presence prevented Beethoven going into the country during the summer; all he managed was a day or two in Baden, as we know from a note to Dr Troxler, an eminent Swiss historian, then in Vienna:[3] "The post from Baden is the most wretched of all: it resembles the whole Austrian state." He explodes over and over again about "this accursed war"—to Breitkopf: "We are short of money in Vienna for we need twice as much as formerly—Curse this war";[4] and to the publisher George Thomson, in Edinburgh who had commissioned some accompaniments to Scottish songs: "Nous vivons ici dans un tems ou toutes les choses s'exigent a un terrible haut prix, presque on paye ici trois fois cher comme avant."[5]

A treaty of peace between France and Austria was signed at Schönbrunn in October 1809, and things gradually became easier; Beethoven wrote to Breitkopf in November that "we are enjoying a little peace after violent destruction, after suffering every hardship that one could conceivably endure. I worked for a few weeks in succession but it seemed to me more for *death* than for immortality. . . .'[6]

The many hardships he had undergone did not affect the quality of his creations, though the quantity dropped. The E flat ("Harp") Quartet, Op. 74, and the Concerto and Piano Sonata in the same key, were all written during the late summer, the Fantasia, Op. 77, and the Sonata, Op. 78 were composed in October, closely followed by Op. 79 and 81a.

---

[1] Stendhal, *Correspondance*, iii, p. 190 (*Divan ed.*, Paris 1933)
[2] Thayer, pp. 466–7   [3] *Letters*, L. 245, p. 242   [4] *Ibid.*, L. 246, p. 243
[5] *Ibid.*, L. 229, p. 247   [6] *Ibid.*, L. 228, p. 246

The reaction to the disturbances in Beethoven's life came in 1810 and 1811 when the torrent of inspiration dwindled to a trickle. Most composers would be satisfied if they had produced in twelve months the *Egmont* music, the Goethe songs, the splendid String Quartet in F minor (Op. 95) as well as military marches and many folk-song settings; but Beethoven's admirers were disappointed, particularly Lobkowitz, seeing "the years pass away comparatively fruitless". They should. have blamed the unhappy events and his money troubles; owing to the war his income had dropped catastrophically: "Last year, before the arrival of the French my 4,000 gulden were worth something. This year they are not even worth 1,000 A.C. . . . (Assimilated Currency)." Beethoven wrote to Breitkopf, in August 1810, asking for an increase in fees and adding: "You as a more humane and far better educated person than all other music publishers ought also to set yourself the aim not to pay the artist a mere pittance, but rather to . . . enable him to create in undisturbed surroundings what he is capable of expressing and what other people expect of him. . . ."[1]

Financial problems, post-invasion Austria and the general hopelessness of the political scene had a stultifying effect on Beethoven at this time, as they did five years later; but in the rather barren period 1810 and 1811 he was at least only partly deaf and, on the whole, fairly cheerful. For this we must thank two sets of friends with whom he was much involved. First, the Malfatti family, a kind and cultured Viennese household, whose daughter, Therese, Beethoven for a few months hoped to marry; and secondly the Brentanos. The eighteen-year-old Elisabeth (Bettina) and her brother Clemens were both poets, of the new Romantic School, and moved in the highest German cultural circles; at this time Bettina was a favourite of Goethe's, and she promised to introduce Beethoven to him. This led to the composer writing to the poet offering him settings of his verses, and to several long flowery effusions from Bettina herself to Goethe telling him the electrifying effect Beethoven had had on her, quoting conversations and describing meetings and walks with him, all in a highly idealised vein. Later, she went so far as to publish a correspondence and is discredited in the eyes of Beethovenologists, who question her veracity in her own letters and the existence of two-thirds of Beethoven's to her. But the one genuine autograph, of February 1811, shows that Beethoven was really very much attached to Bettina and did use her as a means of communication with Goethe: "If you write to him about me, choose all the words which will express my deepest respect and admiration . . . who can thank a great poet, the most precious jewel of any nation, enough?"[1]

However romantic Bettina's descriptions, there is enough truth in them to show us a side of Beethoven not often seen—the great man, relaxed and happy in the company of a charming girl, unreservedly expressing his views on art and life. There was no question of sexual interest, for Bettina was a well-brought-up young lady with her hand promised to the poet von Arnim. If her affection and admiration for Beethoven led her to romance about her life and to distort the truth about her celebrated friends, she has still provided enough facts about Beethoven to deserve some gratitude from posterity. In the letter known to be genuine, the following passage alone gives us a glimpse of him without which we would be the poorer: "I did not get home until 4 o'clock this morning from a bacchanalia, where I laughed so much that today I have had to weep as much again. Exuberant jollity often drives me very violently back into myself. . . ."[2]

He never admitted to enjoying a bacchanalia to anyone but Bettina, but it is good to know that in difficult times he could still occasionally do so.

---

[1] *Briefe*, 50, p. 60   [2] *Ibid.*

7

Liberation in Sight
1811–1814

Things had begun to go wrong for Napoleon and the fruits of his European victories were not proving as sweet as he hoped. His so-called allies, even Emperor Franz, whose daughter Maria-Louisa he had married in 1810, were unreliable; their peoples were discontented at having to pay heavy taxes for war, send their sons to fight as conscripts, and go short of provisions to feed the French. They were disillusioned when the revolution, with its promise of social justice, was not implemented. Napoleon later recognised this and admitted that if he had "granted free constitutions to those who desired them, and abolished vassalage, the people would have been content, and the struggle a mere contest of princes for supremacy".[1] As time went on, the very classes which had welcomed the French were alienated. Beethoven was a typical example of a bourgeois nationalist, formed by the breaking of feudalism, turning against the creators of his nationalism.

So though in 1811 there was no overt sign of Napoleon's approaching downfall, the seeds were there. Europe was weary of the blockade imposed under the Berlin decrees of 1810. During the summer of 1811 Russia broke the agreement with France by allowing 150 British vessels under the American flag to enter her ports, and Napoleon warned that war might follow. Tsar Alexander, his eye on British naval strength, and on Spain where the French were being unmercifully harassed by guerrillas and hammered by Wellington's army, decided to let Napoleon invade Russia, certain that winter would defeat him. The generalissimo shrugged off warnings with one of the least percipient remarks of his career: "All Europe has the same climate." In theory, Prussia and Austria were to be his allies, but secretly they gave the Tsar to understand that the moment Napoleon weakened they would join Russia against France. The King of Prussia, a very weak character, did not

[1] Delderfield, *Imperial Sunset* (London 1969), p. 28

commit himself; although he disliked French domination and knew his people were restive, he was terrified of Napoleon, and when the latter demanded 30,000 Germans for the Russian campaign, he reluctantly agreed, but put General Yorck, an avowed Francophobe, in charge of these troops.

It was against the background of uncertainty—mobilisation for the invasion of Russia, growing resistance in Europe, and an attitude of wait-and-see in Austria—that Beethoven spent the spring and early summer of 1811. Composition was hampered by the amount of time and energy which he had to spend on such uncreative tasks as his duties to Archduke Rudolph, to whom he was a combination of musical adviser, tutor and piano teacher; there was much hackwork to be done preparing music for press, arranging Scottish songs for George Thomson, and correcting copy which publishers' proof readers had skimped.

Sending back the Songs, Op. 82 and 83, and the *Egmont* overture to Breitkopf, he exploded: "Errors—errors—errors—you yourselves are one large error—I must send my copyist to Leipzig or go there myself if I don't want my works to appear as mere errors." But closed his letter magnanimously with, "Farewell, I hope for improvement. . . . Make as many errors as you please . . . you are still highly esteemed by me. The custom of men is to esteem each other because they have not made even greater errors. . . ."[1]

Between these labours and intermittent ill-health, Beethoven's creativity flagged. However, he accepted a commission for incidental music to a drama for the opening of a grand new theatre in Budapest on the Emperor's name-day in October 1811. The subject was a heroic legendary episode in Hungarian history; Kotzebue, a facile and prolific writer, quickly produced three items to be set, "Hungary's First Benefactor", "Bela's Flight" and "The Ruins of Athens". (Later, somebody remembered that Emperor Franz had twice fled from his capital within five years, so "Bela's Flight" was tactfully withdrawn.) Beethoven, who liked the Hungarians, agreed to co-operate: "I sat down in defiance of my doctor's orders to help the Mustachios who are well disposed towards me", he wrote, and produced the music (which is pleasant, melodious, Gluck-like, but not of his greatest), within a month of returning from a three-week cure at Teplitz Spa.

During his stay at Teplitz he had rested and relaxed. He went there with a good companion, Franz Oliva, a young official who had helped

[1] Thayer, p. 508

F

him in recent years, and he made some new and interesting friends: one was the writer Varnhagen von Ense, Goethe's most distinguished champion—"a man whose thoughts are worldwide and are expressed in language as rich and delicate as cut gems", Heine said of him.[1] Varnhagen introduced Beethoven to Fichte, the philosopher Friedrich August Wolf and the poet Tiedge. They were all Francophobes, and Beethoven, outspokenly "anti-French and pro-German", had much in common with them, and joined in their long and lively discussions about aesthetics and politics. One remark typical of the talk was Tiedge's "You can't see the *man* Napoleon at all, on account of the success that stands in front of him!"[2]

On a return visit to Teplitz in the summer of the following year, Beethoven met a great many even more eminent people—royalty and politicians—who had congregated there in a flurry of secret diplomatic activity. Officially neutral ground, the little spa was in fact a focal point of plot and agitation against Napoleon. Ostensibly the imperial personages or their representatives met for health and recreation, but, on the side, opinions were exchanged and contingency plans laid for action should Napoleon's foolhardy invasion of Russia materialise. It was a virtual mini-congress, headed by Emperor Franz with a large retinue (including Prince Kinsky, from whom Beethoven managed to extract his overdue annuity); the Empresses of France and of Austria, the King of Saxony, Prince Wittgenstein, Prince Maximilian, the Duke of Saxe-Weimar and many more were there. The non-royal visitors included Goethe, Lichnowsky, Amalie Sebald (a singer from Berlin), Clemens Brentano, Bettina and her husband von Armin—all of them very well disposed towards Beethoven.

But he did not appreciate their company; he was feeling extremely unsociable, and suffering intensely from the recent parting with a woman—the "Immortal Beloved" of unknown identity—with whom he had had a brief and passionate love affair. He wrote to Varnhagen that "there is not much to be said about Teplitz, few people and among the few nothing extraordinary, wherefore I live alone! alone! alone!" Although he carried out his treatment, and mixed socially in the spa gatherings, he felt his isolation bitterly, cut off as he was by his sorrow, and of course by his deafness, which had lately become worse. He felt too a lack of "rapport" with the grand people who had flocked to Teplitz, and expressed this feeling in a letter to a small girl who had sent him an embroidered wallet as an offering. "If you want anything,

[1] Heine, *Romantic School*, p. 115   [2] Thayer, pp. 513–14

dear Emilie, do not hesitate to write to me, the true artist has no pride
... I would rather visit you and your family than many a rich person
who betrays poverty of mind."

In spite of his unsociability Beethoven often saw Goethe during this
month in Teplitz. He wrote to Breitkopf, "I spend some time with
him every day. He has promised to write something for me." On
20 July they had a trip together to Bilin, and on 21 July spent the evening in each other's company. Goethe noted in his journal, "He played
delightfully", and wrote to his wife: "Say to His Serene Highness,
Prince Friedrich, that I can never be with Beethoven without wishing
it were in the *goldenen Strauss*. A more self-contained, energetic,
sincere artist I never saw. I can understand right well how singular must
be his attitude towards the world."[1]

But the two great men soon found faults in each other: despite his
love of Goethe's poetry, Beethoven might have said with a very
different genius, Heine, "At bottom Goethe and I are two opposite and
mutually repellent natures. He is essentially an easy-going man of the
world, who looks on enjoyment as the highest good, and though he
has at times glimpses and passing intuitions of the ideal life which he
expresses in his poems, yet he has never conceived it deeply, still less
lived it. I, on the contrary, am essentially an enthusiast, i.e. inspired by
the idea and ready to sacrifice myself for it, and always goaded to lose
myself in the idea. ..."[2]

Goethe told one of his admirers that "Beethoven's talent amazed me:
unfortunately he is an utterly untamed personality, who is not altogether in the wrong in holding the world to be detestable, but surely
does not make it any the more enjoyable either for himself or others by
his attitude." Beethoven on his side thought that "Goethe delights far
too much in the court atmosphere—far more than befits a poet. Why
laugh at the absurdities of virtuosi when poets, who ought to be the
first teachers of a nation forget all else for the sake of this glitter?"[3]

There are several well-known stories about the two on their walks
together: of how, meeting the Royal family on an outing, Goethe
stood back, bowing respectfully, while Beethoven pulled his hat
firmly down and strode on regardless of protocol; and of the composer's remark to Goethe when to the poet's annoyance passers-by
incessantly saluted the pair: "Don't let that trouble you, your
Excellency, perhaps the greetings are intended for *me*!" Whether

[1] Thayer, p. 536   [2] W. Sharp, *Life of Heine*, p. 75
[3] Thayer. pp. 537-8

true or not these anecdotes are too appropriate to be completely rejected.

One sad touch in the Teplitz scene of that July was Bettina Brentano's estrangement from Goethe, due to some tactless remarks of Bettina's which had offended the poet's wife. The enthusiastic young woman could therefore not fulfil her imagined mission of bringing her two great heroes together in person. Her husband wrote in mid-July to a friend that "the atmosphere here is not very pleasant. The presence of the Empress and various Saxon princes divides the company, and so there are few general gatherings. Most people languish in their rooms. . . . Just imagine this, Goethe and Beethoven both here, and yet my wife is not enjoying herself! The first doesn't want to know her, and the second isn't able to hear her. The poor devil is getting deafer and deafer, and it's really painful to see the friendly smile he puts on it." (*Sein freundliches Lächeln dazu ist wirklich schmerzlich.*) [1]

Beethoven's health was poor all through 1812, and the baths and doctors of Teplitz and Karlsbad did him very little good. He stayed on in the spa, however, until October, mainly confined to his room; he was consoled a little by the friendship of Amalie Sebald, the beautiful singer whom he had met the previous year, with whom he exchanged affectionate notes. On top of chest and stomach trouble, borne with grim humour and stoicism, his deafness was getting worse.

There seemed no helpful form of medical treatment available, and Beethoven looked desperately around for some sort of mechanical hearing aid. This led to his making friends with the Court Mechanician, Johann Nepomuk Mälzel, a brilliantly inventive man who made persistent efforts to construct an ear-trumpet which might be useful to the composer. One of his instruments proved satisfactory enough to be used for some eight to ten years, we are told. Mälzel was also engaged at this time in the invention of a metronome, in which Beethoven was interested and encouraged him. The instrument was perfected in 1817 (and is still used in its original form today) but in the spring of 1812 Mälzel had already completed a "chronometer", which he demonstrated at a meal attended by Beethoven, Count von Brunsvick, Stephan Breuning, and others in May. On this occasion, Beethoven was "merry, witty, satirical, 'unbuttoned' as he called it", and improvised the canon (WoO 162) "Ta ta ta ta!" which was sung there and then by all present. This canon was to achieve immortality as the theme of the Allegretto of the Eighth Symphony, which the composer was working

[1] Brentano, Bettina, *Unbekannte Briefe*, p. 178 (Bern 1970)

on at the time, and it demonstrates how trivial incidents of every day life could inspire original ideas that flowered into whole musical movements.[1]

In the winter of 1812, Mälzel, who had already won fame by his "mechanical Chessplayer" and other ingenious inventions, opened an exhibition the main attractions of which were his Mechanical Trumpeter, and his new "Panharmonicon". The Trumpeter performed a French cavalry march with signals and martial tunes which Mälzel accompanied on the piano. The Panharmonicon combined military band instruments with a bellows all enclosed in a large case. Keys were touched by pins in a revolving cylinder, as in a musical box. Mälzel was indefatigable in devising original and surprising gadgets to amuse the sensation-hungry Viennese. He had made cylinders for the Panharmonicon which played Haydn's Military Symphony, Handel's *Timotheus* and Cherubini's *Lodoiska* overture; and he figured that if he could add some striking new piece bearing the glorious name of Beethoven he would have a tremendous success with it all over Europe. Mälzel believed in linking his inventions with a topical sensation, and when news came of Napoleon's defeat in Russia and the burning of Moscow, he planned and carried out a striking exhibition of the conflagration. The Battle of Vittoria, which had been fought in June and proved the turning point of the war in Spain, struck the inventor as a suitable subject for his machine, and he invited Beethoven to co-operate with him in a "Battle Symphony" which he hoped would be performed in England and make their fortunes.

Beethoven, who admired the English for their dogged stand against Napoleon, agreed. Mälzel produced a plan for the work which brought in the turmoil of the battle, the sounds of triumph, drum rolls, trumpets, flourishes, "Rule Britannia" and "God Save the King", with background applause. Together the inventor and composer worked on the "pièce d'occasion"; it was not put on a cylinder, but arranged for orchestra, and proved to be the most popular piece of the day. Listeners were amply compensated for its musical weaknesses by the noisy spirit of jubilation which it conveyed.

At the same time Beethoven was completing the Seventh and Eighth Symphonies on which he had been at work for over a year. It has been suggested that the Seventh reflected the spirit of the War of Liberation,

[1] Elliot Forbes queries Schindler's dating of this story, as given by Thayer, but we let it stand. Beethoven's use of short canons on social occasions to make a point or a pun would make a whole chapter, and so would the musical ideas in the canons, hitherto unresearched except for Professor R. Klein's pamphlet "Beethoven canonen", Vienna 1970.

the rising resistance of the peoples against oppression, which was sweeping Europe; but as the symphony was completed before Napoleon's defeat in Russia it could not have been influenced by the events of the following year. Like the "Eroica" Symphony, it contains within it all the experience of battle and human resilience accumulated in Beethoven's consciousness over the years; and it goes further than the "Eroica" in its prophetic mood—victory had not been won, but it was on the way; the A major symphony expressed confidence in the bright future, whether that future was to be won by fighting in the field, as suggested by the galloping rhythms, the timpani and trumpets of the first and last movements, or by the calm faith expressed in the haunting Austrian pilgrim tune of the third movement.

The Eighth Symphony is even more prophetic, looking forward to peace and gaiety in a sunny world. Beethoven's prophecies unhappily were not fulfilled, but in 1812 nobody was to know how the rulers of Europe were going to sabotage the future. They all combined to abuse the tyrant Napoleon and to promise freedom for mankind when he fell, and it was tempting to believe them.

We do not know whether Beethoven's mistrust of princes left him sceptical about the real prospects for freedom and fraternity. In 1813, the Allied rulers did their utmost to persuade the people that they were the standard bearers of liberty: no sooner was Napoleon's shattered army in retreat from Moscow than his former allies called for his destruction. Heine wrote ironically about the artificially fostered patriotic enthusiasm: "We were ordered to be patriots and we became patriots, for we do all that our rulers bid us. . . . When Providence, snow and the Cossacks had destroyed Napoleon's best forces, we Germans got our orders from the highest quarters to free ourselves from the foreign yoke, and we flared up with manly indignation at the servitude we had borne too long, and inspired ourselves with the good tunes and bad poetry of Koerner's songs, and fought and won our freedom; for we do all that our rulers bid us."[1]

Count Wittgenstein, a Russian general whose men were often flogged into battle, grandly proclaimed: "Germans! We open the Prussian ranks to you. There, the son of a labourer is placed beside the son of a prince. All distinction of rank is effaced in these great ideas: King, Liberty, Honour, Country."[2] It became fashionable among autocrats and generals to use the once dirty word Liberty freely in

[1] Heine, *Romantic School*, p. 211
[2] Delderfield, *Imperial Sunset*, p. 26

addressing the underprivileged, though after the battles there was no more heady talk of equality.

But the formula worked in 1813 and volunteers flocked to the barracks, students formed corps, secret societies came into the open, women gave up their jewellery for national funds, patriotic zeal abounded. The King of Prussia gave in and declared war on France on 17 March. Austria joined the anti-French front in July. A Swedish army arrived to attack the French from the north, led by Count Bernadotte who had waited for a favourable moment to turn on his old comrade-in-arms.

The whole of Europe had thus combined against Napoleon, but it was many months before he was driven back to Paris. An army of devoted young French conscripts entered Germany again, and fought the Allies at Lutzen, Bautzen, Leipzig and Hanau—battles where the blood-letting exceeded even the earlier holocausts.

In Vienna the seemingly unending war was watched with tense anxiety, because of the large numbers of Austrians involved—besides those switched from the Russian front there were new regiments sent into battle in the Rhineland. The concert at which *Wellington's Victory* was performed, along with the Seventh and Eighth symphonies, on 8 December 1813, was given "for the benefit of the sick and wounded Austrian and Bavarian soldiers who fought in the battle at Hanau". From this and a repeat performance, war charities received 4,006 florins, after expenses which were minimal, as the players had given their services free. Beethoven made this clear in a letter to the *Wiener Zeitung* thanking the "honoured participants of the Academie" for their services. He mentioned particularly Herr Schuppanzigh, at the head of the violins, Herr Salieri, "beating time for the drummers and salvoes", Spohr, Mayseder and Hummel, in different parts of the orchestra. "I should have been as willing as Herr Hummel to take my place at the big drum", remarked Beethoven, "as we were all filled with nothing but the pure love of country and of joyful sacrifice of our powers for those who sacrificed so much for us." He thanked Mälzel for "the opportunity, long and ardently desired ... to lay a work of magnitude upon the altar of the fatherland."[1]

The letter was not printed, because Beethoven suddenly quarrelled with Mälzel—a sad story, which led to a lawsuit, much ill-feeling and an end to the hopes of visiting England with the Battle Symphony. There is no need to go into the ins and outs of this, which like Beethoven's

[1] Thayer, pp. 564–7

other lawsuits have been well covered in other biographies. It was an unfortunate weakness that, feeling himself injured, he would rush into action to prove his rectitude to the world. What mattered at this time was that the Battle Symphony brought him enormous fame and popularity, and the temporary satisfaction that goes with success, even though the symphony was far less worthy of acclaim than most of his other works. His friend Tomaschek wrote that he was "very painfully affected to see a Beethoven, whom Providence had probably designed to the highest throne in the realm of music, among the rudest materialists. I was told, it is true, that he himself had declared the work to be folly and that he liked it only because he had thoroughly thrashed the Viennese with it." Thayer is convinced that this was so, and the musicians who played it also regarded it as a stupendous musical joke.[1]

However this may be, the success of the symphony and Beethoven's resulting popularity cheered him immensely; he felt truly in touch with the world again, and his urge to be socially useful had been satisfied by giving voice to the general feeling of his people, and helping the war victims at the same time.

As allied successes followed each other rapidly in the winter of 1813, Beethoven's successes too came thick and fast: four more concerts entirely of his works were given within six weeks. In February 1814 he wrote to Count Franz Brunsvik, "No doubt you are delighted about all the victories—and about mine also." Reporting a concert in the great Redoutensaal, he adds, "In this way I shall gradually work my way out of my misery . . . I hope you live contentedly; that is certainly no small gain. As for me, why, good heavens, my kingdom is in the air. As the wind often does, so do harmonies whirl around me, and so do things often whirl about too in my soul."[2]

Out of that whirling of harmonies and ideas, the music of the third period was to take shape, and the kingdom of the air brought to earth for the benefit of the earth's people: for exactly ten years from the date of that letter the Ninth Symphony was completed. But it was to be a decade of much storm and stress for Beethoven's soul.

[1] Thayer, p. 565   [2] Letters, L. 462, p. 445

8

Prospect of Peace
1814

Beethoven had reflected the optimism of his fellow countrymen during the war of national liberation, in the Seventh and Eighth Symphonies and in *Wellington's Victory*. His cheerfulness continued in 1814; apart from his deafness—with which he had more or less come to terms—it was to be the best year of his life, thanks partly to his better health, and the recognition which he at last enjoyed; but mainly to the prospect of peace and a bright future.

As Thayer says, "only as the imagination is able to form a vivid picture of the horror of the war years, can it conceive that inexpressible sense of relief, the universal joy and jubilee which outside of France pervaded all classes of society . . . at the fall of the usurper, conqueror and tyrant". There was an all-prevailing trust "that men's rights, political and religious . . . would be gladly and gratefully accorded to them. . . . Nothing presaged the near advent and thirty years' sway of Metternichism." No one dreamed that within six years the rulers "would solemnly declare all popular and constitutional rights to be held no otherwise than as grants and indulgences from crowned heads", "that they would snuff treason in every effort of the people to hold princes to their pledged words. . . . This was all hidden in the future; the very intoxication of joy and extravagant loyalty then ruled the hour."[1]

Whether or not Beethoven ever shared the feeling of "extravagant loyalty", he was deeply affected by the joy; he wanted to give these sentiments musical expression and looked around for appropriate themes and motives. Schiller's "Ode to Joy" had been in his mind for some time and he now made a note, "Freude schöner Götterfunken Tochter—work out the overture!"[2] This seemed an opportune time to set the poem: the real joy of liberated Europe would take the place of

[1] Thayer, p. 596   [2] *Ibid.*, p. 597

the abstract joy of Schiller's verses, and the work would be dedicated to Emperor Franz, symbolic figure of liberator, and played on his name-day.

This plan had to be put aside for the moment, as Beethoven had other more immediate concerns. One was the revision of his opera *Fidelio* which he was generously letting the superintendents of the court theatres have for their benefit concert in May. His friend Treitschke, at this time "stage-manager and opera-poet" of the two theatres, wrote that the superintendents recognised that "there was no opera, German, French or Italian, likely to draw a remunerative house. . . . The sensation caused by Beethoven's newest music suggested *Fidelio*."[1]

The composer's only condition was that the opera should be thoroughly revised, and that Treitschke should make the changes in the text. In the usual confusion of his room he had lost his only score of the opera, and had to write in January to Count Moritz Lichnowsky to ask for the loan of the Count's score: "I know of course that your copy is not quite correct, but it is better than none at all. People now want to have it performed here at the court theatre, but I can't find my score. I believe I sent it off to Leipzig."[2]

By the end of February both poet and composer were at work on the opera, and Beethoven dashed off letters to Treitschke as manuscripts went to and fro: "March 1814:, . . . I have read with great pleasure your corrections for the opera; and now I feel more firmly resolved to rebuild the desolate ruins of an old castle."[3] Again, in March: ". . . It is better to have to deal with artists than with the so-called great ones (who are very very small)—My thanks for my opera will rush to welcome you wherever you are. . . ."[4] "April . . . To produce the opera in a fortnight is out of the question; I am still convinced that it will take us four weeks . . . I assure you, dear Treitschke, the opera will win me a martyr's crown. . . ."[5]

Several things held up the revision. One was Beethoven's benefit concert on 24 February 1814—("the accursed concert which I was forced to give partly because of my wretched circumstances has put me back with regard to the opera")—at which the Seventh and Eighth Symphonies were played for the first time, along with the Battle Symphony. The newspapers praised the Battle, but remarked of the Eighth, "it did not create a furore"; this greatly annoyed Beethoven who considered it much better than *Wellington's Victory* which always

[1] Thayer .p. 572   [2] *Letters*, L. 460, p. 443   [3] *Ibid.*, L. 469, p. 450
[4] *Ibid.*, L..467, p. 448   [5] *Ibid.*, L. 479, p. 454

brought the house down. After the concert, however, he was appeased by being given cherries by some girls in the street, who refused to be paid because, they said, they had seen him in the concert hall "where we heard your beautiful music".[1]

Other delays in *Fidelio* were caused by the many concerts which had to be attended to: young people, especially, often included Beethoven's works in their concerts; law students, medical students, regimental groups all wanted to play his music and it often had to be arranged and prepared for them. But the main hold-up was due to political events.

During April 1814 the allied armies were marching on Paris, and news of their arrival there was expected any day. The court opera direction decided to celebrate the event by an appropriate performance, and nine leading Viennese composers were asked to provide music for a *Singspiel* by Treitschke, entitled *Gute Nachricht*, to be given when the good news broke. Beethoven's contribution was the final chorus, to the words "Germania, wie stehst du jetzt im Glanze da". He also offered a setting of *Kriegslied*, a poem by J. K. Bernard, a lively young journalist who later became a close friend. This aria was not performed, but the cantata was played on 12 April, the day after the Allies' arrival in Paris, and was such a success that it was repeated seven times.

Gute Nachricht, the preparations for yet another "Akademie", and the absurd, ill-advised lawsuit against Mälzel about who was the owner of the Battle Symphony, all delayed Beethoven's completion of *Fidelio* which everyone was urging him to hurry up and finish. He only just managed to get it ready by Monday 23 May, the day of performance. Rehearsals had begun in April, before the score was finalised, and the last rehearsal was on 22 May; but the new overture (in E Major) had been written only the night before (21 May) and the parts had not been copied in time for the opening night, so the overture to *The Ruins of Athens* was played instead. Apart from this, all went well. Beethoven conducted, with Kapellmeister Umlauf guiding everything behind his back, "as the composer's ardour often rushed him out of time".[2]

The singers, led by Mme Milder-Hauptmann (the original Fidelio of 1805) in the title role, and Signor Radichi as Florestan, rose to the occasion and there was tumultuous applause. Beethoven was "stormily called out already after the first act, and enthusiastically greeted", according to the *Sammler* newspaper.

Another performance of *Fidelio* was given at a benefit concert for Beethoven during the summer of 1814. Friends in the newspaper

[1] Thayer, p. 576   [2] Thayer, pp. 580–3

world wanted him to have as much publicity as possible to ensure the success of this "benefit", and a small cultural journal, *Friedensblätter*, gave his name prominence by publishing his song "An die Geliebte" as a supplement a week before the concert. It was accompanied by an editorial "word to his admirers", pointing out that "the general enthusiasm aroused by the immortal opera *Fidelio*" proved that "true greatness and beauty can reach sympathetic spirits and feeling hearts, without surrendering its responsibility to the future".[1] The writer was Josef Karl Bernard, who has already been mentioned as a lover of poetry and music and an admirer of Beethoven. Bernard had worked for Castelli, collaborating with that prolific littérateur on his papers *Thalia* and *Sammler*, contributing quantities of verse, satirical or sentimental as occasion required; he was now editing *Friedensblätter* (which, probably owing to its liberal tendencies, failed after eighteen months, but was an attractive little paper while it lasted).

Bernard persuaded Beethoven to give him songs for publication as supplements, and he always included glowing reviews of the composer's concerts and new works. In August 1814 he published a German translation by the poet Rupprecht, of William Graham's ode to Beethoven, to show that as far away as Scotland the Master was appreciated. The ode begins: "Hark! from Germania's shores how wildly floats/ That strain divine upon the dying gale", and the following lines show the appeal which the music (most probably the dramatic and melodious second period sonatas) had for the cultured northern listener, soaked in the romanticism of Sir Walter Scott:

> What magic hand awakes the noon of night
> With such unearthly melody that bears
> The raptur'd soul beyond the tuneful spheres
> To stray amid high visions of delight?
> Enchanter Beethoven! I feel thy power
> Thrill ev'ry trembling nerve in this lone witching hour.

The publisher of Scottish folksongs, George Thomson, sent the poem to Beethoven, who passed it on to Bernard for his journal; it was something of a scoop for the editor, and shows Beethoven's regard for him. Bernard's intelligence, enthusiasm and very radical political views had indeed endeared him to the composer; and, a few years later, as journalist and man-about-town Bernard was to be a very useful contact with the outside world.

[1] *Friedensblätter*, 16 July 1814

During 1814, however, Beethoven had no need of a public relations officer. He certainly could not complain of popular neglect. His music was acclaimed wherever it was heard, to judge by such contemporary reports as that of the *Wiener Zeitung* on the "benefit" concert of 24 July: "The house was very full; the applause extraordinary; the enthusiam for the composer who has now become a favourite of the public manifested itself in calls before the curtain after every act."

During the summer Beethoven escaped from the city to Baden, some thirteen miles out, among the foothills of the Alps. In the quiet of the little spa, with its pretty yellow-washed buildings and its parks and gardens, he rested from the hectic activity of the spring. Here he composed two beautiful though not specially "grand" works—the Piano Sonata in E minor, Op. 90, dedicated to Count Lichnowsky, and the *Elegische Gesang* dedicated to his friend Baron Pasqualati (whose house on the Mölkerbastei he had shared at two earlier periods) in memory of the Baron's wife who had died three years before. This lovely little elegy for four voices with instrumental accompaniment is rarely played, which is a pity, for it has unusual spiritual beauty, more characteristic of the "last decade" than of 1814.

In July, while Beethoven was relaxing in Baden, it was announced by the Emperor's new prime minister, Metternich, that the Peace Congress would meet in Vienna on 14 August. The City prepared to welcome the Very Important Persons who were expected; Beethoven set to work to compose suitable pieces for their delectation, such as *Germania* ("a piece of flattery intended for the royal personages at the coming Congress", says Thayer) "Der Glorreiche Augenblick", a cantata acclaiming the peace makers, and "Ihr weisen Gründer", a setting of words by Bernard. None of these works were very memorable, but they served their turn. The Cantata was performed between *Wellington's Victory* and the Seventh Symphony, on 29 November, in the presence of two Empresses, the King of Prussia and other royalties, with many of Vienna's foremost virtuosi in the orchestra. The critics agreed that the cantata "ccntained some fine numbers and was worthy of the composer"—but it has not been heard since. The verses were poor and platitudinous, mainly concerned with exhortations to Vindebona (Vienna) to rise to the occasion and honour the assembled princes. These, one may suppose, were duly satisfied by the tribute.

Royalty was certainly well represented at the Congress, and the array of old-time monarchs must have caused some misgivings among observers who hoped for a new order of things in Europe. There were two Emperors with their consorts, four kings, three princes and their retinues; also 247 members of reigning houses, accompanied by military leaders (Wellington included), 700 diplomats; bankers, journalists, wives, mistresses, interpreters, cooks, valets, equerries and coachmen. Vienna's population was swollen by over 10,000 visitors, for whom hospitality and entertainment were lavishly laid on. There were concerts, masquerades, sledding parties, fireworks, balloon ascensions, and of course receptions and balls galore. Talleyrand remarked that "the Tsar loves, the King of Denmark drinks, the King of Wurtemberg eats, the King of Prussia thinks, the King of Bavaria talks, and the Emperor of Austria pays". Too true! The Court paid 500,000 gulden a day to feed the guests, besides supplying carriages, with 1,400 horses ready in the Hofburg stables. The Festival Committee appointed by Emperor Franz had a hard task, observing the orders of precedence among the touchy grandees and keeping them happy. A vast number of spies were employed to keep check on the visitors, and the police opened, read and re-sealed 15,000 letters every day, while the Emperor studied reports of scandalous incidents.[1] Suitable music had to be provided, and *Figaro*, Handel's *Samson*, and Spohr's *Germany Liberated* were performed at the opera.

Beethoven was well to the fore: *Fidelio* was chosen as the first opera to be played to the Congress celebrities, a considerable honour for the composer. It was repeated at least twenty times, always to full houses. A friend of Goethe's from Weimar, Carl Bertuch, wrote in his diary that he had been to *Fidelio*, on 28 October, and commented, "Profound, marvellous music"; he went again on 27 December and made a note "Chorus of prisoners excellent. Entire treatment very skilful."[2]

This was a typical opinion, echoed by Aloysius Weissenbach, a professor of surgery and writer from Salzburg, who tells us that, "completely filled with the gloriousness of the creative genius of this music", he decided to visit Beethoven. This was the beginning of a long friendship, although, as the surgeon himself was deaf, conversation had to be carried on by shouting at each other. Weissenbach was immensely impressed by Beethoven's personality: "His character is in complete agreement with the glory of his talent", he said. "Never have I met a more childlike nature paired with so powerful and defiant a will; if heaven had bestowed nothing upon him but his heart, this alone would have made him one of those in whose presence many would be obliged to stand up and do obeisance. . . . That heart clings to everything good and beautiful by a natural impulse which surpasses all education by far. . . . There is nothing in the world, no earthly greatness, nor wealth, nor rank, nor state can bribe it."[1]

If Beethoven could have been tempted to succumb to the "social caress", the last months of 1814 would have been the time. His music was heard and applauded by the assembled potentates (though a gala concert of his work had to be postponed once because, according to a secret police report, "the English are so religious that they will not go to a concert on a Sunday. Therefore the musical Akademie of Herr van Beethoven was postponed from Sunday to a workday"). He was fêted and honoured whenever he appeared, and the Empress of Russia, for whom he wrote a Polonaise (Op. 89) gave him a private audience and 150 ducats. His biographer, Schindler, wrote that "the end of the second period (of his life) showed us the composer on a plane of celebrity the loftiest ever reached by a musician in the course of his artistic strivings". Later, Beethoven "told with a certain pride how he had suffered the crowned heads to pay court to him and had always borne himself with an air of distinction".[2]

The most brilliant parties which Beethoven attended were held at Razoumovsky's palace, but these came to a sad end on New Year's Eve: the Tsar borrowed the splendid mansion for a reception of his own, and adjoining it a large wooden annexe was put up with a table spread for 700 guests. In the small hours of 31 December, this annexe caught fire and it, and most of the palace, was completely burned down. The Tsar, who was indirectly responsible for the tragedy, lent 400,000 roubles towards the cost of rebuilding the palace, but even that was not enough, and poor Razoumovsky never recovered his losses; he gave up his home and social life, disbanded his quartet, and died a few years later mainly of a broken heart.

This was only one personal and immediate disaster of the Congress; but there were also grim long-term effects on the Viennese nobility. The prolonged carnival proved so expensive that many of them became bankrupt. Moneylenders and bankers came to their assistance, thereby accelerating the process of middle class take-over from the aristocracy which had been in process for several years. As their fortunes melted away, the nobles became dependent on the financiers, industrialists and traders. To pay their debts, princes sold their palaces

[1] Thayer, p. 595   [2] Ibid, pp. 600-1

to the new masters: 388,000 florins were paid by Banker Sina to Prince Fries, all of which went to the prince's creditors.

Even so solid a noble as Waldstein sank terribly into debt and ruined himself by wild speculations; and this was not at all unusual. Culturally as well as socially all this had wide-reaching effects: "Public taste changed, following the congress, which impoverished the city and which altered its way of life profoundly", says one historian.[1] Artistic and musical patronage became the prerogative of the bourgeoisie; literature, drama, music, art, architecture were all affected. It is true that the old regime would not recognise the change: cultured people had always been titled, so the Emperor presented bankers with the appellation "Fürst" or Count, and pretended things were as they always had been; hence the prevailing superficiality of Viennese "high life" and culture in the post-war years.

Respectability and frivolity, characteristics of the new Austrian well-to-do became those of Austrian "culture"; by mutual agreement between "Biedermann" (as the typical Viennese bourgeois came to be nicknamed) and Emperor Franz, everything new, daring or democratic was strongly discouraged, while the insipid, shallow and conservative prevailed.

However, in 1814 this was not yet evident. Most people believed that between the receptions and balls, Congress representatives were getting on with the business of ensuring progress and a lasting peace in Europe; in reality each statesman—Metternich, Talleyrand, Castlereagh and Hardenberg the Prussian—was working to get the most for his own government, regardless of the common interest or of the rights of the nations which had been promised constitutions, if not independence. In the effort to put the clock back to the pre-Napoleonic era, the Congress wrangled on for many months. Talleyrand's witticism, "*Le congrés danse mais il ne marche pas*" ("Congress dances but does not go forward") summed up the situation at the end of 1814. Beethoven looked on, regardless of the honours heaped on him, with a detached, somewhat cynical eye. To Kanka, his legal adviser in Prague, he wrote: "I shall not say anything to you about our monarchs and so forth, or about our monarchies and so forth . . . I much prefer the empire of the mind, and this to me is the highest of all spiritual and worldly monarchies."[2]

He was still troubled by financial problems, real or imagined, and in the same letter told Kanka, "You can hardly conceive how I am sighing for the end of this business (the Kinsky settlement) as in everything

relating to my financial affairs it compels me to live in a state of uncertainty—not to mention how it injures me in other respects. You
yourself know that a man's spirit, the active creative spirit, must not be
tied down to the wretched necessities of life." He complained that he
could not work as he wished "by means of my art for human beings in
distress".[1] In another letter, "the vexations and the struggles which all
doing and striving in Vienna entail cannot be paid for!!!!!"[2] On the
other hand, he was evidently enjoying the hectic social whirl, and he
sums up the state of things neatly in a note to his pupil the Archduke
Rudolph on 30 November: "I am still exhausted by fatiguing affairs,
vexations, pleasure and delight, all intermingled and inflicted or
bestowed upon me at once."[3]

"Pleasure and delight" had been all too rare in Beethoven's life, and
were to become even rarer. The fleeting moments of happiness due to
personal success during these months, and high hopes of a shining
future, were all that he had to thank the Congress for. They were good
while they lasted; but disillusion was all the more bitter when it came.

9

Post-war Depression

1815–1817

In March 1815, while the Congress deliberated and danced, Napoleon Bonaparte escaped from Elba and landed in France. The war was after all not over, and the partitioning of Europe perhaps premature; but the hundred days of Napoleon's last-ditch stand made little difference to Vienna. The Congress trailed on, though Wellington and other generals left to rejoin their armies, and the two Emperors and the King of Prussia stayed in the city till the end of May. Their representatives signed the final Act of the Congress on 9 June, by which time everybody of importance had gone home—the princes and their retinues in happy anticipation of soon mounting the Spanish, Neapolitan, Piedmontese or other thrones designated for them by Metternich. In Germany, the French autocracy was replaced by local aristocracy—in Karl Marx's words, "despotism was given naturalisation papers. The Germans thus exchanged one Napoleon for 36 Metterniches, and the Congress had ensured reaction for 33 years."[1]

Vienna was left to the settlement of bills and to its memories and hopes. The red carpets were rolled up and stored away, the shutters closed on the great ballrooms. Razoumovsky's palace stood deserted, much of it a blackened shell, occupied only by ghosts of the glorious music-making of earlier days.

Razoumovsky was a symbol, his situation a premonition of Vienna's state of culture to Beethoven and his republican friends, who saw the new Ministry take over with some foreboding: for it was already clear what the general lines of policy were to be. Franz II had resumed the control of his former empire, and his realm once more extended from the Vistula to the Danube, from Galicia to Venice and Naples. He was determined to rule as an absolute monarch, and was well supported in this by Metternich and his henchmen. Their policy consisted in

[1] Karl Marx, speech at Brussels, 22 February 1848

propping up "Legitimacy" (the Habsburg dynasty) and in laying the
spectre of revolution which still haunted them. They re-established the
secret police which Joseph II had used to protect his liberal measures, to
enforce their new reactionary laws and intimidate those who might
have claimed the promised constitutions and civil rights.[1] On the
whole, the majority of the war-weary peoples submitted surprisingly
quietly to the yoke that was reimposed on them; but there were
sections who did not. There were signs of unrest even during the Congress, when young people in Vienna demonstrated in support of the
demands for Italian freedom voiced by the Carbonari (considered most
dangerous revolutionaries).

It was natural that political demonstrations should take place in the
capital, to draw the attention of the mighty men assembled there to the
wishes of the people whose fate they were deciding. It was also to be
expected that the police, both public and secret, should pursue the
demonstrators. A great many students were picked up, with or without
cause, on the charge of agitating, or associating with agitators; and the
older citizens of radical opinions who remembered the difficult days
of the 1790s were shocked at this revival of repression. We have evidence that Beethoven was among them, from Anton Schindler, his
biographer, who himself was arrested.

Schindler, the musical son of a Moravian teacher, in his last year at
the Law Faculty of Vienna University, tells his story as follows: "We
have come to the time when the Carbonari had begun to agitate. . . .
Anyone who moved from one place to another aroused the suspicions
of the police. These suspicions were augmented by the sympathies,
somewhat too loudly expressed, for Napoleon, when they learned of
his escape from Elba. Young people were particularly vocal in these
expressions, and the author was no exception. There occurred a riot
among a small fraction of the Viennese students—a riot which in itself
was insignificant, but which nevertheless drew the attention of the
officials, so that one of the most venerated professors was removed
from his post."

In February 1815, Schindler tells us, he accepted a teaching post in
Brunn (now Brno, Czechoslovakia): "Hardly had I arrived there when

---

[1] Cf. Friedrich Engels, *The Role of Force in History* (London 1968), p. 29. "The Congress
had carved up Europe in such a fashion that the complete ineptitude of the rulers was
revealed to the whole world. . . . The smallest dynasty was given more consideration than
the largest nation, Germany and Italy were split up into small states once again. Poland
was divided for the fourth time, Hungary remained subjugated and one cannot say the
people were wronged, for why did they put up with it?"

I received a summons from the police. I was asked what connection I had with the rioters at the university in Vienna and was requested to give information about certain Italians in whose company I had often been observed."[1] Schindler's papers were not in order, and the document listing the lectures he had been attending was missing, with the result that he was hauled off to jail.

From all we know of Schindler, he was a most law-abiding person, rather unimaginative, and certainly no dangerous firebrand; it must have been most upsetting to him to be taken for such, and a relief when, after some weeks "it was established that I was not a propagandist and I was released". But a whole academic year had been lost, and he was out of a job.

Very soon after his release, a mutual friend introduced him to Beethoven, who had heard about his adventure. As always keenly interested in the victims of tyranny, the composer invited Schindler to meet him "at a certain place where the master wanted to hear from my own lips the events that had taken place in Brunn".

"As I talked", Schindler tells us, "Beethoven revealed such warm sympathy and concern over my unfortunate experience that I could not keep back my tears."[2]

Thereafter Schindler met the composer regularly "in a remote room of the tavern 'Zum Blumenstock' where Beethoven came almost every day to read the newspapers. It was a sort of cell of a small number of Josephinists[3] of the truest dye. Our composer was not in the least out of place in this company, for his republican views had suffered as a result of his becoming acquainted at this time with the British constitution."

One may justifiably question this last assertion: Beethoven was certainly no less republican because of his interest in Britain. He consorted with Josephinists because they were at this time partisans against the rigid police state imposed by Metternich. He was anti-Habsburg to the end of his days. Schindler, on the contrary, for all his devotion to Beethoven always respected the Establishment and disapproved of "the Master's" insulting remarks about it—to the extent of later cutting them out of the conversation books.

After a while Schindler began to go for walks with Beethoven, and gradually became entrusted with secretarial work for him. His services were a boon, at a time of much correspondence with publishers and with lawyers and officials about the guardianship of Beethoven's

---

[1] Schindler, *Life of Beethoven*, p. 203   [2] *Ibid.*, p. 204
[3] "Josephinists", those who admired Joseph II and his reforms.

nephew. Schindler became virtually an unpaid private secretary, and was from that time intimately associated with Beethoven as general factotum, confidant and almost as a member of the family—besides posthumously as his biographer. Schindler was well equipped to write the composer's life, and his book reflects his devoted zeal. He was often scolded or snubbed by "the Master", but fortunately he was of a rather solemn, very equable temperament, and refused to be upset by Beethoven's explosions, countering exasperation with philosophical calm and heavy humour.

Beethoven was fairly cheerful during 1815, sharing the still prevalent optimism, which gave the government the benefit of the doubt. People knew that in the post-war period devastation had to be made good, prices adjusted, the economy normalised; though there was dislocation, unemployment and poverty, there were still high hopes of reform, civil rights and educational advance. Beethoven gradually came to see that these were unlikely to materialise, with the evident resurgence of reaction; he revealed his misgivings in a letter to Breitkopf in March 1815: "Since I last wrote to you from Teplitz [in 1812] how much has happened—and far more evil than good!" And although much of the letter refers to his personal problems, it is clear that he is preoccupied by the political scene. Echoing Sarastro's last words in *The Magic Flute*,[1] he writes, "As for the demons of darkness, I realise that even in the brightest light of our time these will never be altogether chased away", and concludes: "Your present political conditions do not please me much either, but—but—but—children before they grow up must have dolls to play with of course. And that is all there is to be said on the subject. . . ."[2]

*   *   *

Beethoven's music during this period reflected the short-lived optimism. During 1815 he worked on the Piano Sonata in A, Op. 101, serene in its lovely lilting first movement, cheerful in the surprising March in F, and exultant in the Finale. Both this sonata and its predecessor, Op. 90 in E minor, have expression marks in German, for the first time in Beethoven's works—which suggests that he wished to assert his nationality in opposition to the lightweight Italian music

---

[1] "Die Strahlen der Sonne vertreiben die Nacht, zernichten der Heuchler erschlichene Macht". ("With darkness dispelled by the radiance of day/The wiles of the wicked are driven away"), *Magic Flute*, Finale.
[2] *Letters*, L. 533, pp. 500-1

then coming into vogue. In mood and treatment they stand between the "second period" works, such as the Seventh Symphony and the self-assured Piano Trio in B flat (Op. 97), and the introspective and questing music of the "third period".

The next works of this year, also mid-way in spirit between the second and third periods, were the Violoncello and Piano Sonatas, Op. 102, written in July and August 1815. These also reflect the hopeful mood of the thoughtful "Austrian patriot", typical of that moment in time.

There is, however, more hope than certainty in these beautiful works, in which Beethoven breaks new ground harmonically and rhythmically, and prepares the listener for the heart-searching music of the last decade.[1] Critics differ in their judgment of the 'cello sonatas: to quote only two, A. E. F. Dickinson describes them as "moody", "peculiarly personal . . . with high musical appeal", yet R. H. Kauffer complains of "the brutality, inflexibility and lack of poetic relief" of the final fugue of Op. 102, no. 2. This suggests a failure to see what the composer wanted to convey: at this time, he felt it essential to assert that life with its mystery, beauty and even its brutality was an adventure worth living. Op. 102 shows Beethoven at a time when he was still able to enjoy an exterior life; neither his own problems, nor the European scene were so dark as to efface the sunshine of hope; but after the autumn of 1815 for a long time to come, clouds constantly overshadowed his life, and brightness when it broke through was a spasmodic illumination, of lightning, or of the fire of defiance and anger— rarely of spontaneous happiness.

For this many factors were responsible, and one of them was the social and political scene. As time went by, the Austrian government failed to show any interest in bettering the life of the people, either as individuals or *en masse*. Winter came, and spring, 1816, and nothing was offered by way of relief to the hungry and the poor; no reduction of taxes and bureaucratic restrictions on the professional man, no solution of the difficulties of the artist. On the contrary these all increased. Beethoven was plagued by financial problems which he had hoped would be solved by the advent of peace, but which seemed in late 1815 to increase through the petty restrictions imposed by an inefficient bureaucracy.

Beethoven fulminated against this, time and time again. On 16 May

[1] Cf. Martin Cooper, *The Last Decade*, pp. 132–3, for analysis of musical development between "first" and "third" periods.

1816 he complained of the pass to which things had come, in a letter to Johann Kanka of Prague: "Owing to our present circumstances I am losing on all sides, and my income is barely sufficient for three months, let alone for twelve. . . . That is how things are now in this anarchical monarchical Austria!!!!!!!"[1]

He had lost a considerable proportion of his income through devaluation, through the death of Count Kinsky and the bankruptcy of Prince Lobkowitz. There was little ready money about, owing to the decreased demand for his kind of music, which was neither performed nor commissioned on the former scale. Since the Congress, dance music, light Italian operas, and *Singspiele* of the most frivolous type, were all the rage. The government (as Stendhal commented) encouraged "music, suitable to the taste of the age, which diverted the mind from politics", and "pleasures of a more sensual kind which are less troublesome to a government".[2]

Beethoven's cry from the heart was that nobody wanted serious German music any more. He stormed against the decadent Austrian taste which prevented him from earning a decent living, and against the bureaucracy which made life so difficult and disagreeable. Early in November 1815 he wrote to Antonia Brentano: "Truly our situation has again become distressing. . . . Among the individuals (the number of which is infinite) who are suffering, there is also my brother (Caspar Carl) who on account of his poor health has had to retire on a pension."[3]

An official document dated 23 October survives, refusing Caspar Carl leave of absence from work. On this, Ludwig has scribbled, "This miserable product of financial officialdom was the cause of my brother's death. . . . A nice memorial provided by those vulgar superior officials."

Caspar Carl died on 19 November 1815, leaving his son Karl in the joint care of his wife Johanna and of Beethoven. The latter considered Johanna an immoral woman who should on no account have any responsibility for the boy. His quarrel with her over the guardianship led to endless misery and to long legal proceedings, and greatly affected Beethoven's health. The position of adoptive father, to which he dedicated himself, meant a heavy emotional and financial burden, although—deprived of domestic love and attachment—he welcomed the responsibility and personal reward of paternity by proxy.

---

[1] *Letters*, L. 630, p. 575
[2] Stendhal, *Life of Haydn* (London 1817), p. 8
[3] *Letters*, L. 570, p. 531

Although in 1816 the terrible problems of the guardianship had not yet arisen, the charge on Beethoven's finances was considerable; he worried continuously about his situation, which he blamed, typically, on his *bêtes noires*, the cultural state of Austria and the inefficient local and national government.

In July 1816 he wrote to his Leipzig publisher about his difficulties. "We will not say anything abour our other—world—affairs, or rather, our national affairs. Eurus [the East wind, referred to by Homer as pernicious] will always and ever be with us, producing a stagnant swamp!!!"[1] To Antonia Brentano, in Frankfurt, he introduced Simrock's son with the words, "He can and will tell you a good deal about my present situation and what is more, something about Austria, your native land. . . . Our government shows more and more that it will have to be governed, and . . . that we have not by any means experienced the worst."[2] And in a letter of 28 December, he grumbled again about the bureaucracy and its inefficiency. Sometimes he was merely sarcastic as ". . . if you can do something for my brother (Johann) without overthrowing the Austrian Monarchy, I hope to find you willing."[3]

He joked with the publisher Steiner in mock-official security police jargon: "As for the Adjutant (Steiner), he should be put *in carcere* at once and told to prepare himself for tomorrow's court sitting . . . he is charged with great crimes against the state. . . . He has even failed to observe the rule enjoined upon him to be silent about important affairs of state. (Signed) . . . The Generalissimo."[4]

In January 1817, after discussing ironically the title of the piano Sonata, Op. 101, about to be published by Steiner ("call it the sonata in A which is difficult to perform"),[5] Beethoven dealt another indirect blow at his pet aversion, the Austrian censorship: "Since the Adjutant by recently indulging in tittle-tattle has again disclosed his treacherous and seditious opinions, his right ear must be sharply seized and pulled today—and this must be done immediately"; and "even if it should be proved that he *is perfectly innocent yet the treatment must be given*, so that fear and dread of committing any crimes in future may be instilled into him".[6]

---

[1] *Letters*, L. 642, p. 586   [2] *Ibid.*, L. 660, p. 601
[3] *Ibid.*, L. 700, p. 631   [4] *Letters*, L. 706, p. 634
[5] Beethoven refers to the *Wiener Musikzeitung*, which called the Seventh Symphony "The Symphony in A which is difficult to perform . . ." and adds, "This is the most lavish praise that can be bestowed."
[6] *Letters*, L. 750, p. 662

There is something very Kafka-esque about all this, and indeed about the whole situation of the musician in the bureaucrat-ridden, spy-infested setting, with its prevailing bribery which also did not escape Beethoven's acid pen: "The Lt.-General must butter up the Generalis-simo, who in turn must butter up other people . . . I am obliged to make presents of this kind so that the carriage wheels may be oiled to take me to my destination."[1]

At this stage Beethoven could still mock at the censor and secret police. A few years later, as we shall see, the composer's comments became bitterer, as the all-entangling net spread and caught people he liked and respected, damaging them and their work, suffocating creative expression and interesting ideas with mediocre conformism. In view of the effect this had on Beethoven it is worth looking at the system and its results in some detail.

Spying and informing had, as we have seen, been a feature of the Austrian regime ever since Joseph II. It had been increased for the suppression of "Jacobins" in the 1790s, but during the war years had not been so much in evidence owing to a sufficiency of war-time rules and regulations. During the Congress it was reintroduced and reached grotesque proportions, but was aimed mainly at the foreign visitors, to safeguard the Emperor against international plots or diplomatic conspiracies.

After the Congress, the Minister of Police, von Hager, worn out by his exertions in keeping track of suspects and of supervising the moun-tains of papers submitted by the police, died of overwork; he was succeeded by his assistant, Count Sedlnitzky, a thirty-seven-year-old Silesian nobleman, helped by Baron von Choltitz.

Hager had been criticised for being too mild, and Sedlnitzky promised to do better. He professed total loyalty to the Habsburg throne, and declared to Metternich that he always considered the enemies of legitimacy as "enemies to the peace of Europe and of my monarch". His priorities were the same as those of Gentz, his opposite number in Prussia: "First, freedom (that is, security) for the life of the state, then freedom for the Church, then freedom for all who can use it."[2]

The secret police worked closely with the civil police, and thus Sedlnitzky was extremely powerful; he could keep tabs on provincial suspects through the local police forces, and could also send his agents

[1] Ibid., L. 751, p. 663
[2] Emerson, Metternich and the Political Police, p. 42 et seq.

to the far ends of the Habsburg Empire to root out subversion. Between 1815 and 1818 he succeeded in ferreting out the diplomatic secrets of several other powers; in 1817 his agents went through the portfolio of the English *chargé d'affaires* in Vienna, and they regularly purloined the keys to codes in Russian and other embassies. This irregular treatment of allies was applied on the pretext that friends must always know what friends are up to.

Metternich's eagerness to find out about friends as well as enemies was hard to surpass: everybody was watched—former revolutionaries from France in exile, humble Habsburg subjects travelling abroad, Germans of Jewish origin, and most members of national minorities in Vienna all suffered petty persecution along with Austrians associating with them. Informers were well paid and delivered a mass of documentation, though they were occasionally foiled, as when Prince Esterhazy's servants refused to give them information about unorthodox friends of their master.

The mail was closely watched and often seized regardless of its content, and the Vienna police archives were jammed with the most trivial intercepted letters and statements. The Bureau responsible for reading all private correspondence (the "Secret Cipher Chancellery") was so important that the Emperor cherished it under his direct control and eagerly awaited its hauls. One wonders what he thought of some of Beethoven's outbursts, if they came to his notice!

All this intense political security work, which must have cost millions of W.W. Kronen (Viennese currency), seemed quite unnecessary to the average Austrian, who only wanted decent living conditions and freedom after the restrictions of the twenty years of war; the persecuted minorities merely desired the civil rights to which they were entitled as Habsburg subjects—and their aspirations, in no way threatening at the time, were bottled up, to burst forth in 1848 and destroy much of the system the persecution was designed to preserve.

Of all the oppressed, the peasants were probably the worst off, as they suffered both from the controls of the landowners and of the Vienna police. Joseph's improvements had been swept away by Franz, and though serfdom had officially been abolished, most peasants still owed hard labour service and heavy dues and were severely restricted in their movements. On top of this, the police system was now introduced in the countryside by the "district captains" and their subordinates, in case of any signs of unrest.

All this, Beethoven and his friends knew and often discussed with indignation, as we find in the conversation books which the composer began to use at this time. For instance, when the peasants of Prince Palffy's estate rose in desperation, Franz Oliva wrote on the note-pad: "In Hungary, near Pressburg there is a peasant revolt which seems to be very serious; today 3 battalions of the garrison plus 12 cannons have been brought in. It seems that 8,000 peasants from Count Palffy's estate are involved, and a battalion of the Alexander regiment has gone over to them. The Count's heavy oppression is responsible—in many ways it's worse than slavery."

A little later, we find J. K. Bernard writing, "The Count Palffy's peasants have rebelled against their officials and thrown them out because they have been so harshly suppressed."[1]

Beethoven's conversation books and correspondence contain many disgusted comments on the state of Austria, and also remarks showing that he knew things were better in parts of Germany (though worse in Russia), and that he admired Napoleon's measures in France and the constitutional government of Britain. He saw the latter as providing a guarantee of liberty, and Parliament as a democratic forum, and he seems to have thought that, since there was no regular police force there, as in Austria, the British people were far freer than his own countrymen. For those who know something of the history of repression and the extensive use of government spies and informers in England at that time, it is somewhat ironic to read the accounts of Beethoven's enthusiasm for British freedom. Schindler tells us, "he admired the political institutions of that country above all others . . . Lord Brougham's speeches often drove the troubled clouds from his mind";[2] (Beethoven had the *Allgemeine Zeitung* delivered to his house especially to read the parliamentary debates). Dr Stumpff, a friend who lived in London, reported him as saying, "the English appreciate all that is strong, good and beautiful". To Cyprian Potter, also from London, he expressed his great desire to see the House of Commons, and said, "You have heads on your shoulders in England." Potter said, "he rushed into politics and called the Austrian government all sorts of names".

Beethoven often spoke so vehemently and loud that his friends had firmly to hush him up: in the conversation book of December 1819 we find the word "Freyheit" written by Oliva, followed by the remark, "Don't speak so loud—you are too well known. The worst of these

[1] Conversation Book (C.B.), I, pp. 198, 204, ed. G. Schünemann, Berlin 1941
[2] Schindler, *op. cit.*, pp. 221, 248

public places is that one is so hemmed in; everything listens and hears. . . ."[1] On another occasion, Beethoven writes, "Can these people hear what I am saying to you?" and the answer is "Nein, you are talking softly",[2] but this was exceptional. He spoke his mind and did not really care who heard him, in spite of his friends' concern.

★   ★   ★

The years 1815–18 were the least creative of Beethoven's adult life. From 1818 onwards he produced, in a steady flow, piano sonatas, the Mass in D, the Ninth Symphony, the late quartets; why then the silence during this time? It was not, as is often assumed, due to the problem of Karl, although he was plagued with worries about the boy's future and his own domestic affairs. He was not yet afflicted by the torments of the lawsuit which overwhelmed him between 1818 and 1820. Karl was still reasonably settled in the boarding school of the warm-hearted and reliable Del Rio; and his sister-in-law Johanna had not yet gone over to the offensive in her efforts to take charge of Karl. His health was certainly poor, his colic and rheumatism bad enough to stop a man of less determination from writing; his deafness had increased alarmingly too. These factors explain to a certain degree his inability to create: but for years past, especially during the war, he had suffered severe sickness and deafness, and yet he had not ceased to write, except during 1810 and 1811, the years of invasion and national depression. His deafness became total and incurable in 1819, the year he was working on the Mass, but it did not prevent him from achieving that, nor from writing the Ninth Symphony and the last quartets.

The silence of the unproductive years 1816, 1817 and 1818, can, I suggest, be explained by social and economic factors hinted at in several letters of those years (some already quoted); to Kanka, for instance, in March 1817 where, after complaining of illness and poverty, he writes: "For indeed I am poor—owing to the times? to poverty of spirit, and to what else?????— . . . I must add that *everything* around and near us compels us to be *absolutely silent*. But this must not be the case in the bond of friendship . . . and loudly I proclaim myself your friend . . .";[3] to Dr Bühler, at about the same time: "At no. 1241 on the third floor lives this poor persecuted and despised Austrian musical drudge";[4] and he signs another letter "the Generalissimo (in thunder and lightning but a little more subdued than usual)". And in a

[1] Thayer, p. 683   [2] C.B., I, p. 92
[3] *Letters*, L. 771, p. 676   [4] *Ibid.*, L. 795, p. 694

cri de cœur to Zmeskall, in August 1817: "I often despair and would like to die . . . God have mercy on me, I consider myself as good as lost. . . . If the present state of affairs doesn't cease, next year I shall not be in London but probably in my grave. . . ."[1]

The cause of Beethoven's loss of inspiration was partly illness and domestic worry, but principally "the present state of affairs", the dreadfully depressing condition of the country and the attendant evils: suffocation of freedom, stagnation of the economy, decadence of culture; tyranny reigned supreme and there seemed no sign of popular resistance in Austria to provide a ray of hope.

Beethoven was acutely conscious of the atmosphere in the outside world, and to write at all, let alone his best music, he needed fresh air, the wind of freedom which had inspired his great works, optimism and joy—none of which were to be found in Vienna at that time. He wrote what he could: canons, with topical words, often satirical, such as "Reden ist wie Silber, Schweigen ist lauter Gold" ("Talk is like silver, Silence is gold") and "Rede, rede, rede" ("Talk, talk, talk—but only to a friend!"); settings to Scottish songs; and several melancholy philosophical *lieder* with words appropriate to his mood, such as *Resignation* ("Out, my light") and *Hoffnung* (Hope)—in spite of its name, introspective and full of aching sorrow. In all those months, there is only one work where his genius breaks defiantly through despair—the Sonata in B flat, Op. 106—the *Hammerklavier*.

As a composer of our own time, suffering much the same conditions of social frustration as Beethoven, said not very long ago: "Artistic creation today is unthinkable. . . . For each free creative artist, shame and fear of the success of dictatorship, gaining strength in the national spirit, destitutes him and deprives him of the liberty he most needs. This forms the basis of anguish and reproach which finally leads to the death of inspiration and genuine intellectual work. . . . Creation, above all an art of freedom, withers where a law of force and violence reigns. . . ."[2]

The dictatorship of Metternich's Austria was not as total nor as brutal as that in twentieth-century fascist Greece, at least in Vienna; but the knowledge that men were being imprisoned and persecuted for their beliefs, and that the censorship was suppressing all free opinion, had the same effect on Beethoven as on Theodorakis. He said in a letter to Archduke Rudolph, "in the world of art as in the whole of our great

[1] *Letters*, L. 805, p. 471
[2] Mikis Theodorakis, Arcadia, Peloponese, April 1969 (on Record of music to Z)

creation, *freedom* and *progress* are the main objectives". And it is clear that when these objectives were made impossible he suffered extreme frustration and disgust. But towards the end of 1817 Beethoven summoned all his willpower and creative energy to utter a cry of revolt and express his anger and grief *and* his supreme confidence in life. The "Hammerklavier" Sonata is an assertion of the human spirit triumphant. It embodied the artist's will to overcome his own troubles, and his knowledge that in spite of present hardship the forces of progress would win in the end.

The "Hammerklavier" Sonata is the voice of "the Inspired Man", who, in Blake's words "comes in the grandeur of Inspiration

> To cast aside from Poetry all that is not Inspiration,
> That it no longer shall dare to mock with the aspersion of Madness
> Cast on the Inspired by the tame high finisher of paltry Blots,
> Indefinite or paltry Rhymes, or paltry Harmonies,
> Who creeps into State Government like a catterpiller to destroy;
> To cast off the idiot Questioner who is always questioning
> But never capable of answering."[1]

---

[1] William Blake, *Milton*, Book the Second

IO

Students in Revolt

1817–1818

Of all Beethoven's afflictions, far the most poignant was the deafness which not only prevented him hearing music but cruelly cut him off from his fellow men as a whole. For an individual as highly sociable and as socially conscious as Beethoven this was especially hard, and he fought a daily battle against isolation, suspicion and pessimism. Because of his basic vitality and determination, and of the mixture of resignation and defiance which he adopted in face of his scourge, he survived; and thanks to his many cultural and social interests, and to the human relationships he was able to maintain, his life in the post-war years was never empty, though often very hard.

By the middle of 1817 he was so deaf that he could only with great difficulty hear what was said to him, nothing of general conversation, and music hardly at all. He had tried many cures and various forms of hearing aids to little avail—in fact, a written conversation with another deaf Rhinelander, named Sandra, reveals that ear trumpets and the like did more harm than good. Beethoven writes: "Baths and country air can help a lot. Don't use machines too soon, by not using one I have managed to preserve my left ear more or less." Sandra says, "I have not used any machine up to now, but I will have to sooner or later."

Beethoven: "It's best to write (instead of speaking) whenever possible, it saves the hearing, which is distorted by machines."

Sandra: "You mustn't laugh at me if I tell you that for the last week I have pinned my last hopes on a very old medical book—the remedy is no more or less than the use of young tips of fir branches—I will write it out for you in full."

Beethoven says he has tried "Gallvanisieren"—"but I couldn't stand it". Sandra writes, "Give me the full address of where you live, I'll send you the whole recipe. It is quite possible as the treatment is completely natural that we may both be so fortunate as to recover our hearing."

Beethoven: "It's a miserable plague, the doctors know next to nothing, and you get tired out in the end, especially when you always have to make such efforts. . . ."

Sandra: "I bought this book by chance on the Tandel market for 20 x. It's by a famous sixteenth-century doctor—the ancients were no fools. What he says about my ailment is exactly right. I have paid out more than 800 ducat pieces (on treatment). I used to be a travelling salesman."[1]

Beethoven's friends offered suggestions and advice: Oliva wrote in December 1817, "You take fresh horse-radish straight out of the earth, and rub it on cottonwool which you stick in your ear. . . . His wife recovered her hearing in 4 weeks that way."[2] But nothing helped Beethoven.

He continued to play the piano privately and his Broadwood, given by the maker, was fitted with a contraption to help him hear himself play, but, according to visitors' accounts, not to much avail. He gave up playing to people and rarely went to concerts; and though he insisted on trying to conduct the revival of *Fidelio* in 1823 this ended in disastrous confusion and was a disappointment which he never got over.

However, all through these years he carried on a social life, restricted though it was, receiving visitors at home and meeting friends regularly at coffee-houses and restaurants.

Conversation was carried on almost entirely through note-books made of folded paper which he took everywhere, along with a big carpenter's pencil, and handed to anyone he received or met or who accompanied him on his walks. There are amusing descriptions of the composer stopping in mid-street to write down a remark or get an answer to a question in his booklet.

The illegibility of some of the entries is not surprising, nor that of the roughly scrawled musical notation, jotted down as an idea flashed across his mind, between sums, addresses, names of shops, items of food.

The conversation books of which some 138 survive[3] are a fascinating record of Beethoven's daily life and encounters. They reflect his passing moods, needs and interests, and throw vivid light on his character and the personalities of his friends.

They are not only the mirror of the daily life and doings of a group of very unusual people, but of the society about them and beyond.

[1] C.B., III, pp. 170–2   [2] C.B., I, p. 91
[3] Of the original 400 "Konversationshefte" over 250 have disappeared, presumably destroyed by Schindler who considered these as of no interest or unsuitable for posterity. The remaining books are now housed in the Staatsbibliothek in Berlin.

They discuss art, philosophy, the state of culture at home and abroad, and all sorts of musical matters. Of course Beethoven's affairs are mulled over, decisions taken or abandoned, pages and pages filled with business concerning his nephew Karl and his schooling. And constantly, at short intervals, occur the questions of politics, censorship and music, that were in the forefront of Beethoven's mind.

At the time the written conversations begin, the end of 1817, the handwritings we get to know best are those of Franz Oliva and of Johann Karl Bernard. The latter, after working on various journals became editor of the *Modenzeitung* in 1818, and owing to his outstanding ability and drive was in 1819 appointed editor of the *Wiener Zeitung*. He usually came hot-foot from his office, bubbling over with the latest news and scandal which he wrote down for Beethoven's benefit.

Being a newspaperman, Bernard was much concerned about the censorship and he often described his problems when items were banned, or his ingenuity in getting round the ban. Someone described him as "the most intelligent and critical brain we have in Vienna", and his razor-sharp intelligence was certainly needed in presenting the facts in those news-dark days.

In the winter of 1817 we find him telling Beethoven about the student risings in Germany. There had been widespread unrest over the lack of autonomy in local government and in the universities, and this had been canalised into protest by the Tugendbund, a fiery band of nationalistic students. The Austrian censor was determined that their ideas should not contaminate the Habsburg provinces. Sedlnitzky put into operation plans to suppress anti-government journalism, both directly and through friendly regimes in northern Germany. (These plans were later embodied in the Carlsbad decrees of 1819.) Subversive literature was to be replaced by orthodox propaganda of the ruling class and the Church. Needless to say, the students went on protesting. In mid-October 1817 they held a festival on the Wartburg hill near Jena, by the castle where Luther was imprisoned in 1520. Luther's crime had been to lead a band of professors, doctors and students to the gate of the city of Wittemberg and to throw on a specially kindled bonfire the books of canon law and papal decrees, declaring, "Now the real struggle against the Pope begins!" On the present occasion, the students tossed books by reactionary authors, and unpopular papers emanating from Habsburg Vienna on to a huge blazing pyre, to the accompaniment of rabble-rousing speeches. This scandalous affair was,

H

of course, played down by the Viennese press, at the demand of the censor, though details infiltrated the provincial newspapers; the *Salzburger Zeitung*, for instance, reported that "the large assembly of German youth which gathered for this year's commemoration was not confined to students from Halle, Leipzig and Jena. About forty students from Kiel were there, to bring German greetings and handshakes from the distant eastern region."[1]

J. K. Bernard filled out the story for Beethoven who followed it with keen interest, and from his inside knowledge added comments on the movement and the clubs springing up all over Germany. "They (the authorities) simply do not understand the young people", Bernard wrote in the conversation book: "The whole generation feels the same, even the young officers . . ."—"The speech by the student Rittmann is most remarkable." As for the repression brought in by Gentz, the police chief in Berlin, "it is the most absurd thing imaginable". Equally absurd, he thought, was the formation of a public society for Truth and Right, against the fanatically devoted secret Tugendbund.[2]

Feelings were at fever pitch and there were many incidents, small riots and arrests. On 31 October, the Salzburg paper said, students from Jena opposed the performance of *Die Weihe der Kraft*, a play by the reactionary playwright Wiener: "the police and gendarmerie with the secret help of the military forcibly arrested the disturbers of the peace; twenty of the troublemakers wore red caps, all alike, bearing a small white cross. These look very like the former French Jacobin caps [*bonnets phrygiens*]. As students do not wear them in everyday life it was assumed that those wearing them must belong to a secret society. . . . These students will be tried and the red Jacobin caps will be part of the evidence against them."

In December the Jena students turned their attention to another "renegade" writer, Kotzebue—known to be a Tsarist agent—and broke his windows. Fuel was thrown on the flames by the writer Joseph Goerres who preached nationalism in his book *Germany and the Revolution* and stormed against "edicts wholly at variance with reason". While deploring chaos, Goerres foretold violent revolution unless his recipe of national independence was adopted. Though no democrat, he was persecuted for his plain speaking and had to take refuge in France. (Oliva told Beethoven in 1819 that "Goerres is ruined for ever because he dared to speak the truth".)[3] Other intellectuals were hounded for much less, and despite protests that they were not connected with the student movement; for instance, Herr von Massenbach, professor at Heidelberg, "imprisoned for suspected sympathies with the students of Tübingen and Heidelberg who had rioted at Heilbronn" in November.[1]

Early in 1818 the representatives of the Holy Alliance met, with those of Russia and Britain, ostensibly to settle the affairs of France, but the meeting was used as a platform to denounce the German universities as hotbeds of revolution. Kotzebue was there, working for the Tsarist secret service, and sent reports to St Petersburg inveighing against professors and students, authors and journalists. The Congress agreed about the dangers of subversion, and repressive measures were increased.

All this only enraged the students more, but tended to drive conspiracy deeper underground. The most hated anti-patriotic figures were marked down for revenge, and this culminated in an event that brought the whole wrath of Metternich's government down on the mass of the students: the assassination of Kotzebue in March 1818 by a young man from Jena, Karl Sand. This happened at Mannheim and caused a huge sensation, particularly in Vienna. The wretched writer was stabbed to death by the student, who then tried to commit suicide but failed and was taken to prison. Sand had been a volunteer in the anti-French campaign of 1813 and had been to the fore in throwing books by Kotzebue on to the blaze at the Wartburg. According to one of the long and detailed newspaper reports, "Sand had been going about for over six months with the plan of murdering Kotzebue in his mind. It had cost him many tears . . . but the man had to die. The deed had been done in the general interest of Teutonia" (as Sand dubbed Germany).[2]

The press gave ample coverage to the story, with all the gory details. Many reports were obviously rather sympathetic to Sand: "From today nobody will be allowed to see Sand. His fine figure and spiritual calm aroused general compassion and everyone crowded to see him. . . ." Sand was something of a martyr for his cause, and might become a legend: "He speaks only of religion, and even when in the severest pain he is gentle and patient. . . . The deed cannot be put down to madness, . . . he shows no sign whatever of insanity." He read Körner's patriotic poems; "he also had on him a copy of the *Literary Weekly* in which Kotzebue had abused a popular satirist in Berlin, and insulted him and the students by calling him 'coarse and repulsive as a student of Erlangen'".

[1] *Salzburger Zeitung*, 15.11.1817   [2] *Salzburger Zeitung*, 22.3.1818

There were many different versions of Sand's attempted suicide; all reports agreed that he "rushed into the street and wounded himself twice" with a dagger, but each put different words in his mouth: "Mankind is avenged!" according to the *Allgemeine Zeitung*; and "God be thanked—it is done!", the *Carlsruhe Zeitung* of 23 March; the *Oestreiche Zeitung* reported, however, that Sand made a longish speech: "He shouted, 'The traitor is fallen, the Fatherland is saved, *es lebe Teutonia hoch!*' then cried out, 'I am a murderer, yes, but all traitors must die. I thank God that he has allowed me to perform this deed!'" On Sand was a note "written in the language of an overstrained mind, full of misguided ideas about Freedom".[1] The youth was held in prison for over a year, then beheaded. A fellow student, Loning, attempted to kill another Russian agent, Ibell, but failed, and committed suicide in prison.

The episode was typical of the overheated romantic nationalism which possessed the young people, and it achieved little except to add interest in the movement, among sympathisers, and alarm among the ruling circles. Metternich made it the excuse to introduce the drastically repressive Carlsbad decrees—the least appropriate way of dealing with a situation caused by the denial of rights to patriotic people who had believed in past promises.

The government's posture was an unfailing source of irritation and a perennial topic of conversation in Beethoven's circle. Bernard wrote on the pad, in December 1817, with a groan over the ignorance of government officials, "they are the only ones who don't know what is happening, or understand the spirit that is moving people". . . . "There are 38 sovereign overlords in Germany now, opposed to the strength of the people". . . . "In fifty years they (the people) will make real live republics for themselves". . . . "The French are more practical, and the English more speculative than the Germans. That's why we are behind. But the Germans only need unity to be in the forefront."[2]

Another very critical visitor was Friedrich Kanne (according to Schindler "this unequalled eccentric", "personification of scepticism"),[3] author of many plays and short operas who exploded on to the pages of Beethoven's note-book in a rash of exclamation marks: "They are terrified of thinkers!" . . . "What about His Eminence the Pope? what about the King of Spain? and France? and Prussia? Goerres!!!" (How one wishes that Beethoven's reactions had also been written down!)

Castelli, a mutual acquaintance, has described Kanne's friendship

[1] *Oes.Z.*, 3.4.1818   [2] C.B., I, p. 65   [3] Schindler, *op. cit.*, pp. 202, 368

with the composer. "When Kanne came to Beethoven a ray of happiness fell across his face. They belonged to each other. Kanne's hair was even shaggier and wilder; his gnarled face even more adamantine, his form even broader, knobblier, chunkier than the composer's. But he had the same great dark eyes. An Atlas of learning walked about in his dirty old green coat. The unkempt eccentric tore up many of his own studies on history and music. He was a nomad who could be found any day walking from the Prater Ring to Wieden, from Wieden to the Josephstrasse, or the Landstrasse. He did his work going along the street; on his walking stick there was a mechanical device which enabled him to fit a little writing-table on to it; if he had an idea, he would dig his stick into the ground wherever he was . . . and begin to write, notes, verses, thoughts, whatever came to mind. Woe to anyone who looked over his shoulder! It was pathetic to see these two unhappy Titans who loved each other, wandering through the Burgthor, dumb, unable to speak to one another."[1]

But Kanne managed to communicate his fiery indignation through the writing-pad. In 1817 we find him scribbling, "There is no such thing as a healthy nation!" and in a general discussion about the government he contributed the opinion that "the Deputies are rotten cowards with no strong national sense. They stick with the authorities because of their salaries. Sie sagen Ja, Ja, und wieder Ja! Where does that lead to?" Bernard chimed in here, "The whole city council is on the side of the Philistines." But, he said, "I shall not leave Vienna because it's only in Vienna that one can really live."[2] To which Beethoven for all his abuse of the city no doubt grudgingly agreed. With all its shortcomings it was only there that he felt at home.

The stifling censorship was a constant irritant: educated and enlightened people bitterly resented not being able to read the books they chose, or risking arrest for possessing them. Oliva writes in December 1819, "I got hold of some interesting reading today: I got it from someone who made me promise nobody else should know what it is. . . . The police go round to all the bookshops . . . even works printed in Austria are banned now, they take away copies, even the whole stock of an edition; it's frightful how the Obscurantists have the upper hand here."

Referring to the absurdity of banning scientific books, "I know of one such example," writes Oliva, "a book on statistics which was printed in Prague and was still allowed here a few months ago."[3]

[1] Castelli, *Reisenovellen*, 1835   [2] C.B., I, p. 77   [3] C.B., I, p. 201

Bernard castigated the authorities for the way the country's affairs were run. "The banker Rothschild from Frankfurt has arrived here and is quartered in eleven rooms. He went to see Prince Metternich immediately. Metternich and Hardenberg (the Prussian Minister) give full protection to the Jews. . . . These big bankers have all the ministers of Europe under their thumbs and can make trouble for the governments whenever they please. There can be no political solutions now without their help." (At this point Bernard wrote some rude remarks about the police, which Schindler cautiously deleted.)

"Such a way has been taken by European politicians that nothing can be done without money and bankers. They have no ideas at all about anything; ideas disappeared with the conquest of Paris. The ruling nobility has learned nothing and forgotten nothing." Czerny chipped in here with: "The Kaiser often leaves the most important things to lie for 2 or 3 years without settling them. . . . It's the same everywhere . . . difficult to exist."[1]

Another day Bernard wrote that "before the French Revolution there was great freedom of thought and political liberty here" (he was thinking of the good days of Joseph II). "The bad government and its enslaving mistrust of the people has bit by bit brought about our present oppression. The governments are not in touch with the needs of the time, but if they want to exist they will have to change in the end. . . ."[2]

When they were not debating politics, Beethoven and his friends talked about music, lambasting the decadence of taste, lamenting the decline of culture in Austria; often they discussed Karl and the complications ensuing from Beethoven's guardianship (to which we will come in the next chapter); and an ever-recurring subject was of course that of Beethoven's own musical work. The conversation books reflect his friends' serious concern about the composer's inability to produce during 1817 and early 1818. How is his work going, what was he writing, they ask. "When shall I get my songs?" and so on.

Everyone was happy when at last, after eighteen inspirationally lean months he found an incentive for embarking on a great new work—important enough to satisfy the most demanding disciple and stifle any critic who might suggest (as some did) that the composer was played out and could write nothing but accompaniments to Scottish songs! The incentive was the news that the Archduke Rudolph was to be installed in March 1820 as Archbishop of Olmütz. Beethoven made up his mind to honour his pupil and celebrate the occasion with a solemn Mass, and the decision provided the motive power needed for renewed creativity. He worked steadily and sometimes furiously on the tremendous task of the Mass in D for the next three years. Only the *Credo* was ready by 1820, and the rest not till 1823; but this was not important—what mattered was that he was creating on a grand scale again, in spite of the unconducive atmosphere and the prophets of despair.

The escape into work on the Mass was Beethoven's salvation at this time. He was disgusted and disillusioned by the society around him, and life in the morass of domestic, financial and legal problems in which he was floundering would have been almost unbearable had his mind not been at frequent intervals on something higher. As it was, the business of the lawsuit and the guardianship, sordid and unfortunate as it was, contributed to his total human experience; the peculiar suffering and bitterness of the struggle, and the heart-lifting relief of final success were eventually embodied in the music of the years ahead.

I I

Problems of Education
1819–1823

However much one might prefer to pass over the events relating to Beethoven's nephew, they have to be outlined in order to explain much strange and wild behaviour, a good deal of friction between friends, and recurring passages of despair and fury in the limited musical output.

In brief then: Beethoven had been awarded guardianship of Karl in 1816 by the *Landrechte* Court which was open only to appellants of noble family (the Van prefixed to Beethoven's name being cited by his advocate as proof of aristocratic lineage). The boy's mother, Johanna, deeply resentful, appealed in 1818 for a reconsideration, on the ground that Beethoven was a commoner, and the first decision therefore invalid. The case was sent to the *Magistrat* (the Viennese Lower Court) which gave judgment for Johanna in January 1819. Beethoven immediately went, through his lawyer Dr Bach, to the Court of Appeals, which, to cut a long story short, ultimately pronounced in his favour in the summer of 1820.

Throughout the years of the proceedings Beethoven was consumed by his personal feelings for Karl, his fear of deprivation, the conviction that he was being hounded to give up what he most cherished by opponents who were wickedness personified. To defeat them was, he felt, an imperative moral duty. The agitation and anxiety made him ill, and drove him to uncouth behaviour and strange utterances. Several books have had something of a *succès de scandale* in their attempts to expose the seamy side of Beethoven's life, but they do little credit to their authors' sense of proportion. It would be more seemly, one feels, to lament the tragic circumstances which left the composer in charge of his nephew in the first place, entangled him in a web of recrimination and bitterness, and led to great expense of spirit, time and money on all sides.

It is not particularly helpful to blame the deaf and ailing genius for his eccentricity, nor to elevate Johanna to the rank of martyr. More useful could be an attempt to understand Beethoven's behaviour and to gauge the effect of the searing experience on his personality and work. Why did he fight with such furious determination for Karl? Life would have been far simpler if he had washed his hands of the boy; he would certainly have got on with more writing and been saved a great deal of trouble and expense. But that of course is unthinkable, knowing what we do about Beethoven, and looking into the reason why.

Two factors compelled him to plunge into the case as into a life-and-death struggle. First, his intense need for human, personal love, of which he had, he felt, always been deprived. We find him expressing this need in many of the songs, often chosen for their words crying out for love: "Ach, die hart verteilende Liebe!" ("Ah, love, the cruel divider") of *Turteltaube*; "Nur wer die Sehnsucht kennt, weiss was ich leide" ("Only he who knows longing, knows what I suffer"), by Goethe; "Denn ach! mir mangelt Gegenliebe" ("For ah! I hunger for mutual love") by Bürger. Second, he was impelled by his overpowering sense of duty, of high moral mission. He was determined that a child for whom he was even partly responsible should have the best, and attain the highest that life could offer. The intense desire to do the right thing was a near obsession. This is often shown in the lofty moral tone of many songs, from Gellert's "Geistliche Lieder" to "Der Mann vom Wort". Only the very highest standards satisfied him, and it is heartrending to witness the misery that his idealism subsequently caused.

"The sole objects of all my efforts and desires", he wrote to the *Magistrat*, "are the best possible education for the boy . . . I know no duty more sacred than supervising the education and rearing of a child." Hence what Fanny Del Rio (daughter of Karl's headmaster) called "the passionate pursuit of the education of his nephew", a good education such as he himself had never had the chance to enjoy.

Throughout his life Beethoven had made strenuous efforts to make up for the inadequacy of his early schooling. In spite of overtime given to music he read indefatigably in what he considered uplifting books (no trivia for him!)—the classics, Shakespeare, oriental philosophy in translation, and the leading contemporary German, French and Italian writers in the original. Schindler tells us that in "the Master's" library he had Schiller, Goethe, Wieland, *Macbeth*, the Bible, constantly to hand; and we know that his Homer and Shakespeare were dog-eared from continual use, and heavily underlined. From the conversation books it appears that he read authors as widely assorted as Ovid, Schelling, Plato and Byron; of the latter, he noted "Der Vampire . . . von Lord Biron 40 x bey Schaumberg", in December 1819. Bernard, a few months after this recommended *Der Korsair*—"das wildeste und Phantastischste" imaginable, "but without magic". Byron has the most fantasy and deepest feeling of all living poets, Bernard said, adding the biographical note: "He gets two guineas for every verse he writes. Lives wherever he pleases, in Greece, Italy, Asia, France, etc. Easily the most famous poet in Europe. . . ." Later, Bernard commented that "Byron writes like a man with a guilty conscience, dark, wild and frightening—but full of spirit and imagination . . ." and he suggested *The Vampire* for an opera libretto.[1]

Such conversations were frequent and show that Beethoven's mind was much occupied with literature, poetry and philosophy. In his note-books he often scribbled book titles, authors' and publishers' names, and prices. Sometimes the titles are for immediate practical use, such as *Pesther Kochbuch* (Hungarian cookery book) or *Hausärztherkund* (Home doctor); others have serious or melancholy implications: *Friedrich Christians Vermächtnis an seiner Söhne*; Goldkorne's *Kleine Bibel für Kranken und Sterbender*; Hufeland's *Makrobiotik. 2 Theile, Berlin 1820".[2]

His friends often helped the composer in his self-education by lending or recommending books. Bernard suggested the Life of Cellini, Friedrich Kanne offered him Schelling's *Lectures on Academic Studies*, and Schleiermacher's *Monologues*. Bernard provided information about the local public library, where Beethoven possibly thought of reading, but which compared unfavourably with libraries elsewhere: the Vienna library only opened for three hours a day, and was shut for twelve weeks' holidays in the year. "They should be open from 6 a.m. till 10 p.m. every day", in Bernard's opinion, "so that they can be used by people who are working during the day. In Paris they are open until midnight!"[3]

While struggling untiringly to improve his mind, Beethoven felt he

---

[1] C.B., II, p. 32

[2] Trans: *F. Christian's Legacy to his sons; Little Bible for the Sick and the Dying; Makrobiotik—the science of prolonging life.* Hufeland was a well-known physician in Berlin.

[3] C.B., II, p. 173

must be equally indefatigable in raising Karl's *Kultur* to the highest possible level. It was hard work at first. Although everybody agreed (perhaps to please his uncle) that the boy was unusually bright, healthy and talented, Karl showed little aptitude for learning or for obeying the school rules at Del Rio's or anywhere else. Emotionally deprived by the loss of his father at the age of eight, and being subsequently kept from his mother (for that was what Beethoven's conception of guardianship involved) Karl was insecure and hostile to discipline and lessons. For four years (1816 to 1820) his uncle worried about his progress, grieving at the poor school reports and Karl's lack of interest in higher things. He longed for the boy to be a musician, and did his best to encourage any latent talent, taking him to concerts ("I request you [Del Rio] to let me fetch him at about 11 tomorrow for I want to take him to an interesting recital") and giving him lessons himself. This proved unrewarding, as Beethoven's worsening deafness made tuition almost impossible, and Karl's pianoforte studies were eventually entrusted to Carl Czerny. His uncle, however, continued to take a close interest in the boy's playing, and gave Czerny advice on how to teach him (which might to such an expert as Czerny have seemed unwarranted interference had it not come from "the Master"). In a letter of 1817 he urges Czerny to "be as patient as possible with our Karl ... if you are not patient he will do even less well because (although he must not know this) owing to the unsatisfactory time-table for his lessons he is being unduly strained.... Treat him so far as possible with affection, but be firm with him."—"In regard to his playing for you, as soon as he has learned the right fingering and can play a piece in correct time and the notes too more or less accurately, then please check him only about his interpretation; and when he has reached *that point*, don't let him stop playing *for the sake of minor mistakes*, but point them out to him when he has finished playing the piece. Although I have done very little teaching, yet I have always followed this method. It soon produces *musicians*, which, after all, is one of the chief aims of the art."[1]

Beethoven wrote frequent notes to Del Rio asking him "to ensure he (Karl) puts in time for practising the pianoforte", insisting that "la musica merita d'esser studiata", stressing "his great talent", and asking for leave of absence for Karl: "I have to go through some music with him and take him to some musical performances".[2] In spite of all this, Karl never became a good pianist, but he developed a nice critical sense and some of his later comments about music and musicians were really perceptive.

It was Karl's general education which chiefly worried his uncle, who went to great lengths to find what he considered suitable institutes or tutors for him. Beethoven was hard to please, and found fault with every school in turn. At the beginning of 1818 after two years at the Del Rio establishment, the boy was taken away, ostensibly because Johanna managed to get in to see him there (even, on one occasion, dressing up as a boy to get inside), but probably because Beethoven did not think the school good enough for his precious ward. He had Karl to live with him and with the help of a Professor Hohler found a tutor. He told Frau Nanette Streicher, an old friend and good counsellor on his home problems, "I must be grateful to Heaven that everywhere I find people who . . . are ready to help me . . . I have come across one of the most distinguished professors at the university here, who is arranging and advising me in the very best way about everything connected with Karl's education."[1]

In spite of this expert help the arrangement did not work out well. Life in Beethoven's house, the alternate indulgence and severity, the prevailing confusion and the constant quarrels between master and servants, cannot have been easy for a sensitive youngster, already pretty insecure. Beethoven suffered too, from an overpowering sense of responsibility towards the boy and deep suspicion of all around him —the tutor who did not come home all night, the servants who were on Johanna's side—and was intolerably crotchetty and overbearing. The boy resented this, the servants were up in arms, and Beethoven himself was restless and miserable, his only solace the devoted Nanette and God ("I appeal to him in the last resort.")[2]

When Beethoven moved to summer lodgings in Mödling Karl was sent to the village school, which was run by the Pastor, Johann Froehlich. This was a failure; according to Froehlich, Karl was unmanageable, while in Beethoven's view the pastor was a scoundrel in league with "the Queen of Night". Karl was again privately tutored, this time for the Vienna Gymnasium entrance examination, which he took in August 1818. He was admitted, and seemed to settle down to his lessons, with extra tuition in French, piano and drawing, while still living at his uncle's house in the Landstrasse suburb.

In September, Johanna made an application to the *Landrechte* to have the boy under her care. This was rejected in October, but Johanna was determined to try again. Karl knew of her persistence, and he reacted to it by running away from Beethoven to her in December. On the strength of this, and asserting that the boy was not properly cared for, she again applied to the Court, which this time referred the case to the *Magistrat* (Commoners' Court). This court held a preliminary hearing, then deferred the case to a later session in January 1819. In the meantime, Beethoven was still responsible for Karl's schooling, and was once more faced with the problem of finding somewhere suitable for his studies.

There is no hard evidence to show why Karl left the Gymnasium to which he had been admitted in September. It may be that the Headmaster considered that he had blotted his copybook by running away from home, or that in other ways he did not come up to the strict standards of the Gymnasium; or perhaps Beethoven decided to remove him in disapproval of the form of education he was getting, and of the curriculum, typical of such Austrian schools.

These institutions were described by a contemporary observer (who called himself Charles Sealsfield to avoid trouble with the authorities), as "throughout Austria the same. The director of the Gymnasiums and the Lyceums . . . is also a priest. They are under the control of a counsellor of the Government to whom they make their reports. The elementary schools are equally under the supreme direction of a clergyman . . . answerable to the Government."—"The youth who has run through the elementary schools passes into the Latin schools or Gymnasiums."

At Karl's age (nearly fourteen) he would have the following curriculum: "He reads extracts from Latin authors and the elements of the Greek language; two hours in the week are allotted to religion, mathematics, geography and history. Each Gymnasium has one prefect, six professors and a teacher of religion. . . . In six years the youth . . . is advanced to the university."

"The school books for all these different classes", Sealsfield goes on, "are compiled in Vienna under the superintendence of the Aulic commission of studies. They are subject to such alterations as a new created counsellor of the court thinks fit to suggest, according to his own or his Emperor's notions. These school-books are the most barren and stupid extracts which ever left the printing press. The professors are bound, under penalty of losing their places, to adhere literally to these skeletons."[1]

[1] Sealsfield, *Austria*, pp. 77–9

One can imagine Beethoven looking at some of Karl's textbooks and deciding in disgust that this was not at all the education he wished him to have. He may also have realised what Sealsfield noted about the effect of this schooling on a young hopeful who "has gone through the academical course of these studies" and "knows a little of everything but on the whole nothing. He has regularly forgotten in the succeeding course what he had learned by heart in the preceding. A free exercise of the mental powers, a literary range is impossible, nay, against the instructions of the professors." This would hardly appeal to Beethoven, whose mainspring in life was "the free exercise of the mental powers". Nor would the fact that "the youth during the time of his studies is watched with the closest attention. His professors are *ex officio* spies. . . . His predilections, inclinations, his good and bad qualities, every movement is observed and registered in their catalogues, one of which is sent to the Government," another deposited in the school archives. "This observation increases as the youth advances into the higher classes, and a strict vigilance is paid to his reading . . . if he applies himself to law . . . his principles about the natural rights of man and of government are extorted under a thousand shapes and pretences."

Beethoven, looking ahead to Karl's future, and longing for him to become a broadminded, free-thinking individual, knew that any independence of outlook would be squashed by this regime; and he must have agreed with Sealsfield what the end product would be: "The youth, having finished his academical course . . . is entirely in the hands of the Government. . . . Has he given the least cause of suspicion, shown the least penchant towards liberal ideas? Then he may be sure that the higher his talents, the less his capacity to serve his Emperor. . . . An unguarded word is sufficient not only to preclude his advancement but to deprive him even of his station."

Small wonder then, if Beethoven thought it better for Karl to leave the forcing-ground for young ultras and breathe the freer air of a private school. Outside Vienna, "private teaching was not allowed", but in the capital it was permitted and there was a choice of several schools. Del Rio took Karl for a few weeks in January 1819 to tide him over till a permanent place was found, and in February the boy was sent as a boarder to the school of one Johann Kudlich. This proved so unsatisfactory that by the end of May his uncle had taken Karl away, writing to Bernard on 18 June that "I will never again send him to Kudlich who is either a rascal or a weak fool!!!!!!"[1] But where to

---

[1] *Letters,* L. 950, p. 816

send him now? Del Rio quite naturally refused to have the boy back,
and there was another hiatus in the poor child's education. Beethoven
applied for a passport for Karl, hoping to send him to Professor
Sailer in Bavaria (where, Bernard said, "he would be in the best of
hands", Sailer being a distinguished scholar and a great admirer of
Beethoven). But, as frequently happened in Austria, a passport was
refused. At last, in July 1819, Karl was given a place as a boarder at the
institute in Vienna run by Joseph Blöchlinger, a Swiss who had worked
with the famous educationalist Pestalozzi, and who had a good
academic reputation. There Karl probably learnt as much as he would
have anywhere in Austria at the time.

The *Magistrat* decreed on 17 September in favour of Johanna, and
Beethoven immediately flung himself into the battle to win back the
guardianship. He engaged Dr Bach, a very able lawyer, to act for him,
and was encouraged by Bach to high hopes of success. None the less,
during the last months of 1819, the suspense and anxiety reduced
Beethoven to a very nervous and excitable state; he found it difficult
to work, and we find his friends urging him to get on with the Mass—
"Können Sie sich denn nicht losmachen, um Gotteswillen für Sie und
die Kunst!" ("Can't you finish it, for God's sake, for yourself and
Art")[1] and "Mit der Messe sind Sie noch aufgehalten" ("Are you held
up again with the Mass?")—writing fussily and indecisively to publishers, abusing his acquaintances, worrying over Karl's health. He
picked quarrels with everyone, including Blöchlinger, who did not
always prevent Johanna from visiting her son at school (which she was
entitled to do) though he tried to keep on the right side of the composer. Beethoven accused him of being false, weak and dishonest, and
even wrote that if Frau Beethoven were allowed to see Karl, "legal
proceedings will be taken against you as a seducer of my nephew into
low company".

Blöchlinger seems naturally to have been somewhat alarmed. He
went to see Beethoven and concurred with everything he said: Karl's
mother, he agreed, was "a canaille, no better"; and "Unhappily", he
added (surely a little unnecessarily), "the boy seems to be going the
same way. He lies every time he opens his mouth." Oliva commented
that "Blöchlinger seems to be a garrulous fellow who behaves wrongly
through misguided ideas, rather than because he is bad. I think he is
cowardly, so he doesn't behave as firmly as he should towards Karl's
mother."

[1] *Letters,* L. 959, p. 829

The conversation books give us a curiously vivid picture of Blöchlinger, the respectable, rather grey, cold Swiss pedagogue (Beethoven called him "the ice-house" and "that glacier"), anxious to be on good terms with the important parents—a type not only found in Metternich's Vienna.

Relations improved between the two men after the lawsuit was wound up in July 1820. Judgment was given for Beethoven, made co-guardian with Court Councillor Dr Karl Peters, and the composer was thereafter in a much more amiable frame of mind. One day the Headmaster went to visit him, evidently hoping to impress with his lofty account of his educational methods, his ideas on life, religion and politics, which he wrote in the conversation book: "One must do all the good one can in this world without thought of self; otherwise one is more or less sick in spirit. If our own conscience does not reward us we are greatly to be pitied." Talking of country life, he observes, "there one is closer to Nature. Here, eating and recreation occupy one too much to allow full consciousness. One must sacrifice all that, otherwise one is lost."—"Today so much is threatening. We live in difficult times. We must wait and watch patiently . . . and do what we can each in our own circle."—"Religion comes into it, and the so-called Liguorians[1] have started practising Gnosticism again; people join in and agree with it because they do not know what to do for the best."

Knowing Beethoven's interest in politics, Blöchlinger airs his views in unexceptionable terms: "Everything was much better before 1813", he says. "Later the aristocrats won power again in Austria, and now the republican spirit is only a glimmer in the ashes . . . I don't believe a union of German States is thinkable, though it would be the best thing for us. . . . Anyway, not till the numerous monarchs give up their privileges. . . . If we could only get rid of the Russian influence then it might be possible." He adds, probably in defence of the Tsar against abuse by Beethoven, "Alexander does a great deal for his people."[2]

Blöchlinger talks a good deal about Pestalozzi, follower of Rousseau, whose experimental school had become famous in Europe, and whose name still survives and is honoured, though in his own day his ventures ended in debt. Beethoven was interested in the idealism of Pestalozzi

[1] Liguorians: members of the strict Catholic sect, the Congregation of the Most Holy Redeemer, founded by A. M. de Liguoris in 1732.
[2] C. B., I, p. 323

who gathered into his schools the destitute children of the poorest class, first in Switzerland then in France. The schools at Yverdon and at Mirtel were based on Pestalozzi's idea of a system of "social harmony and happiness" combining useful practical work with elementary learning. Teresa Brunsvik worked in the Yverdon school, by the Lake of Neuchatel, for a while, and perhaps this was another reason for Beethoven's interest. We find him asking Blöchlinger about the teacher who, at seventy-four, was still running his school though "poor, reviled and slandered", and Blöchlinger remarks: "His methods are only agreeable to a few people, because he lives too much for mankind for others to want to imitate him, so they prefer to laugh at him. . . . The difference between him and many schoolmasters of our day is the same as the difference between Christ and the Pharisees. . . . Most of his writings, especially his economics, are banned here, as I know from personal experience."[1]

It seems that Blöchlinger left Pestalozzi's idealism behind when he came to teach in Vienna, for the pupils in his institute were very different from the deprived children of Yverdon, and he evidently taught them on the accepted academic lines. Beethoven questioned him closely on the running of the school, probably with Karl's slow progress in mind, and Blöchlinger defended his system energetically, and offered excuses for its shortcomings: "The teachers can't if they have 150 pupils guarantee that every one of them understands the subject. . . . To improve the curriculum one should subdivide each class and have one teacher for 25 pupils, but this is not possible . . . I am mostly at home. One has to keep an eye on things . . . to have a good influence." But Kanne, in another conversation, said "teachers here are too lazy. Your nephew is not properly developed, that's my bitter conviction. . . . The pupils learn too much by heart. . . . Nobody ever grows up by learning by heart alone."[2]

As to Karl's material wellbeing, Blöchlinger assures the anxious "parent" that the school meals are adequate and that he believes in the staff eating with the pupils in an egalitarian manner: "The pupils should know they are having the same food as the teachers."

Karl's comments throw a rather less rosy light on the school diet and some doubt on Blöchlinger's generosity. The boy complains of the watered-down milk and the shortage of bread at meals: "The housekeeper used to test the milk by sticking her finger into the can. It used to be much better, we got as much bread as we wanted—at 11 everybody was given a big piece and we could eat as much as we liked at table. Now we can't get bread in the morning, but go hungry from 7 till 1 o'clock, and only get two pieces at table. In the evenings only one piece although we most of us think bread is the best thing we have to eat at that meal"—"When I had scarlet fever I should have starved if you hadn't sent me extra food."

Another time he tells his uncle, "they all say that I look fatter when I go back after the week-end". Beethoven pressed Karl for details about the school, which were readily forthcoming: "The servant wants to leave Blöchlinger—because of hunger—. . . rice soup but without meat as they haven't got any. . . . Green vegetables with bacon. Mutton bones, gruel, salad."[1]

The trivia jotted down by Karl add up to a funny and not very flattering portrait of his Headmaster. "He insists on drinking coffee without sugar in the staff room, and won't provide sugar for the teachers. When they started bringing their own as a hint, he made them drink cocoa, and took his coffee into another room." One boy wet his bed at night, and Blöchlinger gave him a beating and would not let him have any supper but thin soup for several days. "I don't think that was fair or sensible", commented Karl. Nor, one might add, worthy of a follower of Pestalozzi.

A little light relief is provided by the story of Frau Blöchlinger's birthday party, which Karl announced in June 1823: "At the beginning of July he is going to celebrate the Name Day of his illustrious spouse with a party. As he can't afford to pay the expenses himself every pupil has been ordered to ask his parents for a contribution." Karl had been somewhat embarrassed at having to ask his mother as well as Beethoven for a donation. "Everybody thinks she should not be asked to contribute. I was surprised he gave me such a task."

Why was Blöchlinger organising this event, Beethoven wanted to know, and Karl writes, "Partly to surprise his wife, partly good business. At first he had the idea that all parents living in the town should send some food as well as money. *Ein Art Piknik* (A kind of picnic). I believe he isn't thinking of anything except to have a good day's drinking without paying for it . . . on such occasions he always drinks the whole night through." Karl adds the reflection that "in the end what Palay (one of the teachers) prophesied will be true: 'The Institute carries in itself the seeds of its own destruction.'"[2]

A few days later the boy reports that "up to now only two contribu-

[1] C.B., III, pp. 336, 378   [2] C.B., III, pp. 325, 326

tions have come in, though we worked the whole week to get them—
one of 10 fr. W.W., the other of 5 fr." Beethoven is obviously worried
at having to pay up and wants to know how much is expected of him;
Karl assures him that "nobody will give more than that—you give
whatever suits you. But the ones whose home is in the town are being
begged to send food as well." How much food, his uncle asks. "Every
family will probably send according to the number coming to the
party, and as a lot of them are very keen to show themselves off he will
get enough in the end." In fact, some days later we learn: "Now
everybody has contributed and the sum collected comes to 300 fr. But
the parents still have to send food." Karl tells his uncle proudly that "on
the birthday I have to recite the famous speech from *Hamlet*, To be or
not to be, in English." And as the day draws near, he says he can't come
home next evening because of the party. "What party?" Beethoven
asks. "The party I had to invite you to" (Karl, slightly reproving of
such forgetfulness). "Actually it's on Saturday evening. It goes on all
night and I have to be there to tidy up after it." We may assume that
his guardian gave a contribution (though probably not of food) but
did not feel bound to attend.

Two more observations finish off the story of the party: "These
new shoes? Blöchlinger's wife bought them as I needed some for
dancing at the *Fest*". Finally, "On the day of the party I was up till
sunrise."[1]

However unwillingly Beethoven contributed to the funds, he must
have been glad to see Karl so innocently excited and happy, and his
heart certainly swelled with pride to know that Karl was reciting
Hamlet—surely a sign of the cultured man he so much wanted the boy
to become.

*   *   *

Karl was in spite of everything acquiring a modicum of culture and a
degree of useful learning at the institute, as can be seen from pages in
the conversation books covered with his tidy handwriting and sensible,
often shrewdly practical remarks. We find him talking about Greek
drama: "They had theatres where 80,000 people could sit and listen.
Their building methods must have been amazing. In our modern
theatres not a tenth of that number would be able to hear. . . ."[2]

Karl quotes Homer (in Greek) and Ovid and Goethe, and discusses

[1] C.B., III, pp. 347, 372   [2] *Ibid.*, III, p. 384

Beethoven's cherished collection of books, slightly superciliously: "Our library is very deficient; we'll have to see about improving it. . . . It's a shame—when one volume is missing from Goethe's works the whole set is ruined . . . Schiller too." His uncle must have grumbled about the cost of "improvement", for Karl writes, "I believe it's better to give money to a bookseller than to a fashion-house."[1]

He helped Beethoven to do his accounts, and worked out percentages and premiums, which the composer found beyond him—the only way Beethoven could do multiplication was to write out the single figures vertically as many times as necessary and add up the column; Karl must have saved him hours by the application of schoolboy arithmetic.

By 1823 the boy was qualified to take the entrance examination for the Polytechnic, and was admitted to the college (which he entered in 1825). Beethoven had new problems as the lad grew up, began to go out and to bring home friends whose standards of culture and behaviour were not what he would have liked for his precious nephew. But, at least, the worst anxieties were over, and in 1823, secure in his possession, he enjoyed Karl's company and—*pace* the psychologists—the boy's affection.

Difficult though Beethoven was, and great (and often unreasonable) though his demands were on Karl, it does not strike one, reading the conversation books, that the boy was constantly harassed or unhappy. On the contrary, having grown up and adjusted to his strange surroundings Karl had evidently taken his place in Beethoven's circle, and, like the other loyal friends, played his part in making life bearable for the deaf genius with patience and humour. He helped in many ways —taking messages, supervising copyists, drafting and writing out letters; but there is no reason to suppose he overstrained himself, and his remarks, anecdotes and comments throughout 1823 and 1824 show a good relationship which did not suffer seriously when Beethoven found fault and exploded in abuse. There were certainly quarrels, but like many family disputes they were almost immediately made up with explanations on both sides and more likely cleared the air than made for permanent hostility. It is a pleasure, after reading Karl's apology or explanation of a tiff, to come across such remarks in the conversation books as "I'm enjoying myself already here at home", and *"Bester!*[2] We study, we sleep, we eat, drink and laugh—what more do you

---

[1] C.B., III, p. 384
[2] Trans.: "My dear fellow!" or "Old Boy!"

want?"[1] And Karl's contributions to the table talk are generally cheerful and lively.

However, as time went on Karl obviously increasingly felt the lack of freedom under his uncle's roof and the constraint on his choice of friends. It was natural that he should rebel and want to assert his independence, and Beethoven's obtuse refusal to understand this led directly to disaster.

Several pages of the conversation books bear witness to Karl's interest in gambling (to prove himself adult and sophisticated), and in stories of suicides, which were not uncommon in this age of economic crisis and *Weltschmerz*; and it is with a sense of foreboding that one reads Karl's admiring description of the young rakes in Paris who "spend their last but one franc at the gaming table, and their last on a pistol to shoot themselves"; and of Count Palffy, who "spends his time at the bank playing for high stakes. . . . He lost 20,000 florins in one night recently. . . . At the time of the Congress he lost a million in Paris and the Emperor had to pay out for him."[2] Beethoven is treated to an account of one Mikailovitch "who committed suicide after an unhappy love affair" and one can imagine his pitying contempt—to squander the precious gift of life for a woman was for him unthinkable, and even in his most harrowing moments he would never have contemplated suicide. But it was the fashionable way out of their troubles for romantic young men of the Austrian and German upper classes, who read *Werther* and Foscolo's *Jacopo Ortis* and felt that life in the ugly, decadent new industrial age had nothing to offer except unpleasant pressures and demands. It is not surprising that Karl who considered himself definitely one of the young *élite* should have dreamed of such a melodramatic escape from his difficulties and debts. One might have hoped that the example of his uncle (for whom life must often have seemed intolerable), and the "moral" teaching of Blöchlinger and Del Rio, would have given Karl pause; but too many pressures were at work —lack of freedom at home, bureaucratic restrictions outside, the political and intellectual suffocation in Vienna; these, with the shortages of money in his pocket and the problem of finding cash for the expensive clothes and amusements he longed for, caused him anxieties which, with his fundamentally insecure character, he could not face. That he eventually rushed out and made an unsuccessful attempt to take his own life—dramatically, *à la* Childe Harold on a romantic rocky crag

[1] C.B., IV, p. 342
[2] It is not known whether Karl gambled, but he was certainly heavily in debt in 1825-6

outside the city—was perhaps not extraordinary. But it was a terrible and unnecessary tragedy which broke Beethoven's heart.

However, the years we are considering were a period of relative calm, when Karl's presence and personal affection provided an element of satisfaction which sustained the composer through the stress of writing some of his most demanding and very greatest music.

12

The Sublime and the Ridiculous

1820

Throughout the years of the lawsuit, with their background of severe economic crisis, Beethoven had been worried and depressed. The legal settlement in his favour, and the slight recovery of the Austrian economy after 1819 lifted some of the load from his heart; and though his deafness and the oppressive atmosphere of the police state still greatly affected him, we know that his creative genius had revived, and reading between the lines of letters and of the conversation books we can glimpse a calmer frame of mind. In February 1820 he wrote on his pad, in heavy pencil, a quotation fitting his mood: "The moral law in us and the starry sky above us—Kant!!!" Those words rang in his mind as he worked at the Mass, and in the months that followed he temporarily regained inner peace, and much of his zest for life.

It is true that the completion of the Mass was proving arduous—it should have been ready for the Archduke's installation in March 1820, but in fact took two more years to finish; and during that time he was engaged off and on in a dreary wrangle with publishers over the sale of the work, which he offered to several at once in a most unethical manner. Beethoven seems to have had a double standard of morality when doing business, strange in someone so strictly moral in personal matters. One can only put it down to his near-obsession with getting as much money as possible, not for himself but to ensure Karl's future.[1] He also had the feeling, we know, that he was underestimated, and that the world owed him a much greater reward for his work than he ever got.

His behaviour in this case was irrational, as it was indeed in many more trivial domestic things, and it may be accounted for by the

---

[1] Every florin he could save was put aside for Karl's future. 4,000 florins were invested in bank shares for Karl, which Beethoven refused to touch, even when in apparent poverty during his last few years of life.

severe stress under which he worked when producing the Mass. Schindler has given us a glimpse of the "pathetic, impressive, almost terrifying picture of the state to which his labours lifted him".

In his country lodging at Mödling, in August, forgetting to eat his meals, he locked himself in a room and struggled with the composition of the Credo. "Behind a locked door, we heard the master singing parts of the fugue ... singing, howling, stamping. After we had listened a long time to this almost awful scene and were about to go away, the door opened and Beethoven stood before us with distorted features ... looking as if he had been in mortal combat with the whole host of contrapuntists, his everlasting enemies."[1] The servants were evidently very much upset; Schindler wrote in the notebook, "They say you stormed terribly during last night, is that true? ... Don't lock yourself in at night, no stranger will come into the room, but the housekeeper must be able to get in. ..." To an objection by Beethoven, Schindler replied, "In that case you must expect the food to be overcooked and burned, and unappetising, and not roar at them."[2]

Beethoven in the main, however, was happy and relatively calm when in retreat from the town and its pressures, and Mödling was one of his favourite places. He recommended it to the painter von Klöber ("You must have a good look at Mödling, because it's very beautiful, and as an artist you must be a lover of nature")[3] and he stayed there for several summer months, in 1818, 1819 and 1820.

The house, built round a courtyard with vine-trellised and white-washed walls, is in the centre of the village, on the main road. In about ten minutes he could be out in the open country. Behind the handsome parish church with its noble twelfth-century bell tower, a path (still today) leads up the steep wooded hillside, and, bearing left a little way up, stops at the edge of a rocky precipice; there one can see across a valley to hills on the other side, a wonderful view of rocks and gorges and distant Alps. Bernard showed him the way, as we learn from a conversation in 1820: "Which path do you want to take? ... a track goes up behind the church, right between the rocks, and it's extremely pleasant." On reaching a spectacular viewpoint, the walkers stopped, and Bernard wrote on the pad, "One feels quite a different person in the country. ... This is where there ought to be an institute. ... Let's found an Institute for philology, philanthropy, poetry and music here in Mödling—and have that cook to cook for us!"[4]

[1] Schindler, I, pp. 270–1   [2] C.B., I, p. 263
[3] Thayer, p. 703   [4] C.B., II, pp. 253, 255

We know that Beethoven was a great rambler and walked his friends off their feet in earlier days at Döbling; he kept up the habit throughout his life. Even at the age of fifty-two he tired out the teen-age Karl, according to the boy's entry in May 1823: "We have come a good long way. . . . In the evening I can walk really well, but the heat at midday is too much for me. . . ."[1]

We are reminded of Hazlitt, at about the same age as Beethoven then, of whom his friend Patmore wrote: ". . . we walked over to Salisbury (a distance of 12 miles) in a broiling sunshine", and remarked on "the extraordinary physical as well as moral effect produced on Hazlitt by the sight and feel of the country".[2]

For Beethoven walking was a necessity; he needed it for his health and for inspiration. A note in April 1820 reads "4 in the morning, go for a walk or study"; he could happily ramble about at dawn as he did round Teplitz in 1812 when he caught a bad cold from the morning chill, or during the midday heat, or at night when the starry sky inspired some of his most beautiful ideas, in the second Razoumovsky quartet, as we know, and in many works from the Moonlight Sonata to the Ninth Symphony. The song "Abendlied", composed in 1820 to words by the poet Goble, expresses very literally what the night scene evoked for Beethoven—vast skies, twinkling stars, the human soul soaring away from earth and its troubles towards the Creator through the multitude of planets. The words were after his own heart—as so often, they were not great poetry but full of lofty thoughts about the soul:

> As it sees those constellations,
> Looks back on familiar lands,
> It is striving, it is seeking,
> Out of gloom and darkness breaking—
> Earth seems narrow now, and small:
> Upwards to the stars, my soul!
> Though on earth the storms are raging
> And the wicked reap reward,
> Look aloft, my soul, adoring
> There the constellations' Lord.
> Tyrants can no more oppress you,
> Terror never more distress you—
> With a vision clear and bright,
> Soaring up to heaven's light.

[1] C.B., III, p. 321   [2] P. P. Howe, *Life of Hazlitt*, p. 328

The musical ideas in "Abendlied" closely fit the words, and these ideas frequently reappear in greater works—trills and triplets expressing the glittering stars, rich chords conveying the majesty of the night, sequences of ascending runs and arpeggios representing the soaring and hovering soul. It is clear that Beethoven's thoughts even in such comparatively early works as the "Kreutzer" Sonata, the G major Piano Concerto, the Violin Concerto, were dwelling on the wonders of the universe, giving a glimpse, in the music, of the firmament and man's relation to it and to the Creator. Later, in the Mass, this message comes across clearly, and in the Ninth Symphony it is unmistakable:

> World, dost feel thy Maker near?
> Seek him o'er yon starry sphere
> Brothers! O'er the stars enthroned, adore him . . .

The rising wind passages, flute, oboe, clarinet, bear humanity up and away towards regions of love and light, the timpani suggesting the distant troubles left behind. And the violins in the slow movement winding and floating in ethereal beauty tell the same story of the soul in its search for peace.

The vision of the spiritual striving towards the Creator is, however, in the Mass and the Symphony, as in the song, bound up with the human condition—"Tyrant's oppression", war and its horrors, mankind's escape to freedom, men as brothers—are in all these works actually expressed in words, and elsewhere in the great body of Beethoven's serious music clearly implied.

This is perhaps what makes him so universal a musician: he saw mankind, life and nature as one whole, the individual as part of one undivided creation. This was what he wanted to convey in the Mass, and after having been isolated from life during the barren post-war years it was an almost superhuman task for him.

★   ★   ★

Few great artists have lived their lives in quite such a turmoil of trivia, produced their masterworks against such a background varying from the sublime to the ridiculous as did Beethoven. This turmoil is vividly reflected in the conversation books, where notes for a symphony, or ideas for the Mass (such as "*Posaunen* [Trombones]—4 in unison") jostle references to the knotty and tiresome problems of everyday life.

One of these was the perennial housing problem which conditioned Beethoven's life and work in Vienna. When in the country he could

relax, but in the city he was always restless, constantly on the move or
wanting to be. Since 1814 he had changed homes six times, and at the
beginning of 1820 he was living in Josephstadt, so as to be near Karl,
with another address in Alten Blumenstock, within easy reach of
J. K. Bernard. Nevertheless, by the summer he wanted to move again,
and throughout July and August the note-books are peppered with
entries in his hand jotting down addresses from newspaper advertise-
ments for houses. Between romantic country walks and creative work
he went house-hunting with the faithful Oliva. We know that Oliva
was useful in many ways; he called the barber, advised on cobblers,
intervened in domestic quarrels; but the most arduous chore was helping Beethoven to find lodgings.

They would trail together round the suburbs, usually fruitlessly, as
the following passage from the conversation book of August 1820
shows:

Oliva: "It's raining atrociously. . . . The man following us knows
about everything, he's plain clothes police."

"Where did you get the address from? the house is being rebuilt and
everyone has to get out of it. . . . You must have got the number
wrong. . . . The *Magistrat* is rebuilding this house and everybody is
being turned out. . . . Let's go to Herr Embel (of the housing depart-
ment). He will know all about it. . . . Everyone knows that this house
is being pulled down. It seems to me you have made a mistake in the
number, the Müller house is 691 so you could easily have got it wrong."
Beethoven was obviously unwilling to admit his mistake, but they
went to the office in the courtyard to find the Overseer. "Here we are,"
says Oliva, "we ask here for information."

"He says the house is being pulled down, and has the newspaper to
prove it." At last they find the right place: "The Müller House. . . .
This room, 600 florins. . . . I like the little room best and if you got it for
400 fl. it would not be too dear. You'd have plenty of space."

Beethoven would not make up his mind. Alternately (and typically)
vacillating and obstinate, he argues about it through page after page of
the pad. Oliva says, "If you could last out, it would be best for you on
the Landstrasse, at least it's healthy there, which is important for you."
Beethoven objects and suggests something cheaper. Oliva points out,
"That one has very little room, and the saving is almost nil. . . . But I
don't believe you could bear it—the rooms are too low—. . . You
would save a little but not be satisfied. . . . It would be stuffy. . . . No
suburb except the Landstrasse. . . . You won't find anything better than

what we have seen already. . . . You ought to describe the other house to me. . . . But you must decide today otherwise the lodging will be gone. . . ."

A few days later, Oliva asks, "What have you decided about rooms?" Getting a negative answer, he insists, "Time's passing—you won't get anything in the end. . . . The landlord promised to wait two days, and on Sunday there was someone who wanted it. He could certainly not wait. You won't find anything else now which will content you—but in my view you really must make up your mind if you are not to land up in real difficulty."

And so it went on, with occasional comments on Vienna's housing in general, much of it taken up for military purposes ("there are so many barracks in Vienna, and even so the suburbs have military quarters as well").[1]

Beethoven eventually settled for Oliva's recommendation of 244 Landstrasse and moved in there in October 1820. In his new lodgings, in the big house of the Augustinians near their church, he settled down to work. "Late in the fall," says Schindler, "returned from his summer sojourn at Mödling, where like a bee he had been engaged busily in gathering ideas, he sat himself down to his table and wrote out the three sonatas, 109, 110 and 111 in a single breath, as he expressed it to Count Brunsvik, 'to quiet the apprehensions of his friends touching his mental condition'."[2] He stayed in this house for two years and was visited there by friends and by many foreign musicians; he worked steadily on the Mass, the Bagatelles, Op. 123, and the Diabelli Variations. The conversation books show that his most constant visitors were his close friends, Bernard, Kanne, Czerny and Oliva (until he left Vienna for Russia). They were his eyes and ears on the world from which he was so much excluded. As he was unwilling to go to the theatre and could not hear music at concerts, they kept him up to date on the pro-grammes, and on the opera, which all agreed was at a low ebb and almost entirely Italian.

There were few instrumental or orchestral concerts, now that the nobility had disbanded their musical ensembles. Performances of Beethoven's works were infrequent, but whenever one occurred one or other of the friends would attend and write his comments after-wards in the note-book. Oliva scribbled down in April 1820: "I forgot to tell you that the Dilettanten (amateurs) scraped their way through your symphony yesterday—they left out half the third movement; the fugal movement was only played once, then they came to where the violins play pizzicato and straight into the Finale ..." (a very odd way to treat the C minor Symphony!) "The symphony was spoilt through bad conducting, and probably through the nervousness of most of the players. . . . But I was glad in spite of it all to find that their terribly poor performance could not destroy the beauty of the symphony—it made a visible sensation on the whole audience." [1]

Mosel, the critic of the *A.M.Z.*, wrote at about this time that "musical jugglery has taken the place of sensitive performance, everywhere the symphonies of Mozart, Haydn, Beethoven have disappeared". A new series of symphonic concerts, "excluding virtuoso music and bravura singing" was launched during the year, but unfortunately for the works performed the orchestra were amateurs, reading at sight (it was no doubt one of these that Oliva reported). [2]

His friends often took Beethoven out to eat, or to his favourite beer houses, the Kamel or the Schwann; but the shadows of the ubiquitous secret police was apt to dampen conviviality. Beethoven himself did not care who heard his opinions, but his companions did not want to be arrested for subversion, so we find Oliva (already quoted) shushing him up, and Karl whispering "Silentium! Die Stöcke haben Ohren" [3] ("Walls have ears!") The conversation keeps clear of politics, and centres on local gossip and musical chit-chat: "Czerny ist fuchsteufelwild (hopping mad)", says someone, "because he is losing his best and prettiest pupil—she is marrying von Hervals"; Bernard describes how the Princess of Salerno slept all through the opera in the royal box; and how Count Lichtenstein says "if his boys won't learn anything he will get them made ambassadors—how else can he manage the expense of living?" Young Mozart is in town, and is criticised for not having called on Beethoven.

Very often they write comments on the other customers, which one reads with a strong feeling of actually being there: "That one sitting opposite us who looks so stupid is the son of Simoni the singer", says Oliva. "That hunchback over there used to live in Nürnberg. He's called Plotz."—"That's Kallman, a Jew, who used to supply the French, sitting with his back to you next the mirror."

Beethoven remarks, "This pub is only for *leckermauler* (gluttons)," and Bernard says, "It's an old firm with wide connections. A *picling* which is much better here costs 12 kr., at Keepings you'd pay 24 kr."— "These people have all spent their lives in this grocery cellar, and never

[1] C.B., II, p. 398   [2] Thayer, p. 771   [3] C.B., II, p. 286

been anywhere else. It's their world, that's where they are happy. Schiller says, 'What I should be without you, Muses, I know not, But it terrifies me when I see what so many people are like without you.' And Mephistopheles in Faust: 'If you disdain art and science, the highest achievements of men, You will soon come to the end of the road and become a brother of swine.'"[1]

A scene in a tavern is enacted before our eyes in a conversation book of April 1820. Oliva is telling Beethoven about a new opera, *The Fall of Baal*, by Weigl. "A boring piece of rubbish with a few stage effects, but splendidly produced and acted, thanks to which the first Act was loudly clapped; the second was a flop; it was too feeble, boring and bad. The third act could only carry on by the efforts of Weigl's friends. . . . The opera will have the same fate as all his others."

Some suspicious character was hovering nearby; to Beethoven's query who it is, Oliva replies, "Police in disguise, prowling around. . . . He is dressed up as a military. . . . It's all part of the Inquisition. . . ." There is an incident, and one of the customers is removed by a gendarme. "The one in blue asked his name", Oliva writes, "and then said he had orders to arrest him; so the other resisted him, and then the first man called the one in grey, a police sergeant, and he arrested him and took him away."

The café is full, and Oliva points out the interesting characters: "The young man over there in the blue coat, when he was eighteen married an old woman, the fat one there, for her money; he was young and handsome then, now he's prematurely old and grey."—"That dark fat lady is the wife; that other one used to run after the girls." They are getting warmed up, Oliva ordering more drink: "I've taken your glass . . . the wine is excellent . . . unusual for the Prater." Beethoven writes, in his almost illegible scrawl, "The one opposite us is a dried-up old fish."

Oliva orders some food. Beethoven may have wanted shellfish, for the next remark is: "They are not good at this time of year." Another choice was "noch nicht fertig" (not ready yet). Beethoven was evidently becoming restless. Oliva writes, "He went away because you were kicking the table with your feet. . . . He had already seen earlier that he was not in a good place."

The coffee house or tavern was not the place for serious conversation, and it was in the seclusion of Beethoven's room that politics and religion were discussed. While Vienna went its decadent, censor-ridden way, stirring things were happening in Europe: there was a democratic rising in Naples, and in Spain the people were demanding the abdication of their king, and restoration of the promised Constitution. Beethoven was eager to hear about these events and Bernard and Kanne kept him supplied with news:

Kanne: "A number of students came into the inn yesterday, they drank a flask of beer and broke it. Don't say so too loud! but I'll wager that the students were drinking the health of the Spanish insurgents."

"Have you seen the *Allgemeine*? It is really good about the insurgents. The King called for help from England through Gibraltar, but in vain!" Kanne is disgusted with the Austrian government's attitude: "And we Patriot killers, we Austrians are not able to help them. . . . You are still a Patriot in your roots," he tells Beethoven.[1] Bernard brings good news, heard at his office: "The King of Spain has agreed to the Constitution. . . . The Austrians will never be comfortable in Venice, it's time we pulled out of there. . . . Constitutions make men free." Jubilantly, he goes on: "The Spanish business will make a sensation. . . . When the Constitution has been set up we can make a trip to Madrid. . . . The Bourbons are on the run everywhere. . . . A tree which bears no fruit should be cut down and thrown on the fire. . . ."[2]

Another day, Bernard explains why things happened as they did in Spain and gives a little lecture on inflation: "All Europe's in the same state. In Spain it was the worst. For two years the poor got no wages, the officers had to beg, and in the navy they were dying of hunger. . . . Because of bad financial management, the over-spending of the court, and the great demands from the poor, all Europe has become like Spain—debts everywhere. It's like with families and individuals where there are no more means of help." To get out of their difficulties, Prince Palffy and Count Stadion have set up lotteries, Bernard says; "the whole of Europe is going to the dogs . . . Germany must be maintaining thirty-eight courts and perhaps a million princes and princesses, while the soldiers working on the earthworks get 6 groschen (farthings) a day even though we have received so many millions in reparations from France. . . ."[3]

They all agree that "Napoleon should have been let out for 10 years," and Bernard says that "if he returned to France today he'd have an easier job than in 1814".—"The Swiss guards will soon be thrown out of Paris, nobody wants foreign troops there any more." From Spain

[1] C.B., I, p. 359   [2] C.B., I, pp. 372, 387   [3] C.B., II, pp. 58-9

the news is that "the King has appointed Quiroga and Riego [constitu-
tionalists] as A.D.Cs. . . . The only ambassador to wish Spain well was
the American. . . . Dr Pradt says the King of Spain would much prefer
to be back in Valençay prison" (where he had been interned since the
war).[1] During September, Blöchlinger visited Beethoven and rather
sourly observed that "today people's heads are full of bloody revolution", adding that "Troops have been ordered to Naples, it's a fact."

Oliva reports the rumour that "the three great monarchs [Austria,
Russia, Prussia] are meeting in Teschen, and while they are there will
sign a new Declaration of War against the Constitutionalist powers. . . .
The Carbonari have dedicated their daggers and weapons to the Virgin
Mary, and propose to use them openly to defend their freedom against
their enemies."

Schindler's comments were: "If it's decided that the Deutschmeister
Regiment must go to Italy we shall lose Count Ertmann and his wife,
which will be a severe loss to our matinees in Czerny's house." And
(typical Schindler): "If Count Herberstein had lived a few years longer
I should certainly have become a Diplomat. . . . At least a second
Talleyrand, of course! I'd have finished the revolution in Naples at
once through a diplomatic bloodletting . . . Solche Scheisskerls! (What
shits!)"[2]

In early November, Beethoven had a visit from a Dr Müller, a
philologist of Bremen, who commented on his outspoken interest in
all that was happening. "His sense of cosmopolitan independence . . .
might have been the reason why, over and over again, he continued a
conversation begun earlier, in restaurants where he often had his frugal
lunch, and expressed opinions freely and candidly about everything,
the government, the police, the manners of the aristocracy, in a
critical and mocking manner. The police knew it, but left him in peace
either because he was a fantastic or because he was a brilliant artistic
genius. . . ."[3]

(Müller, being an outsider, was evidently less worried by the rash
talk than the Viennese friends who were at risk and shut Beethoven up
so firmly in public places.)

Whenever the composer's health allowed, he went out to read the
newspapers; and even when he was very ill he followed the peoples'
struggles for freedom. When things were going favourably he was
stimulated and better able to create; it was natural that his inspiration
should flow more abundantly when his main objectives "freedom and

[1] C.B., II, p. 60   [2] C.B., II, p. 84   [3] Thayer, p. 765

progress" appeared to be gaining ground anywhere in the world. He would have sympathised fully with Hazlitt who, at this very time of Spanish and Italian risings, wrote: "Since the voice of Liberty has risen once more in Spain, its grave and its birthplace, and like a babbling hound has woken the echoes in Galicia, in the Asturias and . . . Extremadura, why, we feel as if we 'had three ears again' and the heart to use them, and as if we could once more write with the same feelings (the tightness removed from the breast and the pains smoothed from the brow) as we did (once before). . . ."[1]

Beethoven knew too, as Byron did, that "Freedom's battle once begun/Bequeathed by bleeding Sire to Son,/Though baffled oft is ever won." The very fact that the battle was again being waged, that people still had the courage, the heroism, the passion enabling them to fight for freedom, aroused Beethoven's own courage and passion; and this is one reason why 1820 was one of the years in which he was able to write such great and human music as the last three piano sonatas, and the Diabelli Variations, through which the revolutionary wind breathes or blows, sometimes rising to gale force.

[1] Hazlitt, in *The Examiner*, 25.6.1820, *Works*, xviii, p. 341

13

Artists against Metternich
1821–1823

The relatively good health and spirits which Beethoven enjoyed in 1820 did not last long; 1821 and 1822 were years of illness, passed in semi-retirement. In January 1821 the *A.M.Z.* reported that "Herr von Beethoven has been sick with a rheumatic fever. All friends of true music and all admirers of his muse feared for him. But now he is on the road to recovery and working actively."

However, a few months later his activity was again curtailed, by an onslaught of jaundice: "In my case . . . an extremely objectionable disease," he wrote to Archduke Rudolph, in July, "largely to be ascribed to my distressing situation and particularly to my economic circumstances. I hope to overcome these eventually by the most strenuous exertions."[1]

His health improved while he was in Baden later that summer, and he was able to indulge his passion for roaming the country. One evening he went too far afield and got lost, looking so peculiar, bareheaded and in his old coat, that he was arrested as a vagrant. Nobody would believe him when he kept yelling that he was Beethoven. The police locked him in a cell till 11 p.m., when the "tramp" insisted that Herzog, the Musical Director of the suburb Wiener Neustadt, be called to identify him. The Commissioner of Police got out of bed, went out and woke up Herzog and they went to the watch-house, where the composer was identified, released with fulsome apologies and sent back to Baden in an official coach.[2]

This adventure may have contributed to violent attacks of colic which sent Beethoven rushing back to Vienna. "Since last year and until now I have been constantly ill," he told Franz Brentano in October 1821, and it was not till mid-November that he was able to write "Thank God, I am now feeling better, and at last good health

[1] *Letters*, L. 1054, p. 920   [2] Thayer, p. 778

seems to be returning to revive my spirits so that I may again start a new life devoted to my art."[1] But his hopes were dashed in the spring of 1822 by "gout on my chest for four months", and he tells Ries in July that he has been unwell for more than half a year. He was financially worried too, owing to his inability through illness to write remunerative works, to the expense of keeping Karl as well as himself, and to the high cost of living. There had till recently been a food shortage in Vienna, indeed starvation in the country districts (Theresa Brunsvik was much involved in famine relief in nearby Hungary), and prices of food and other commodities had soared, and remained high. Beethoven begged his publisher in Berlin during the winter to "send the manuscripts free of charge, for we poor wretches in Vienna have to pay dear for everything except the air we breathe".[2]

For many months he had written nothing except a few new songs, Bagatelles for Piano (Op. 119), and some arrangements of former work, because of having to concentrate on the Mass (for which he had as yet no contract, though negotiating with seven publishers) and the compulsion to work on a new symphony.

In December 1821 he wrote to Franz Brentano, agent for Simrock in Frankfurt, explaining his plight ("I have been compelled to write a great many potboilers") and Brentano sent him a considerable sum—nominally as an advance on the Mass, which Simrock hoped to publish; and the letters of 1822 are mainly concerned with similar publishers' loans or advances and make dreary reading. On a more cheerful note is the agreement with Diabelli, the Viennese minor composer and music publisher—"the fee for the variations would be 40 ducats at most, provided they are worked out on as large a scale as suggested"—showing that he was taking up a reasonably well paid and not too demanding commission.

Diabelli had supplied a short and banal waltz theme to fifteen composers, including Liszt and Schubert, who each produced one variation. Beethoven, after refusing to enter the lists, finally complied with *thirty-three*—"the greatest piano variations ever written", according to Tovey. They provided ample evidence to those who had thought he was played out, that Beethoven's powers of imagination and inventiveness were as great as, or even greater than ever.

At the end of September 1822, after a "cure" at Baden his health at last began to mend, and the following months were to see a great flowering of creativity. Several things contributed to the improvement, including good progress on work in hand, a revival of *Fidelio* in November, and a reconciliation with his brother Johann, after a long domestic estrangement.

Johann was able to help him financially, became a regular visitor and a tireless adviser on money (which he understood) and on artistic matters (of which he was totally ignorant).

If they had not been bound by family ties, Ludwig and Johann would certainly never have been close friends. Johann, as can be guessed from his portrait, with its tight lips and calculating eye, was the opposite of his brother—no idealist, but worldly, money-grubbing and vain. Karl remarked in March 1823 that "*Der Bruder's* hair is quite white when it isn't dyed. . . . He dyes it black. . . . He says you ought to let him dye yours dark too. . . ."[1] (One can imagine Beethoven's reaction.) Johann, however, had a kindly side, and was genuinely anxious to help Ludwig; he offered to approach important people, and write them letters though he was unable to spell; he invited his brother to stay with him on his country estate, and visited him constantly, entertaining him with news of the outside world.

In January 1823 we find Johann and Schindler discussing the situation in Europe which had become tense, owing to the revolutionary risings in Spain and Italy: "According to the paper there will be war between Spain and the Allies." Schindler chimes in, "The Cabinet is wavering frightfully between war and peace. One doesn't know yet whether to expect good or bad. Yesterday's *A.Z.* had a most extraordinary report on the Ministry's position: it showed the gap between them all—the King against the war, on the one hand, and the Ministers for it, on the other."[2]

The question was whether Austria should intervene in the Spanish Peninsula where, since Riego's rising in 1820, democratic forces had been in the ascendant and a Constitution established. France was threatening to invade and restore reaction; Britain was watching Portugal (and sent an army to safeguard her interests *vis-à-vis* her "oldest ally") but not intervening in Spain. Schindler reports that an incident between an English ship taken by a Spanish privateer was seen in Vienna as "a secret intrigue of Parliament, to hide their real plans with a false alarm. . . . We know that they just recently signed a trade agreement with Spain."[3]

Beethoven followed these remarks with much interest, and obviously encouraged them, for there is a great deal on the subject in the conversations of 1823. On 23 February, J. K. Bernard brings the latest news from his office: after joking about the King of Naples whom he had seen at a masquerade the night before, he goes on more seriously: "In the Cortes the Spaniards listened angrily to the messages of the united monarchs when they were read out. The Cortes declared that they would make no change in their constitution." Diplomatic personnel of Austria, Prussia and Russia had been arrested, according to a report of 27 January. "The ambassadors have demanded their passports, but they have not been given them yet. The people's anger was extraordinary—especially now when we are calling out troops."[1]

Schindler writes in mid-February that "the Royalists have increased in numbers and are approaching the capital. The Constitutionalists have captured a corps of Royalists, 130 Franciscans among them. All the same, the support for the Cortes seems to have declined considerably.... Foreign newspapers foster the idea, because they count on the Royalists soon entering Madrid."[2]

On 25 February Schindler says "People here are rising in revolt: the United States are said to be getting involved in war with England, so since yesterday the price of coffee and sugar has gone up a lot. It's all commercial speculation, nothing else. The State's credit depends on many factors such as Spain." Schindler opines that "our mixture of different nations ensures Austria peace for a long time, though even this has its limits. They will never unite, and singly they are not to be feared.... Even Kaiser Joseph saw this during his thirty years' reign." Beethoven said something derogatory about the present Emperor, and Schindler wrote that "to a certain degree it is a good thing for the country that he has no plan to follow, but only acts according to chance...".[3]

Disgust with the Austrian regime dominates many conversations: Schindler blames the Viennese character: "The Viennese is spoilt, has no feeling for Law or Nature. The Hungarian is naturally rough but flexible. I speak from experience not hypothesis. The revolutionary feeling is rooted in his heart.... It has gone so deep there that it is now the usual thing; in Prussia, Saxony, France too...".[4]

The stirrings in Europe and the general discontent reported by Schindler, stimulated Beethoven. He held to his opinions, voiced them loudly regardless of friends' warnings, and pretended to be immune to abuse. None the less it was rather hurtful to learn of the rude things

[1] C.B., II, pp. 406-7   [2] C.B., III, p. 28
[3] C.B., III, p. 39   [4] C.B., III, pp. 355-6

said about him by Abbé Joseph Gelinek (one of his first Vienna acquaintances, and a rival in piano contests in the 1790s). Gelinek had always been jealous of him, and in 1814 had told Tomaschek that Beethoven's compositions were lacking in internal coherency, being made up of ideas on scraps of paper.[1] His remarks in 1823 were more dangerous. One visitor refers to him as "the arch-enemy Gelinek", and Czerny told Bernard, who passed it on to Beethoven, that "Abbé Gelinek was mocking you violently in the Camel (Inn). He said you were a second Sand, that you insulted the Kaiser, the Archduke, the Ministers . . . and that you would finish up on the gallows . . . Czerny says he is a very evil man."[2]

Beethoven may have mocked the regime, but he still kept on good terms with individual members of the nobility. We find him in the early summer of 1823 in conversation with Baron Pronay, a friend of Lichnowsky, who leased him a villa on his beautiful estate at Hetzendorf. Karl, writing in the conversation book of 11 May, warns, "The Baron is Kammerherr (Chamberlain) to the Emperor. . . ." Beethoven's reaction was, no doubt, "So what?" Karl: "I only meant, you should not talk to him against the government."

The Baron was an old-world gentleman who divided his time between the court, botany and music; he told Beethoven, "The Liguorians are a bad sign of the times in Austria. . . . The King of Naples is coming to Schönbrunn . . . the Court is going to Laxenburg. . . ." He took them round his garden, and wrote on Beethoven's pad, "This is an exotic plant, called Buddleia—after a botanist—Globosa."[3]

Schindler said: "Baron Pronay is a strange Hungarian. I never met one like him. He only lives for Botany and Literature. The house and garden cost him 100,000 gulden, without the vine-house, and he is still trying to enlarge his library and his glass-houses. Princes visit him. . . ."

Beethoven and Karl moved into the rented villa, to Johann's congratulations. Pronay had done all he could to make them comfortable, arranging for a table to be put in the garden as eating in the open air would be good for Beethoven's health. Karl was enthusiastic: "We really live better than the Baron himself!"[4] and Schindler, who often came to visit them, found everything delightful: Pronay was very polite and solicitous, and "makes such beautiful elaborate compliments that I've decided to go to him for lessons". But Beethoven could not stand the courtly politeness; "the Baron made deep bows to him every time they met"—and after a few weeks left Hetzendorf for Baden.

*   *   *

Beethoven's return of health in 1823 brought a return of interest in life, as we have seen, and a burst of creativity.

Not content with working simultaneously on the Mass and on the Ninth Symphony, Beethoven decided in good earnest to write an opera. He was encouraged by the news that *Fidelio* was to be revived in the autumn; and by the Kärtnerthor Theatre's offer of a commission for an opera on any subject he chose. All his friends pressed the idea; Schindler said, "There's no composer in Europe except you who can rescue the theatre from ruin!" Brother Johann urged him on: "Rossini is rich through his operas . . . you would be rich too if you wrote one." Dr Peters pleaded, "Nur noch eine Oper, bitte, bitte" ("Just one more opera, *please*").[1]

Beethoven was not going to write the kind of musical comedy which was then the rage, and such as was turned out in four weeks by a man like Weigl, or two at a time by Kreutzer. He had the greatest contempt for most of the current Italian operas, though he admired their singers; and we can imagine his comments on the sort of show described by the English Professor in his *Musical Ramble*: "My English proprieties were somewhat scandalised at finding a number of young ladies introduced on the stage here in short tight jackets without tail, silk breeches, and stockings equally tight, a dress calculated to delineate the form with excessive accuracy. . . . In the suburban theatres laughter reigns supreme, and the unities of time, place, etc., are all sacrificed to it." The Professor regretted too that "the German opera is not much patronised by the Viennese, who doat upon things which are foreign and despise their own good writers."[2]

None the less, Beethoven was keen to write a serious opera, even if it meant producing it abroad instead of in Vienna. He had thought of many possible subjects, and discussed them endlessly with friends; J. K. Bernard had promised a libretto, but newspaper work held it up; Collin had started on *Macbeth* for him, but had died. However, new ideas poured in. Lichnowsky proposed a variety of subjects—Joan of Arc, Voltaire's tragedies, "any of them—Mahomet, Pheidra, Merope, etc." He (Lichnowsky) had just read a libretto on Alfred the Great—

"it would be an extraordinarily spectacular subject . . . the bridge over the Thames . . . 100 warriors with torches searching for the King . . . something highly romantic. . . ."[1] Beethoven was not tempted by any of these. He turned instead to the greatest poet in Vienna, Franz Grillparzer, and asked him for a libretto.

The two men had known each other slightly as far back as 1808 when Beethoven had shared a house with Grillparzer's parents in Döbling, and now they became firm friends. Although the poet was very different as a man, of the cultured conservative class, opposed to republican and democratic ideas, he shared Beethoven's hatred of injustice and obscurantism. He had suffered personally through the outspoken sincerity of his work, and through his involvement with the "Ludlams-höhle", a group of way-out literati, romantic and rather wild young men. With their leader, Daffinger, Grillparzer had been arrested by Metternich's police for "insubordinate sentiments" and "presumptuous comments". The young poet was no trouble-maker and in his desire to win back official favour, he wrote a poem of thanksgiving for Emperor Franz's recovery from illness; unfortunately he only succeeded in annoying the Imperial invalid, because the poem contained a mention of two women watching by the royal bedside—a reflection on Franz's morals, the censor claimed. In spite of Grillparzer's great gifts he only held menial and subordinate positions in the civil service, till late in life.[2]

At the time Beethoven approached him, he had already written several very successful tragedies: *Die Ahnfrau* (in which, says one critic, "the darkest fatalism is combined with the most romantic beauties and sweetest graces of language and metre"), *Spartakus*, *Schreyfogel*, *Sappho*, *Goldenes Vlies*. He was now completing his play *King Ottokar*, and having much trouble with the censor.

Lichnowsky wrote in the conversation book in April 1823, "Grill-parzer is being persecuted in many ways, especially by the censorship", and Schindler supplied details: "In May, two years ago, Grillparzer submitted a poem about the restoration in present-day Rome; in it he said, where once the proud Roman triumphed, today Christianity stands supported by 10,000 priests—or something like that. Dr Nuntius (the Pope's envoy) complained, and the poem had to be destroyed." Another day, Schindler writes: "G. told me openly all about the amazing things which have happened to him. . . . Nobody else in his

[1] C.B., II, p. 395
[2] Grillparzer, *Selbstbiographie*, Vienna 1925, IV, pp. 207–11

position has suffered as he has. . . . He will read you the poem through which he has earned such disfavour. . . . It was not the Nuncio but a writer here who stirred up the trouble. The King wrote to the police: A real so-and-so that Grillparzer—What a scandal, infamous!"—"He had to defend himself in writing, to the Police. . . . He has been serving ten years already for 400 fl a year. Now there is a post going, but they are dithering and he thinks that through the high command someone else will be sure to get the post. . . . He has also lost the post of Theatre Poet through this meanness. . . . How they pester him! (*Wie chikanieren sie ihn*). He is now writing a great tragedy, *Ottokar*. They will most likely put spokes in his wheel, and as his work is already commissioned abroad there is great hostility to him."[1]

Grillparzer was basically a loyal subject, but under such provocation even he exclaimed that "the system under Metternich and Emperor Franz was a crime against the human race and God", because it sought only to conserve, and was selfishly and stupidly unprogressive. Grillparzer never consciously introduced politics into his writing; but he was an honest artist, and concerned with human truth as he had experienced it; and for such sincerity there was no place in censor-ridden Vienna.

"Grillparzer is very depressed, and persecuted by the court rabble", we read in the conversation book,[2] and find him bewailing his condition to Beethoven, who no doubt had been grumbling about his own troubles: "If you were as plagued as I am. I'm nothing but a clerk. I am lower than the stupidest idiot. . . . At least the Censor can't touch music. . . ."[3]

But Grillparzer would not be deflected from his principles. He was keen to provide Beethoven with a libretto, and meant it to be something which would match the composer's high-mindedness.

Some remarks made in the spring of 1823 show the poet's serious and reflective attitude to his work, in this case the revision of *The Ruins of Athens*: "I am making the changes which you think necessary . . . I recognise that reshaping is needed, but it is not the work of a moment. It's much quicker to carry out the idea than to experience it. So I must naturally ask you for time to reflect on it, turn it over in my mind and think it through at home. . . . As to the idea of representing the present Greek situation, the censors would be sure to come down on it with their almighty No."[4] After some further discussion, he says, "I will

[1] C.B., III, p. 293   [2] C.B., III, p. 401
[3] C.B., III, p. 274   [4] C.B., III, pp. 76-78

think over the material in the meantime. . . . In short, the key is reflection, and I shall not start work without having shown you a plan."

For the future opera, Grillparzer offered a scenario based on the legend of Melusine, proposing to adapt it to Beethoven's style of writing by introducing choral episodes and "powerful finales". Poet and composer discussed it at intervals of a few weeks, either in Vienna or in Hetzendorf; here, Grillparzer was treated with great honour, given three bottles of wine to himself, escorted half-way back to Vienna and his journey paid for by Beethoven out of his meagre purse.

The latter looked forward to composing the opera, but in the meantime he was far too busy to get down to it. On 1 July 1823 he wrote to the Archduke, "I am now writing a new symphony for England, for the Philharmonic Society, and hope to have it done in a fortnight." [1] He concentrated on this big work to the confusion of his domestic affairs and neglect of other compositions. He was in any case not entirely decided about *Melusine*; though enthusiastic from time to time, he showed typical unwillingness to commit himself, and shilly-shallied, making excuses for his lack of decision. "I don't write what I really most want to", he said: "I have to write for the money I need, which doesn't mean to say that I only write for money—that time is past. I hope in the end to write what is highest for me in all art—Faust." [2]

The faithful Schindler, who replaced Oliva as factotum when the latter left for Russia in December 1820, was kept on the run taking notes to Grillparzer, in the intervals of looking after "the Master's" wellbeing, seeing to publishers' business, trying to encourage him and give good advice. He was pedantic and banal, but engagingly open and obviously devoted. (In a conversation of February 1823 he says someone accused him of "wanting to stick a knife into anybody who spoke against Beethoven", so blindly devoted was he.) [3]

Apart from negotiating with Grillparzer and work on the Ninth Symphony, it was a very busy time; the Mass was completed early in the year and a copy presented to the Archduke in March, but to cover his costs Beethoven hoped to get subscriptions to the work from the courts of Europe, and sent Schindler scuttling around the embassies, with limited success. About twenty invitations were issued, and the response was not too encouraging. The King of France subscribed and also sent a handsome gold medal, but the German kings dragged their feet. The King of Sweden, Bernadotte, did not reply to Beethoven's personal letter; perhaps he thought Sweden had done its duty by the composer in making him a member of their Royal Academy in 1822. The Prince Regent of England did not get an invitation to subscribe to the Mass; he had not even acknowledged the gift of the Battle Symphony, sent him in 1814.[1]

There were in the end ten subscribers who each paid 50 ducats and received a copy of the *Missa Solennis*: The Tsar, the Kings of Prussia, Saxony, Denmark and France, the Grand Dukes of Tuscany and Hesse Darmstadt, Princes Galitzin and Radziwill, and the Caecilia Society of Frankfurt. Conspicuous by their absence were Goethe and the Weimar court, the wealthy Prince Esterhazy, and the Kings of Naples and Bavaria.

It seems strange that these immensely affluent people could not afford 50 ducats—the equivalent of about £23—for such a masterpiece. The truth may be that, if they knew anything about Beethoven, they mistrusted his capacity to write serious religious music; he was not known for orthodox piety, (in fact, Haydn had once called him an atheist—unfairly, for his religious views were strong and sincere; but according to the reliable Schindler "rested less upon the creed of the church than in Deism"). Beethoven rejected the Trinitarian dogma, and the Deity of his faith was a personal God and Universal Father—hence his many prayers for divine support. The crowned heads were not to know this; they may well have feared and suspected that he would not be bound by the liturgy, and they would have been right. The *Missa Solennis* is not a church service but a dramatic and poetical interpretation of the words of the Mass.

As Ernest Newman said, "the words and the solemn ceremony and implications of the Mass having provided him with his emotional starting-point, his imagination was then able to play with perfect freedom upon them. . . . A better libretto he could not have found." The *Kyrie* gave all he needed to paint in music a vast panorama of human hopes and fears; *Gloria* sufficed to sing the praises of the Creator; *Miserere nobis* enabled him to reach to the very heart of human pain and sorrow. As for the *Agnus Dei*, it takes on an altogether vaster meaning than the average church-goer would expect: headed "a prayer for internal and external peace", it refers directly back to Beethoven's life experience. "The *Agnus Dei* calls us back from the rapturous vision of the divine to the harsh realities of this earth. The G major of the *Hosanna* . . . turns into the dark B minor of humanity." After warlike trumpet fanfares and drum rolls, we hear the outcry of terrified

[1] C.B., I., p. 144

humanity, of the soloists, followed by shouts of anguish from the chorus. "This is the fury of war which ravages the earth, and Beethoven also reads a realistic meaning into his prayer for peace—peace not only in death, but peace among nations."[1]

This was not the kind of church music to please the Kings of Bavaria and of Naples, nor Emperor Franz (who liked his Masses "the shorter the better"!). They were living in the past, and this was religious music of the future, music which would burst through barriers of dogma and show others—Berlioz, Verdi, Mahler, Kodàly and even Messiaen—that Requiems, Masses and Te Deums can be set to music with a directly human as well as ecclesiastical relevance. Beethoven summed up his message in a few words written at the end of the Mass: "From the heart—may it go to the heart."

For Beethoven and his friends it was something of a tragedy that the Mass was not performed complete in Austria until after his death. Only Prince Galitzin, who arranged for its performance in St Petersburg in April 1824, was able to supply some consolation for Vienna's loss: he wrote that the effect of the music on the Russian public was indescribable, and he himself "had never heard anything so sublime.... It can be said that your genius has anticipated the centuries. . . . It is posterity that will pay you homage and will bless your memory much better than your contemporaries can."[2]

---

[1] E. Newman. Notes on sleeve of record of Mass in D; W. Hess, *Introduction*, Miniature score, Mass in D, Eulenberg ed.

[2] Thayer, p. 925

14

Opera, Symphony and Mass

1824

The Archduke Rudolph received a presentation copy of the *Missa Solennis* in the spring of 1823, but Beethoven worked on additions to it and supervised the copying of the many scores needed for royal recipients, throughout the year. The Ninth Symphony was finished in form by December 1823, and written out in score two months later. It was an astonishing feat to achieve the completion of the two great works simultaneously, particularly as, during most of the year, the composer was afflicted with eye trouble which continued till March 1824. A letter of 23 January 1824 apologises for a tardy reply "as I have been overwhelmed with work".

His experienced copyist had died, and the less reliable successor needed constant supervision. "Everything proceeds more slowly than before, the more so as the score must be copied again as a score . . . everything must be checked by me, and in addition I have been suffering a long time from my eyes."[1]

The close work must have been a considerable strain, especially as it often had to be done by candlelight. This is brought home to the reader of the conversation books where candles repeatedly feature in shopping lists and their price and merits are discussed. Karl, in November 1823, for instance writes, "What do wax candles cost per pound? . . . . How many candles? . . . I think you should only burn wax. When you reckon it up they don't cost more than tallow, because they burn a long time; and then it avoids the harm that tallow candles do to your chest. Hufeland [the author of *Betrachtungen*] writes that one should only burn wax candles."[2]

But wax candles gave no stronger a light, and work continued to be done by the flicker of tiny flames. The words of the song "Lisch aus, mein Licht" (1818) were topical—except of course in the sense that

[1] *Letters*, L. 1268, p. 1113   [2] C.B., III, p. 219

Beethoven's inner light almost always burned bright. It was thanks to this inner flame that the work was accomplished in spite of every difficulty.

The question then arose, when and where the Mass and the new symphony, with its exceptional demands on orchestra, chorus and soloists, should be performed. The condition of music in Vienna seemed to Beethoven extremely unfavourable to his great new work. He wanted passionately to produce his symphony but despaired of receiving adequate support or recognition from his home public. His fear and suspicion that his music was no longer understood by the Viennese, and that he was not admired any more, had grown into a deep-rooted conviction; he thought of north Germany, England, France even, as much more likely to appreciate his new work.

To a certain extent he was right. New literature and music were encouraged by the rising bourgeoisie in those countries outside Austria where the new capitalism had pushed feudalism aside; but Metternich's obscurantist regime clung to old and "safe" culture, discouraged and stifled any serious creative work. Beethoven did not analyse the causes of the cultural barrenness, but he knew that while freedom and change were forbidden the second-rate would prevail, and this had been amply proved in the post-war years.

Since 1816 standards had fallen lamentably, and triviality and tinsel glitter had invaded Viennese concert halls and theatres, along with Italian touring companies and their (very) light operas. This could be blamed on the managers who saw the chance of making money fast, and on the government which supported them and their like in all the Habsburg dominions, in giving the public easy and sensuous entertainment "to divert minds from serious matters and from politics", as Stendhal observed. Beethoven remarked to Rellstab in 1819 that "since the Italians have taken hold here the best art is in jeopardy. The nobility has no eyes for anything but ballet, no feeling for anything but race-horses and dancing-girls."[1] Schindler reported the verdict current in Vienna drawing-rooms in 1816 as "Mozart and Beethoven are old pedants, the older generation were fools to enjoy them. Until Rossini came we did not know what melody could be. *Fidelio* is rubbish; how can anyone endure such boring stuff?"

By 1823 the musical scene consisted of second-rate Italian or third-rate German programmes. Schindler suffered acutely in his position as leader of the Josephstadt Theatre orchestra, directed by the

[1] C.B., III, pp. 53-4

inferior musician Hensler. In 1822 Beethoven had been on good terms
with Hensler, who had given the *Weihe des Hauses* in his theatre; when
Fidelio was performed at the Kärntnertheater in 1822 there was a con-
vivial dinner at which Beethoven met Hensler and Gläser, a very
prolific minor composer. But a discussion in 1823 shows that he and
Schindler had a low opinion of these musicians. Schindler writes,
"You'd be amazed, if you saw Gläser conduct, at his tempi: Allegro is
always Presto; . . . he has never heard of Adagio. . . ." "Last Sunday
Gläser performed his latest work—etwas abscheuliches (something
frightful), everybody told him so, and it has only been given once. . . .
The man is unbearably self-satisfied—he thinks he's nearly as great as if
he had written *Fidelio*, *Medea* or *Don Giovanni*. He uses Hensler to get
every bit of rubbish performed . . . we are not allowed to play good
overtures and symphonies, nothing that is not by Gläser or Rossini. . . .
He (Gläser) has written about 80 operas in 4 years."[1] Hensler made all
sorts of difficulties over performing Beethoven symphonies, which
Schindler urged him to let the orchestra play. "He gives us nothing but
Rossini and Gläser. . . . If only I could get out of this theatre—it
demoralises my musical self-respect." Another cause of complaint
was the time wasted on pantomime effects; but this was inevitable in
the business. Theatres all vied with each other in putting on spectacular
displays, to the neglect of good music or drama. It was not only
Dryden's "many-headed monster of the pit", who clamoured for
sensation—the well-to-do were equally undiscriminating. The native
taste for illusion and magic, pantomime and fairy tale (which had
thirty years earlier had one good result, *The Magic Flute*), led to break-
neck competition between impresarios outdoing each other in magnificence and ingenuity. Mälzel came to their assistance with mechanical
bands and war scenes, and helped to stage Haydn's *Seasons* with suitable
decor—snow, avalanches, rain, thunder and lightning *ad lib*. Fireworks
from the Prater were brought in to provide more excitement.

One production, *Count Waltrion*, featured a whole army of marching
troops and battle scenes where cannons went off, "startling the audience
and creating an atmosphere of terror". There were tournaments,
cavalry charges, storms, shipwrecks, worthy of Cecil B. de Mille. Live
animals were popular; as an unusual attraction, camels appeared on
stage, and in *The Dog of Montargis* the chief star was the producer's pet
dog, performing its tricks. When these shows were described to him,
Beethoven thought it all a travesty of drama, but Karl tried to persuade

[1] C.B., III, p. 10

him to go to the theatre: "You simply must go this week—they have a poodle acting on the stage. We really must see it!"[1]

And Schindler describes one pantomime: "Vesuvius is shown in full eruption, with the rain of fire in puris naturalibus! There are so many stage effects that the whole show is held up. . . ." He adds that in his own theatre "the new pantomime uses an extraordinary number of machines. . . ."[2] One of the current productions, Der Rasende Roland, is said by Dr Peters, to be "so overloaded with spectacle, dances and decorations and machines that the opera suffers". His remark is supported by the Allgemeine Theater Zeitung (A.T.Z.): "There are 54 major characters without counting minor parts—field-marshals, riders, warriors, heralds, arms-bearers, trumpeters, pillar carriers, negroes, negresses, ship's crew, hunters, magicians, genii and so forth. . . ."

The censor had no objection to dramatic spectaculars, nor to the vocal pyrotechnics from Italy which challenged the Austrian theatre. The Italians had escaped from the miseries of Metternichism in their own land, by song and dance, and Stendhal defended them, asking: "Would it offend the gravity of our century, etc., etc., to dare to think that the more hypocritical, hidebound and sad the way of life, the gayer should be the recreations?"[3] The Austrian censor saw no offence: anything, bar blasphemy, that prevented people thinking or talking politics, was passed. The Italians were allowed in, and the Viennese were swept off their feet. As Schindler wrote, "the uninhibited enthusiasm grew from performance to performance until it degenerated into a general intoxication of the senses whose sole inspiration was the virtuosity of the singers". And the critic of the Allgemeine Musik Zeitung described the farewell performance of the tenor Cramolini as "like an idolatrous orgy; everyone there acted as if bitten by a tarantula; the shouting, crying, yelling of 'viva' and 'fora' went on and on". When the Italian company left "the city went into deep mourning; their only relief . . . consisted in ridiculing the German singers".[4] One is reminded of present-day pop festivals, which provide an outlet for the emotions of susceptible teen-agers (and perhaps the pressures of economic crisis, a decadent society and social emptiness in 1820 Vienna were similar to those of our day). And though the Viennese audiences were not young they needed an escape from Metternich's dreary rule. Bernard remarked to Beethoven one day that "the ministry has a

[1] C.B., IV, p. 194   [2] C.B., III, p. 252
[3] Stendhal, Life of Rossini, I, p. 122   [4] Schindler, op. cit., p. 271

firm hold on the theatre. They know nothing except the menial and commonplace. Anything higher is quite outside their range of vision."[1]

Schindler wrote despairingly that "What was left of appreciation of German vocal music has entirely disappeared. . . . For years now hardly a single piece of serious music has been published. We have nothing but piano arrangements of Rossini's operas. All is barren. What next?"[2] With hindsight, the answer to Schindler's "What next?" would be— the rise of the romantic composers for whom Beethoven had opened the door: Schubert, Weber, Liszt, Schumann, Brahms, Wagner. But when Schubert visited Beethoven in 1822 and sat tongue-tied in the great presence, or when Beethoven heard the infant prodigy Liszt perform, there was little to indicate that they would make musical history each in his own way.

Weber had, in fact, received some recognition—for of the very few German operas performed in post-war Vienna, his *Freischütz* was one. It had been reasonably successful, thanks to its romantic German character which was in tune with the fashionable reactionary romanticism, approved even by Metternich.

It was representative of the medievalism which depicted the ordered society of feudalism, "the colourful heraldry and gallant court, surrounded by the shadowy mystery of fairy-tale forests and canopied by the unquestioned Christian heavens, the obvious lost paradise of the conservative opponents of bourgeois society", as Eric Hobsbawm says.[3] It is not an insult to Weber to say this, any more than to condemn Clemens Brentano or E. T. A. Hoffmann for their romanticism. Weber was known as a German patriot with the right ideas ever since, in fury at his country's defeat by Napoleon he had set Körner's patriotic songs to music; he dreamed in his youth at Darmstadt of creating a real German opera, and bitterly reproached his former friend Meyerbeer for abandoning the old ideals, when the latter succeeded in Italy with operas à la Rossini. Although he would not descend to this, Weber had to earn a living, and his chamber music, for solo piano or for strings, more often than not was merely glittering and shallow, in the *style-galant* of the restored monarchies of Europe.

Weber's true gifts were shown in *Der Freischütz*, and were recognised by Beethoven who admired the opera's originality ("I would never have thought it of that gentle little fellow", he said). When

[1] C.B., II, p. 168   [2] Schindler, *op. cit.*, p. 272
[3] Hobsbawm, *The Age of Revolution*, p. 264

Euryanthe was performed in Vienna (with little success—Lichnowsky wrote on the conversation pad, "practically nobody goes to the Weber opera"), the composer visited Beethoven in Baden, was received enthusiastically and "embraced at least six or seven times". He left a lively account of the visit and of Beethoven's talk: "He railed at the theatre management, the impresarios, the public, the Italians, the taste of the people." Weber urged him to make a tour of Europe. "Too late!" cried Beethoven, drew Weber's arm through his and dragged him along to the Sauerhof where they dined."[1]

The story shows how interested Beethoven was in new music and talent, and how generously he could behave towards another composer. His liking for Weber is often reflected in the conversation books, at some times in serious comment, at others in quips and jokes. One subject for joking was Weber's inscription, "As God wills!" on his portrait. Karl, in December 1823, reported the current witticism that "other composers say *as they will*, Rossini says *as the Viennese will*". Schuppanzigh (the fat violinist nicknamed Falstaff) caps this with "Weber says: as God wills, Beethoven says, as Beethoven wills!"[2]

Beethoven was philosophic about the Rossini craze; on hearing of the latest smash hit he rightly remarked, "Well, they can't rob me of my place in musical history." He was even not ungenerous in his comments on Rossini, such as "Rossini is a talented and melodious composer; his music suits the frivolous and sensuous spirit of the time and his productivity is so great that he writes an opera in weeks where Germans take years."[3]

Beethoven's friends were much more damning: "The Kapellmeisters know your work much too little . . . they only know Rossini," said Schindler. "Rossini needs no strength, only *piano* and common crescendo", wrote Bernard,[4] referring to the famous sudden crescendo trick stolen from a composer named Joseph Mosca in Milan (who flew into a terrible rage at being copied, if we are to believe Stendhal's account).

Beethoven was always interested in natural phenomena, and there is no doubt that Rossini was a very extraordinary creature, about whom there was a great deal to wonder at, as well as to criticise. He was a man of the new times, and though a subject of feudal Habsburg Italy he reflected the true *entrepreneur* spirit of the future. First and foremost an entertainer, he looked on the box-office as a natural ally rather than as an enemy of his muse. He wrote some forty operas and cantatas in fifteen years, in his youth producing four or five a year to pay his rent and laundry bills. Stendhal described his method of composing while touring Italian towns: Arriving with a commission for a new opera, he would write it on scraps of paper in the middle of the night, after a hectic social day; and the scraps would be put together next day while talking to his friends. The opera would be ready a few days before the performance, after which Rossini would move on to another town and repeat the proceeding.[1] Wherever he went in north Italy he was awarded "the most rigorous surveillance" by the police, according to a secret report of 1821; this was absurd, for Rossini was quite apolitical (conservative if anything). He no doubt owed his reputation as a dangerous revolutionary to his father's enthusiasm for Napoleon in 1797.

Paradoxically, Rossini's success in Italy was largely due to the heavy-handed censorship, worse even than in Austria: "Except for music, no form of art flourishes," said Stendhal; "in a burning climate, under a pitiless tyranny where to speak is dangerous, music is the only subject of conversation; one cannot have an opinion and discuss it with fervour or frankness about anything except music. When a poet writes satirical sonnets against the regime, the prefect arrests all the local poets as carbonari."[2] Opera was thus the only dramatic entertainment which the people could enjoy in freedom. Rossini cashed in on this by joining a fellow Milanese, Domenico Barbaja, who had made his fortune with gaming houses and dubious deals during the French occupation of Milan, and later ran two opera houses in Naples. Barbaja's mistress was the singer, Isabella-Angela Colbran, who was also the King of Naples's favourite.

When she lost her voice in 1816 King Ferdinand insisted on keeping her on as prima donna, and this spoiling of their one pleasure "alienated the people from his Majesty more than all possible acts of despotism".[3] In the end, Rossini saved the situation which was becoming dangerous for law and order, by marrying Colbran himself and removing her from Naples. They both came to Vienna in 1822 and took the city by storm. Barbaja, who was already there and lease-holder of the Kärtnerthor Theatre, buried the hatchet, in view of the enormous

[1] Stendhal, *Vie de Rossini*, I, p. 147
[2] Weinstock, *Rossini*, p. 107
[3] Stendhal, *op. cit.*, I, p. 236

commercial advantages, and invited Rossini to appear at his theatre.

During the visit to Vienna Rossini went with the writer Carpani to call on Beethoven. For all his easy success, the Italian genuinely admired the music of the great Germans: "What does my work amount to compared with the work of Mozart or Haydn?" he once said to Richard Wagner. "Bach's genius is astounding. If Beethoven is the prodigy of humanity, Bach is the miracle of Heaven."[1] Although he addressed letters to his mother, "All' ornatissima Signora Rossini, madre del celebre maestro, in Bologna", and said "he did not see why he should not have the same rank as a general or a minister",[2] he told Wagner, "If I could have studied music in your country I might have written better stuff."[3]

A *bon-viveur*, genial and carefree, Rossini should have got on well with Beethoven. Mendelssohn, who met him in Paris, described him as "big, fat and in the sunniest disposition of spirit—I know few men who can be so amusing and witty as he when he chooses; he kept us laughing all the time".[4] But Beethoven's deafness proved a real barrier, and Rossini's bad German meant that he could not write down his remarks. So the visit did not achieve much except to register mutual goodwill. Beethoven welcomed the foreign guest, congratulated him on the *Barbiere*, and advised him not to write serious opera. The Italians, said Beethoven, "have not enough science to deal with real drama. Indeed where could they acquire science in Italy?" (a dig at the unenlightened regime). Rossini gracefully "expressed the admiration I felt for his genius". He answered with a deep sigh "O! un infelice" (I am an unhappy man). "He wished success to my *Zelmira* and accompanied us to the door, saying once more: 'Don't forget to write many *Barbers*'. Coming away from that meeting I was moved to tears at the thought of the great man alone and in poverty. 'It's his own wish to live like that,' said Carpani (who had accompanied Rossini). 'He is an ill-tempered misanthrope who cannot keep a single friend.'"

That evening Rossini dined at Prince Metternich's (something which would never have happened to Beethoven) with the words "O! un infelice" ringing in his ears. "I felt ashamed at being treated with such deference in that brilliant company," said Rossini. "I had to say what I thought of a Viennese court and aristocracy that ignored the greatest musical genius of the time. The answer I got was a repetition of Carpani's words. . . ." Rossini suggested that the rich families of Vienna

[1] Bonavia, *Musicians on Music*, p. 219   [2] Stendhal, *op. cit.*, I, p. 137
[3] Bonavia, *op. cit.*, p. 218   [4] *Ibid.*, p. 137

might get together and open a subscription to place Beethoven out of the fear of poverty. "But nobody listened to my suggestion."[1]

*   *   *

Acutely conscious of the hostility to him in high places, and believing that it influenced the general public, Beethoven, with his great symphony and Mass completed, looked around him in deep dejection. He saw nothing for it but to have these new works performed abroad—in Germany, or England perhaps. Friends tried to reassure him that Austria would appreciate these compositions and should be the first place to hear them. The singers Karolin Unger and Henrietta Sontag visited him during the winter of 1823, and Karolin wrote in the conversation book: "When are you going to give your concert? . . . if you give it I guarantee the house will be full. . . . You have too little self-confidence. Will you not believe that everyone is longing to worship you again in new works? O Obstinacy!" (Halsstarrigkeit!)[2]

They reminded him of the success *Fidelio* had, when revived in 1822. Dr Bach exclaimed (in writing), "Heavenly *Fidelio*! *Es ist ein Lieblings Speise!*" (It's a favourite dish!) He then said his wife was in love with it. "I am no enemy of Rossini, but when one hears something powerful again after so much twaddle, it's like a refreshing breeze after hot sweltering air. Rossini seems to me like a milk-calf!"[3]

In spite of all cajolings Beethoven was still convinced of Vienna's antagonism to anything new and serious, and he decided to approach Count Brühl, head of the opera house in Berlin. Visitors had told him how much better things were in that city, and of the flourishing condition of culture there: "In Berlin we are very lucky, we live in full freedom and the arts and science bloom more and more, and would do even better if Spontini did not interfere so much."[4] Beethoven's suggestion that the new Mass and symphony should be given in Berlin was enthusiastically welcomed by Brühl.

When the composer's friends heard this, they set to work to collect support for a letter imploring him to have the new music performed in Vienna. In February, thirty distinguished admirers signed an appeal, assuring him of their long-felt wishes for this: "Though Beethoven's name and creations belong to all contemporary humanity and every country susceptible to art, it is Austria which is best entitled to claim

[1] Bonavia, *op. cit.*, p. 216   [2] C.B., V, pp. 105-6   [3] C.B., III, p. 112
[4] C.B., III, 276. Spontini: A later comment (C.B., III, p. 371) reads, "Spontini makes a lot of noise . . . 36 trumpets in the *Olimpia*. . . . It's very empty. Much ado about nothing.'

him as her own." They know, they say, how painful it must be for Beethoven "to feel that a foreign power has invaded this royal citadel (of Mozart, Haydn, Beethoven), that . . . phantoms are leading the dance who can boast of no kinship with those princely spirits . . .; that . . . unworthy dalliance with sacred things is . . . dissipating appreciation for the pure and eternally beautiful." . . . "We know that a new flower glows in the garland of your glorious . . . symphonies. . . . Do not allow your latest offspring some day to appear as foreigners in their place of birth. . . . Appear soon among your friends, your venerators." Beethoven alone, they declare, is able to ensure a decisive victory to their efforts to re-establish German music; they expect from him "new blossoms, rejuvenated life, and a new sovereignty of the True and Beautiful over the dominion to which the prevalent fashion wishes to subject even the eternal laws of art".[1]

Among the signatures, headed by Karl Lichnowsky's, were those of Abbé Stadler, Dr Sonnleithner, Diabelli, First Court Chamberlain Czernin, Kuffner, Czerny—a representative collection of eminent personalities, poets and musicians. Unfortunately, when the letter was published in the *Theaterzeitung* and in Kanne's journal, gossip circulated to the effect that Beethoven had prompted it. He burst out in disgust in the conversation book: "The atrocity of attributing such an act to me sickens me with the whole business. . . . Not a single critic can boast of having had a letter from me, I have never—" Here, words failed him, and he broke off in mid-sentence. Schindler tried to calm him down: "Nobody will accuse you of having been directly concerned with it."[2]

Court Secretary von Felsburg and Bihler, tutor to the royal family, visited him and presented the address. Beethoven said he wanted to read it in privacy. After a while he returned to Schindler and said briefly, "It's very beautiful, it makes me very happy!" The object was achieved. He shed his despondency and found new zest for life. By March he told Schindler that the concert of new works would be given in Vienna in May. Everyone was delighted and began to discuss the details—above all there must be no delay. But Beethoven vacillated, was full of doubts and suspicion. Too many people had a hand in the arrangements—Lichnowsky, Schindler, Schuppanzigh, Karl, brother Johann all of them wrote their advice and suggestions in the conversation book. The many problems, the choice of theatre, conductor, orchestra, were all confused by differences of opinion and by Beethoven's refusal to give a firm answer to anything. In April, Schup-

[1] Thayer, p. 898   [2] *Ibid.*, p. 899

panzigh, Schindler and Lichnowsky made a plot to meet at Beethoven's house with a list of points on which a decision had urgently to be reached, and to get the composer to agree in writing and sign a document confirming the decision. This worked, but as soon as they had left him, bearing away the agreement in triumph, Beethoven saw through the trick and dashed off angry notes to them all: to Count Lichnowsky, "I despise treachery—Don't visit me any more—there will be no concert!" and the same to Schuppanzigh, while he ordered Schindler "not to come again till I send for you. There will be no concert."[1] However the storm, like others, blew over, and a few days later they all met again for a consultation. And after a great deal of further wrangling the date, place and performers of the concert were agreed upon. It was to take place on 7 May, in the Theater-an-der-Wien, with Umlauf conducting, Schuppanzigh leading the orchestra, Sontag and Unger among the soloists.

The programme was a testing one—the overture to *Der Weihe des Hauses*, three movements from the *Missa Solennis*, and the Choral Symphony. The day arrived and the conversation book shows us Schindler fussing over last minute details, and—very important—what Beethoven was to wear; "We will take everything with us now, also your green coat, which you can put on when you conduct. The theatre will be dark and no one will notice it. . . . Oh, great master, you don't possess a black frock coat! The green one will have to do; in a few days the black one will be ready."[2]

Nominally, Beethoven was conducting, but in fact Umlauf, standing beside him, was in control—he told the choir and orchestra "to pay no attention whatever to Beethoven's beating of the time but all to watch him (Umlauf)". The performance, according to the Leipzig *A.M.Z.* was far from perfect. "There was a lack of homogenous power, a paucity of nuance. . . . Nevertheless, strange as the music must have sounded to the audience, the impression which it made was profound and the applause . . . enthusiastic to a degree."[3]

The story has often been told of how Beethoven stood with his back to the audience, oblivious to the storm of clapping and shouting which broke out at the end, until Mlle Unger took his arm and turned him round to face it; completely deaf to the sound, he had to be assured by Schindler in the conversation book that "the reception was more than imperial . . . the people burst out in a storm four times. At the end there were cries of Vivat!", and "When the parterre broke out in

---

[1] Thayer, p. 901   [2] *Ibid.*, p. 909   [3] *Ibid.*, pp. 908-9

applause for the fifth time the Police Commissioner yelled 'Silence'!"

The Police Commissioner was there evidently to watch out for any-thing seditious or untoward, and probably strongly disapproved of the applause for the composer being twice as long and loud as that for the Royal Family (the imperial box, incidentally, was the only empty space in the theatre). Schindler admitted that he feared secretly that the three movements of the Mass would be prohibited, because the Archbishop had protested against it. "After all I was right in not saying anything in advance to the Police Commissioner. By God! It would have happened!"[1]

Schindler had been on tenterhooks up to the last moment. The clergy's censorship had originally forbidden any performance of the Mass, a sacred text, and in Latin, in a theatre; it was only by Beet-hoven's direct personal appeal to Count Sedlnitzky that the ban was lifted—and this on condition that the three numbers (*Credo*, *Kyrie* and *Agnus Dei*) were given in German, and billed as "Three Grand Hymns".

There is no doubt that had the authorities got the whole message of the Mass and the symphony they would not have allowed them to be played at all. But Metternich's minions were probably incapable of understanding this music, which brought such intense joy to the ordinary listener and to future generations, from the Viennese in the parterre to men of our time. Many have felt like Bruno Walter who wrote in 1954 that "it was episodes of special audacity in masterpieces such as . . . to name an example of the highest order, the war-music of the *Agnus Dei*, which filled my heart with an intensely personal satisfac-tion that was over and above my admiration for their greatness".[2]

The prayer "for inner and outer peace" was a summing up of all the aspirations of the people of Europe who had suffered so much in twenty years of war—a dangerously democratic idea to have found its way into a religious text! As for the finale of the Choral Symphony, what a shocking call to humanity to join together in brotherhood, to throw overboard the old mode of thinking which divided men in the past and present.

"All men will be brothers beneath the shadow of thy wings"—the wings of Joy, or of Freedom (for Schiller originally wrote his Ode to "Freedom", but had to change it to get past the censor);[3] the ideas were synonymous to Beethoven; where Schiller refers to the March of

[1] Thayer, p. 910
[2] Walter, Bruno. *Of Music and Music-Making*, London 1953, p. 206
[3] Cf. Vaughan Williams, *Beethoven's Choral Symphony and Other Essays*, O.U.P. 1953, pp. 13 and 45, and A. K. Holland in *The Symphony*, Pelican 1960.

the Stars across the heavens, Beethoven's unearthly military band in the finale suggests to us, and surely did to the liberty-starved Austrians in the audience, the advance of the army of freedom, culminating in triumph with a great shout of joy.

The authorities had hoped to prevent the performance of a new work by the well-known republican. But they failed, and Beethoven's reception at the concert turned into a mighty popular demonstration. It was not often that the people of Vienna had the chance to hear their feelings and deep aspirations translated into music, expressed in "an unapproachable masterpiece" (as Vaughan Williams put it). When the chance came they took it, and showed their appreciation in no uncertain voice.

15

The Last Years

1825–1827

The concert of 7 May, and the repeat performance on 23 May, were the last public occasions of Beethoven's life. The great satisfaction he derived from them was unfortunately clouded by various misunderstandings with friends over the financial outcome. The takings from the first concert were hardly more than the expenses, which had been very heavy. Beethoven was bitterly disappointed, and blamed his advisers, particularly Schindler.

It would be pointless to recount here the recriminations and abuses which the composer hurled at his hapless friend, or to censure Beethoven who, owing to his deafness, was prone to suspicions which sometimes amounted almost to persecution-mania.

These were encouraged by his brother when it seemed to Johann's advantage; and it is clear from many conversations that he was jealous of Schindler's relationship to Beethoven. Karl reported one day that he had heard "that *der Bruder* said in the presence of several people that he was only waiting for the concert to be over, to drive Schindler out of the house".[1]

Poor Schindler had in fact been getting on Beethoven's nerves for some time; he was dismissed from his position as confidant in May and only readmitted two years later. His place was gradually filled by Karl Holz, the second violin of the Schuppanzigh quartet. Holz was well read, musically cultured, a cheerful companion, strong and independent in his convictions and fearless in proclaiming them—a trait which endeared him to Beethoven, to whom Schindler's rather timid conservatism was anathema. (Schindler was so afraid of some of the remarks in the conversation books which he thought seditious, blasphemous or just plain rude that, to the irreparable loss of posterity, he

[1] Thayer, p. 911

deleted or destroyed whole pages where there was an abusive reference to priests or princes.)

Despite all the mishaps and *contretemps* in the course of the May concerts, Beethoven was basically satisfied. He knew that the performance of the Ninth Symphony and parts of the Mass were the highlights of his life. Now that his greatness had been seen in broad daylight and acknowledged by the people of Vienna, he could retire without heeding critics or cliques and let his inspiration guide him without concern for public demand. He still wanted to write an opera, with Grillparzer if possible, and planned a tenth symphony too, but at this time he was absorbed in the composition of the string quartets which had been commissioned by Prince Nicholas Galitzin. Ideas for these sprang up in the quiet of the country around Baden, where he went for the summer of 1824; and in spite of illness in the autumn he had completed Op. 127 in E flat and sent it off to Russia by the end of the year.

He then worked on the A minor Quartet, Op. 132, and finished it in August 1825, and the B flat, Op. 130, was ready by November. At the close of 1825, Beethoven noted the opening theme of the C sharp minor Quartet (Op. 131) in the conversation book, in the midst of remarks about New Year greetings; he completed it in July 1826.

It seems extraordinary that he should have been able to produce these long, elaborate, and heavenly works in less than a year, confidently embarking on a quite new and strange idiom and mastering all the problems with apparent ease, in spite of many day-to-day difficulties. He seemed, in the process of composing, to throw off the worries of daily life—bad health, housing problems, and the guardianship of Karl (now aged nineteen), who had entered the Polytechnic and whose resentment of his uncle's constant interference in his life led to many quarrels.

When Beethoven was composing now he existed on an altogether higher plane of consciousness. He was, as it were, above the battle, having in the Ninth Symphony said his last word on the human condition. Occasionally he did come down to earth with such minor works as the Six Bagatelles for Piano (Op. 123), and the fourth and final arrangement of "Opferlied". This beautiful and elaborate setting of Matthison's Masonic-type poem to which he had always been so attached, shows that he was still under the influence of the ideas of his youth: "*Sei stets der Freiheit Wehr und Schild. Dein Lebensgeist durchatme mild/Luft, Erde, Feu'r und Fluten. Gib mir . . . O Zeus, das Schöne zu dem Guten*" ("Be forever the shield of Freedom, Breathe thy Life Spirit through earth, air, fire and water. Grant me, O Zeus, the Beautiful and the Good"). The song (in E major, the key of Sarastro's great aria) evokes the *Magic Flute*, Eulogius Schneider, the Enlightenment, in every bar.

To show that he was still completely human, in spite of the remote regions in which he spent his working time, he threw out rounds or canons on many occasions, addressed to his friends, to the doctor, to an honoured visitor (Sir George Smart received one on the words "Ars longa, vita brevis"), affectionate, sardonic, humorous—usually all three. To Dr Braunhofer he wrote a three-voice round appealing to him to "close the door to death", and another time, not finding him at home, left a note in canon form on the four words, "Doktor, ich war hier!" It is difficult to think of the Beethoven of these jokes as being the same man as the composer of the *Heilige Dankgesang*; but his sense of humour was as characteristic of him as his moodiness, tempers and moments of exuberance, and like all these, it was reflected in whatever he wrote. The achievements of 1826 were even more amazing than those of the previous year when we consider that it was still more beset with sickness and troubles. In the early spring, rheumatism, gout, stomach complaints recurred, and he suffered again from his eyes. In May he was complaining to Schott of ill-health and pressing affairs; he was quarrelling with publishers and proof correctors; and relations with Karl were strained to such a point that at the end of July the boy attempted suicide.

The shattering effect of Karl's action were described by Stefan von Breuning's son, Gerhard, who wrote: "The pain which he received from this event was indescribable; he was cast down as a father who has lost his much-loved son." Schindler said that "the blow bowed down the proud figure of the composer and that he soon looked like a man of seventy".[1]

Karl recovered in hospital, then he and Beethoven went to Johann's country estate at Gneixendorf, where they stayed from September till December 1826, the composer in a very poor physical and emotional condition, which was not improved by his surroundings and companions. None the less, illness and shattering emotions did not prevent his composing the Quartets in C sharp minor, and F major (Op. 131 and 135) which are among the most wonderful chamber music works of all time. He also wrote a new finale for Op. 130, as the Grosse Fuge was criticised as being too difficult for contemporary performers. He

[1] Thayer, p. 1000

agreed that this could be played as a separate item, by strings, and also arranged it for piano duet.

It would not be fair to suggest that Beethoven was utterly miserable during his three months' stay at Gneixendorf—he must, indeed, have had periods of inner calm and visionary experiences of great beauty to have brought forth his last quartet.

To be in the country was always good for him, and though his brother's estate lay in a rather flat uninteresting area, Beethoven's room in the house looked out on a magnificent view of the Danube valley stretching away to the distant Styrian hills.

Though he did not get on with his sister-in-law Theresa, bickered with brother Johann, scolded Karl, grumbled at the servants (who thought him quite mad when he sat composing in the early morning, gesticulating, singing, stamping, as they tried to tidy his room), he was able to wander at will over the fields, in the freedom of the country-side. He wrote to Schott on 13 October, "the district where I am now staying reminds me to a certain extent of the Rhine country, which I so ardently desire to revisit. For I left it long ago when I was young."[1]

The longing to see the Rhineland again had been increased by letters from Dr Wegeler and his wife Eleonore (*née* Breuning) urging him to visit them. "Has travelling no attraction for you? Don't you ever want to see the Rhine again?" Wegeler wrote, reminding him that "the rocks of Bonn . . . Godesberg, the Baumschul, etc., have been a sounding board for you, from which you have been able joyfully to shape many ideas. . . ."[2]

Beethoven was, alas, not destined to see his homeland again—nor the many places he had longed to visit—Paris, Italy, and above all, England, of which he had a highly idealised conception, thanks to the British Constitutional Monarchy, Shakespeare, Canning's liberal speeches and the past kindness of many English musicians.

During November Beethoven's health deteriorated, and he became still more restless and quarrelsome. The weather was too cold for the long country walks which made life tolerable to him (though it was sometimes an ordeal for the farm hands when he scared the oxen by wild shouts and gestures). He withdrew from the family life of the place, refusing to eat meals with them, hardly ever speaking to his sister-in-law and seldom to his brother.

Johann, to give him his due, tried to entertain him by taking him to the nearby town of Krems, and to Langenfeld (where *der Bruder's* business friends took him for one of Johann's servants!) and both brother and sister-in-law were solicitous over his ailments. But it was obvious that the composer could not stay the winter at Gneixendorf. His health was deteriorating with the bad weather and lack of social stimulus, and he was oppressed by the prospect of a gloomy future, helpless in the case of sickness in the country. Karl's future, too, had to be considered; he was wasting his time playing billiards and having rows with his guardian, and Johann decided he ought to be sent back to Vienna to begin his career in the army as soon as possible. "I see . . . that he would like to remain with us", Johann wrote from Vienna when on one of his business trips: "but if he did so it would be all over with his future, and therefore this is impossible . . . I think it ought to be by next Monday." Both Karl and Beethoven objected to being told to go at such short notice, and the journey was finally fixed for Friday 1 December 1826. Johann's carriage was not available and they travelled in what was described by Beethoven to his doctor as "the most wretched vehicle of the devil, a milkwagon".[1]

It was raw, damp, cold; the composer's clothes were quite unsuitable. He spent the night in a village tavern, in an unheated room without shutters. He contracted pneumonia and took to his bed on arrival in Vienna. In spite of illness, the return to the metropolis seems to have restored his sense of humour, for he at once sent off a comical note to Holz which included a canon on the words "*Wir irren allesamt nur jeder irret anderst*" ("We all of us err, but each of us errs differently").

Holz was alarmed at Beethoven's condition and called Dr Wawruch after two doctors had been summoned and failed to come. On top of pneumonia Beethoven had a severe bout of dropsy and had to be operated upon. His humour did not desert him; on being tapped, when the tube was inserted and water spurted out of his abdomen he remarked, "Professor, you remind me of Moses striking the rock with his staff!"[2] The doctor wrote on the pad, "You bore yourself like a knight." Today it seems almost incredible that this operation (albeit a minor one) was performed without anaesthetic, in the presence of Johann, Karl and Schindler. Karl's entries in the conversation book show that the young man was really concerned about his uncle, and looked after him devotedly during his illness. Early in the New Year of 1827, however, he went off to his army career, and did not reappear in Beethoven's lifetime.

The sick man bore his burden stoically, but apart from the pain, he must have suffered terribly from the premonition of death, in spite of his friends' prophesies of recovery. On 3 January 1827 Beethoven drafted his will, leaving Karl all his property. He knew that he had not long to live, but he bore the knowledge as well as his illness with immense fortitude, and continued to take an intense interest in life. He was delighted to receive a present from his friend Stumpff in London, of forty volumes of Handel's works. He told little Gerhard Breuning, Stefan's son and a faithful visitor, he had long wanted them, "for Handel is the greatest, ablest composer that ever lived. I can still learn from him."

Long before, in 1808 when he first discovered Handel, he had been impressed by his music; in 1823 he told Schultz, a visitor from England, that Handel was the greatest of all composers, and said the same to Stumpff, adding as he went down on one knee on the floor, "to him I bow the knee!"[1]

To be able to read Handel's scores, even in a sick bed, was a joy for Beethoven. The warmth, solidity, melody of Handel appealed very directly to him; in Mozart there was too much tragedy and too much intellect and wit for comfort in his present condition (although the *Magic Flute* was very dear to him he rather disapproved of *Don Giovanni* and *Figaro*), Haydn was too personally close, too much of the schoolmaster to soothe him; Cherubini and Cimarosa, whom he admired and borrowed ideas from in the past, were hardly bedside books. But Handel's straightforward solid German goodness and his proficient workmanship were qualities which found an immediate echo in Beethoven; and he could have had no greater solace than Stumpff's present. Another comfort to him was the stream of visitors, some of whom had been estranged by former tiffs or misunderstandings and now came in a spirit of reconciliation: Tobias Haslinger, Schick, the Streichers, J. K. Bernard (whose libretto had never materialised), Nanette Schecker, the singer. Schindler was once more constantly with him, and Beethoven no longer scolded him; he tried hard to mediate between two doctors, Wawruch and Malfatti, who had been called in and between whom there had been some disagreement which led to a breach of professional etiquette. "Beethoven was ever a dis-obedient and irritable patient," said Schindler. "He had, when under Dr Malfatti ten years before, become dissatisfied with his treatment and commented upon it and him in such a manner as to cause a serious estrangement." Malfatti unwillingly agreed to treat Beethoven when

[1] Thayer, p. 920

called at Schindler's urgent request, and succeeded in temporarily alleviating the poor composer's sufferings with a prescription of frozen punch. But the invalid "began to abuse the prescription and applied himself right bravely to the spirits which soon caused a violent pressure of the blood upon the brain".

Malfatti withdrew his services and it was only after the most heart-felt appeals from Schindler that he agreed to see Beethoven again, but strictly under the condition that Wawruch was the physician in charge. By this time (the end of February 1827) it was obvious that the case was hopeless, and Malfatti, knowing a cure to be impossible, strove to give temporary relief, which was the best way of cheering up the sick composer. On 27 February, Schindler says, "the noble patient thought himself already half saved and wanted to work on his tenth symphony, which he was allowed to do to a small extent".

In a note to Schindler in mid-March Beethoven wrote "Miracles! Miracles! Miracles! The learned gentlemen [probably Wawruch and another doctor, Seibert] are both defeated. Only through Malfatti's science shall I be saved."

But neither Malfatti nor any other doctor could really help, and Beethoven must have known it. He suffered from spells of melancholy, caused not only by the illness, but by anxiety over his financial affairs. He made the effort to write a letter to Stumpff in London, thanking him for the Handel scores, and telling him of his financial predicament: "Doctor, surgeon, everything has to be paid," and he had only enough to pay his rent with a few hundred florins over to live on. He asked whether the Philharmonic Society could help him by giving a concert for his benefit. If so, "I might still be saved from the poverty which now confronts me."

The Society met and agreed to lend a hundred pounds, to be sent (according to the Minutes of 28 February) "through the hands of Mr Moscheles to some confidential friend of Beethoven to be applied to his comforts and necessities during his illness. Carried unanimously."[1] The money was sent to Vienna, and Herr Rau, a bank official, took it to Beethoven at once. "The joyous sensation at the sudden relief from London had a wonderful effect upon him," Rau told the secretary of the Society. "The following day he was in remarkably good spirits and felt himself much relieved. . . . You will find enclosed a receipt from Beethoven for the 1,000 florins (£100) . . . he acknowledged "openly that he considered this money as a relief sent him from heaven. . . ."

[1] Thayer, pp. 1030–36

Schindler wrote on 24 March to Moscheles, "care and anxiety vanished at once when the money arrived and he said quite happily, 'Now we can again look forward to a comfortable day once in a while.' ... Numerous times during the day he exclaimed, 'May God reward them all a thousandfold.'"

His friends in Vienna rallied round too. Baron Pasqualati sent him regular gifts of fruit and drink; so did Streicher, Breuning and Malfatti himself, seeing no reason to deny him, when the end was anyway so near. Schuppanzigh and Linke called, as did Moritz Lichnowsky, Count Gleichenstein and his wife, Theresa Malfatti's sister. Diabelli visited and gave him a print of Haydn's birthplace which he had published. Beethoven showed it to Gerhard von Breuning, saying "Look, I got this today. See this little house, and in it so great a man was born!" Beethoven himself sent Schindler a present of food when the faithful disciple was kept away from his bedside by an accident: "Do take this . . . given from the bottom of my heart."

He was still able in February to correspond with his publisher, Schott, about the dedication of the Quartet in C sharp minor, which finally went to Field-Marshal von Stutterheim who had helped place Karl in the army. He also dictated a letter to Moscheles thanking the Philharmonic Society for their £100. "I pledge myself to return my thanks to the Society by binding myself to compose for it either a new symphony which lies already sketched on my desk, or a new overture or something else which the Society would like."[1]

But he was rapidly weakening, and all that his friends could do to help was to visit him and try to divert his mind from gloomy thoughts. Schindler hit on the idea of bringing him a collection of sixty songs by Schubert, whom Beethoven hardly knew, "because people had lacked trust in him and belittled his name". Beethoven was astonished when told that Schubert had already composed over 500 songs, and expressed the greatest admiration for him. "For several days he could not separate himself from the songs, and every day he spent hours with 'Die Junge Nonne', 'Viola', the 'Müllerlieder' and others. . . . He cried out repeatedly: 'Truly a divine spark dwells in Schubert!' . . . The respect which he acquired for Schubert's talent was so great that he now wanted to see his operas and pianoforte pieces; but his illness had now become so severe that he could no longer gratify this wish."

A week before Beethoven's death, Schindler took Schubert and his friend Anselm Hüttenbrenner, a pupil of Salieri's, to see the sick

[1] Thayer, pp. 1037-40

M

composer. Schindler announced the two young men and asked Beethoven whom he would see first. He said, "Let Schubert come first." Unfortunately there is no report of their conversation. But there is a very full account by Ferdinand Hiller, of the talk Beethoven had with Hummel, the pianist, who came specially from Weimar to see him. "The conversation at first turned on domestic affairs. Beethoven asked about Goethe's health with extraordinary solicitude. . . ." He complained about his own state, "I have been lying here for four months—one must lose patience in the end!" He lambasted "the present taste in art" and "the dilettantism which is ruining everything".

Hiller says Beethoven did not spare the government, up to the most exalted regions. "'Write a volume of penitential hymns and dedicate it to the Empress', he remarked with a gloomy smile to Hummel. . . . The master continued to give free rein to his moody and passionate utterances; when referring to Karl and his scrapes with the police officials, he commented bitterly, 'Little thieves are hanged but big ones are allowed to go free!'"

On a second visit Beethoven showed his visitors the picture of Haydn's home, saying "the cradle of so great a man!"; then he appealed to Hummel on behalf of Schindler—"he is a good man, who has taken a great deal of trouble on my account", and asked Hummel to play at Schindler's benefit concert (which, in fact, the pianist did, ten days after Beethoven's death). He expressed his intention of travelling to London: "'I will compose a grand overture and a grand symphony for them', he said. He would visit Mme Hummel and go to I don't know how many places. His eyes dropped and closed today," wrote Hiller. "It was not possible to deceive oneself—the worst was to be feared."

On 23 March 1827 Beethoven signed a will drawn up in simple form by his old friend Stefan von Breuning. Schindler wrote in a letter to Moscheles, "he feels the end coming, for yesterday he said to me and Herr von Breuning, 'Plaudite amici, comoedia finita est'."

Little Gerhard was there, and later recalled this remark, "expressed in his favourite sarcastic-humorous manner at the departure of his doctors as though to imply, nothing more can be done".[1]

Beethoven died on 27 March 1827, at five o'clock in the afternoon. According to Hüttenbrenner who was in the room, there was a sudden flash of lightning "which garishly illuminated the death-chamber—snow lay outside—and a violent thunderclap. At this startling, aweful peal of thunder, the dying man suddenly raised his head and stretched

[1] Thayer, pp. 1047–48

out his right arm majestically, 'like a general giving orders to an army'. This was but for an instant; the arm sank down; he fell back. Beethoven was dead."[1] This most dramatic of death-bed stories was vouched for by several witnesses. It could certainly not have been more in character.

*   *   *

The funeral took place in the afternoon of 29 March and was one of the most imposing functions of its kind ever witnessed in Vienna. The State had no objection to the composer whom it had so neglected while he lived receiving full honours now that he was dead. The Roman Catholic church awarded him the privilege of its most solemn and ceremonial rights to which he had been averse all his life, although he had when dying accepted extreme unction, under pressure from Johann and his wife, and, according to two witnesses, had thanked the priest for bringing him comfort.

Von Breuning and Schindler made sure that all the arrangements were correct as well as impressive. Beethoven was put in a polished oak coffin, with a gilt cross on the cover, a wreath of white roses on his head. In his folded hands they put a wax cross and a large lily. Eight candles burned on each side of the coffin, and on a table at the foot stood a crucifix and holy water for aspersion, along with ears of corn. Visitors came in a steady stream to pay their last respects. People crammed the courtyard and the crowd in the street outside stormily demanded entrance. "The military assistance from the Alser Barracks, procured by Breuning, was hardly able to ward off the crowd. Even the schools were closed."

Bearing in mind Beethoven's attitude to ritual, and the Establishment's attitude to him, the proceedings strike one as a combination of the deeply impressive and the unreal. The irony of a full-dress religious ceremony after a lifetime of almost heretical anti-clericalism would not have been lost on Beethoven; one can imagine his sardonic smile if he could have seen Barbaja's court singers honouring him with a funeral hymn, and eight Kapellmeister, including Kreutzer and Weigl whom he had so often railed against, bearing the pall, after nine priests from the Schottenstifte had blessed his corpse. But he would have been glad to know that some forty torchbearers accompanying his coffin included his best friends, and some of the greatest of Vienna's intellectuals and musicians—Grillparzer, Haslinger, Bernard, Castelli, Czerny, Schoberlechner, and Schubert among them.

[1] Thayer, p. 1051 fn.

The scene was extremely impressive. The crowd was so huge, and jammed so tight, that the director of ceremonies had the greatest difficulty in organising the procession. Eventually it moved off from the house, led by carriers of crosses decorated with flowers, and behind them members of welfare institutions. Behind these strode the trombonists and the choir followed, singing Beethoven's *Miserere* (written at Linz in 1812), with trombone refrain. All the composer's friends and relatives were in the procession, along with the students of Drechsler (for whom Beethoven had once interceded with the Emperor) and of the Conservatory and many more. Last of all came a "very lovely ceremonial carriage" pulled by four horses supplied by the office of St Stephan Cathedral. The church in Alsergasse, the suburb where Beethoven had last lived, was packed; friends could hardly get in, as the soldiers on duty did not want to admit anyone after the coffin had been carried in: "Those who had fainted from the pressure of the crowd were taken across to the hospital", according to the account in the Vienna archives. The crowd was estimated at 20,000 by young Breuning, 10,000 by Castelli's journal.[1]

After the blessing in the church, the coffin was taken, again followed by a vast multitude, out along the road into the country going beside the bank of the Währing brook to the village parish church. There again the coffin was blessed, and the Währing parish choir sang the *Miserere* (motets). Then the procession started again, consisting now of many of the former crowd, plus the village folk, school-children and local poor people. They walked through the countryside to the entrance of the cemetery.

At the gates, the coffin was put down and the great tragic actor Heinrich Anschütz stepped forward to read the funeral oration which Grillparzer had written. (Only priests were allowed to speak at the graveside.) Inside the cemetery, the priests consecrated the tomb and blessed the corpse for the last time. The coffin was lowered into the earth, and Hummel placed three laurel wreaths, brought by Tobias Haslinger, on the grave.

Grillparzer's words powerfully summed up Beethoven's life, work and personality: "He was an artist—and who shall arise to stand beside him? As the rushing Behemoth spurns the waves, so did he rove to the uttermost bounds of his art. From the cooing of doves to the rolling of thunder . . . he had traversed and grasped it all. He who comes after him will not continue him; he must begin anew, for he who went

[1] Thayer, p. 1054

before left off only where art leaves off. . . . He was an artist but a man as well, a man in every sense—in the highest.

"Because he withdrew from the world, they called him a man-hater, because he held aloof from sentimentality, unfeeling. . . . He fled the world because, in the whole range of his loving nature, he found no weapon to oppose it. He withdrew from mankind after he had given them his all and received nothing in return. . . . But to the end his heart beat warm for all men, in fatherly affection for his kindred, for the world his all and his heart's blood.

"Thus he was, thus he died, thus he will live to the end of time."[1]

---

[1] Thayer, p. 1058

16

Beethoven, Yesterday, Today, Tomorrow

"You have not lost him. You have won him. He stands from now on among the great of all ages, inviolate forever. . . ." After a century and a half, Grillparzer's words still move us by their truth, even more valid now than when they were spoken at the Währing Friedhof gate. Beethoven's immortality and inviolability are well assured; and we certainly have not lost him—for every one of us who loves and respects his music he is there, very much alive, every time it is played. Whether in the simplest works like "Opferlied" and the Piano Bagatelles, or in the most elaborate—the symphonies, the *Missa Solennis*, *Fidelio*—whether in the heart-searching quartets or the triumphant overtures—his messages comes through, clear and authentic, in the voice of a man who refuses to die.

We are fortunate today in being able to approach even the most "difficult" Beethoven and to derive delight and strength from it, unlike his contemporary admirers who could not follow him beyond a certain height. As Thomas Mann said, "in the works of the last period they stood with heavy hearts before a process of dissolution, or aliena-tion, of a mounting into air no longer familiar or safe to meddle with . . .".[1]

It is lucky for our time that cacophony and violent rhythms are so familiar that we can hear even the *Grosse Fuge* without flinching and grasp its amazing beauty and depth unworried, assisted in fact, by the clashing discords and surprising counterpoint.

Beethoven's immortality was assured before Grillparzer pronounced it. All the same, it has been questioned and tested a good many times, and Beethoven's status among the Immortals has varied according to the standards of the mortals through ensuing generations.

The nineteenth century, on the whole, adopted Beethoven as a sort of legend, a romantic rugged lion of a man who wrote melting melodies and stirring martial music. The most telling tributes to his

[1] Mann, *Dr Faustus*, p. 52

genius came from the composers who followed him, Schumann, Mendelssohn, Liszt, Brahms, Wagner; they went along the new paths he had opened, and took full advantage of the liberation he had achieved from the set classical patterns. Romantics in a sense which Beethoven never was, they developed their subjective, ultra-individualistic styles, adding virtuosity and emotional display where hard thinking failed. *Songs without words* and *Dichterliebe, Fantasias* and *Rhapsodies* became the fashionable fare of the Viennese public.

Thanks to local tradition, Beethoven's second-period symphonies were always played fairly regularly; but until the twentieth century he was not properly appreciated. The "last decade" Beethoven was unacceptable as concert material in Vienna; and for a long time the piano sonatas were "regarded as music for the drawing-rooms and second-grade students at the Konservatorium", according to Artur Schnabel. "The G major Concerto was labelled 'the ladies' concerto', and the B flat was unknown." Schnabel said that in the ten years 1889 to 1899, when he studied in Vienna he never head of the Diabelli Variations, or the "Hammerklavier" Sonata (nor indeed of the twenty-eight piano concertos of Mozart!).[1]

Of course, even though there was no cult, and his profoundest music was not known, Beethoven had his champions and admirers in Germany and Austria during the nineteenth century; a memorial monument was put up in Bonn, in 1846, thanks to money-raising efforts by Liszt, who gave concerts all over Europe to that end; Vienna followed suit and offered a variety of effigies in tribute. Beethoven's memory was preserved and his reputation fostered by Schindler, his first biographer, and many friends who published reminiscences of him. Schumann and Brahms saw to it that the symphonies did not gather dust, Joachim kept the chamber music in the repertoire, performed the Violin Concerto, and taught his pupils to revere Beethoven. The composer soon became a subject for learned dissertations by professors and musicologists. The scholar, Nohl, wrote critical studies discussing whether he should be counted among the classical or romantic composers, and decided he was essentially a romantic "of a democratic revolutionary type who expressed religious and aesthetic truths". Wagner, who saw Beethoven as a sort of philosopher-reformer (like himself), countered with articles denying that he could be pigeon-holed in any category: it "diminished" Beethoven to "consider him as a servant of one or other kind of music".[2] In fact,

[1] Schnabel, *My Life and Music*, p. 26   [2] Schrade, *Beethoven in France*, pp. xiv, xxvi

German romantics, from E. T. A. Hoffman on, claimed him in accordance with each individual's ideas; and it was due to anti-romantic reaction that he became unfashionable with later generations.

Outside Germany Beethoven had a steady following right through the nineteenth century, and his symphonies were regularly played at the "Saturday pops" in London. In England, as in Austria, he was mainly admired in cultured upper-class circles for the same qualities as the pious melodious Mendelssohn; Vaughan Williams amusingly refers to their preference for "the Beethovenish Beethoven . . . whom the early nineteenth century called the 'sublime' Beethoven; the Beethoven who made strong men with whiskers brush away a silent tear".[1] The ordinary people of Victoria's England did not recognise him as a composer who belonged to them. "The public is not really conscious of that part of Beethoven's work which raises it above the level of popular painting," wrote Bernard Shaw.[2] "It finds a great deal of Beethoven incomprehensible and therefore dull, putting up with it only because the alternative is either no music at all or something a good deal duller."

Among the British musicians who recognised Beethoven's true greatness were Sir George Grove and Dr (later Sir Hubert) Parry who tried to drag him out of the drawing-rooms and explain the wider significance of his work: "Beethoven serves as a link between the old and the new," Parry wrote. "He accepted all that was best and purest in his art, renewed and transformed it by the fever, passion and sympathetic imagination of his naturally democratic disposition."[3] Bernard Shaw, too, let in some light when he spoke of the Ninth Symphony as "music of my own church"—a direct reference to the democratic message.[4] But on the whole, the writers and critics in England treated Beethoven as a great outsider.

It was different in France, where Beethoven's political tendencies echoed those of so many thinkers and writers. At first there was strong resistance to Beethoven which was overcome largely by Berlioz, who had himself been overwhelmed by his first hearing of the C minor Symphony, and shaken to the depths of his soul by the late Quartet, Op. 131. He fought strenuously on Beethoven's behalf against the "philistines" of the Conservatoire, and held the latter up to ridicule for their ignorance, in his Mémoires, and in Les Grotesques de la Musique:

[1] Vaughan Williams, Beethoven's Choral Symphony, p. 11
[2] G. B. Shaw, Music in London, III, p. 204
[3] Parry, Studies of Great Composers, London 1887
[4] G. B. Shaw, Music in London (Pelican, 1960), p. 177

"A learned theoretician printed his opinion somewhere that Beethoven knew very little about music . . ."—"I heard a Director of the Beaux Arts say that this same Beethoven was not without talent!"

When Beethoven began to be accepted, some intellectuals affected disdain; Flaubert joked, in his *Idées reçues*, "Be sure to gush when one of his (Beethoven's) works is being played." But by 1860 the symphonies were in every Conservatoire concert programme. Thereafter, the French romantic poets and writers not only accepted him but were singing his praises as one of the greatest of musicians and of men. Victor Hugo, Lamartine, the poet Lemayne, Léon Daudet, all saw him as the standard-bearer of art (art liberated and humanised), and also as a heroic romantic personality. Later Hippolyte Taine, the radical historian and critic, wrote of his greatness and nobility as an individual, as well as praising his music in fulsome terms. All these writers, with their intense and very French historical sense interpreted Beethoven in terms of history, or rather as the individual artist in history. This became even more the case after 1870: During the last thirty years of the century France went through a crisis of identity, and the patriotic and socialist thinkers, licking their wounds after the war and the crushing of the Commune, needed a tragic hero, some great genius to raise their spirits and restore their faith in life.

Beethoven was adopted by the French socialist movement. Octave Fouqué in his book *Les Révolutionaires de la Musique*, put him at the head of the great champions of freedom; Edgar Quinet, a leading socialist, used a pamphlet, *Ce que dit la Musique*, in 1885, to present Beethoven's whole musical work from a socialist point of view. Quinet related it to the cause of France which had suffered so much from the horrors of foreign invasion and the tyranny of a right-wing regime. Beethoven's love of freedom was expressed in the Ninth Symphony, where, said Quinet, *Freude* ("joy") meant the universal happiness evoked by the philosophers of the French Revolution. "Ah! It is indeed the Marseillaise of humanity!"[1]

The Fifth and Seventh Symphonies are also "Marseillaises héroiques" in Quinet's view. The movements of the Fifth mirror "our own life, in which men have long been waiting for justice and liberty", and the finale is "an explosion of the public conscience".

We may feel Quinet carried his theory rather too far when he cast the composer in the role of saviour to the French nation, giving them

[1] Schrade, *op. cit.* 403

"the sanity of morals, spiritual rejuvenation, nobility of ideas", which they so urgently need. But Quinet was one of the first to claim Beethoven's moral and political stance in support of the fighters for a better society—justifiably, as we know, and as socialists today could well claim it.

A succession of progressive writers shared this view, and after 1900, as the French socialist movement spread, and intellectuals became more involved in the political struggle, Beethoven was adopted as one of their heroes. In 1903 Romain Rolland wrote his famous *Life of Beethoven*, the first in a series *Vies des grands hommes* (the other great men being Michelangelo and Tolstoi), and in no time it was a best-seller. The composer was held up as a moral inspiration, his will and strength of character as an example to the French people, and through the book Rolland appealed to France to recover the will to live, to seek their intellectual salvation through a new faith. "The atmosphere is sultry", he wrote: "The old Europe grows rigid in an oppressive and vicious atmosphere. A materialism without greatness stifles thought . . . the world chokes in its prudence and vile egoism. . . . Let us open the window. Let in the fresh air again! Let us breathe the breath of heroes."[1]

Rolland was a poet but a political activist too, and in the thick of the battle over the Dreyfus case he brought Beethoven in as the champion of the Dreyfusards. "We are not alone in the struggle," he proclaimed. "Let us march alongside all those who fight, isolated, scattered through all countries and all centuries. . . . Let us remove the barriers of time, rouse the host of great-hearted heroes!"[2] Many of the young radical intellectuals of France became Beethoven enthusiasts, and later one of them, Camille Bellaigue, wrote that the Beethoven cult encouraged him "to believe in the regeneration of present-day man . . . the music is so brotherly and charitable that the people everywhere find in it the shining signs of an immense and universal love".[3] The historian Julien Tierson presented Beethoven as the musician of the French revolution: "Whatever he created was an echo to events in France which had stirred this instinctive Republican." The true Hero of the "Eroica" Symphony is "the people of France", and the work is inspired by French ideas, especially those of the revolution.

It is difficult to believe that Beethoven would have recognised himself in the role given him by these French writers. High-flown rhetoric was not his style, and he might have said of it, as he said of Klopstock's

---

[1] Rolland, *Vie de Beethoven*, p. ii (Paris 1903)
[2] Rolland, *op. cit.*, p. 155   [3] Schrade, *op. cit.*, p. 198

poetry: "It begins at too lofty an elevation. Always D flat major, Maestoso!"[1] But he would have given them credit for being the first to grasp the truth of his political commitment and to proclaim it in the interests of society. Over-lofty and flowery as all this French literature was, its influence was immense and lasted up to and throughout the 1914–18 war. One writer recalled that in the trenches "between the copybook and the flashlight torch in our dirty knapsack we kept the *Life of Beethoven*, treasuring it with veneration".[2]

After the war, with the reaction against hero worship and high moral talk which had failed them, intellectuals tended to cold-shoulder Beethoven. Debussy disliked him, anti-German feeling was strong. Rolland's 1927 version of the *Life* was toned down and less idealistic than that of 1903. The shrine of Beethoven worship was to be found in post-war Germany where a consolatory hero-figure was badly needed. There, more than anywhere, the centenary of his death was commemorated in 1927 with great performances and many important publications. Since then he has held his place at the very summit, claimed by every European and American movement and ideology however unsuitable—from the National-Socialists to the United Nations Organisation, from the Soviet Union to the Council of Europe—the Ninth Symphony being played as an ideological anthem at their state occasions. It may seem ironic that even protagonists of ideas most unlikely to appeal to Beethoven should use his music as a means of asserting the righteousness of their cause: like hypocrisy, a tribute paid to virtue. But it does also show his quite extraordinary universal appeal.

Grandiose tributes to Beethoven, and the image they evoke of a prophet or even a Jehovah, may be gratifying to his admirers, and they have a historical interest too. But they are really of less importance to us than the more mundane approach of working musicians of successive generations, who may find in Beethoven the answer to the perennial problem of the artist's place in society. This, as we have seen, was very much in Beethoven's own mind, and he never had doubts about it. His duty as an artist towards God, Man and himself, was to compose, to say to the world what he had to say fearlessly and in complete sincerity. If it was useful to the world so much the better; it was the world's fault, anyway, if it did not benefit by it. In this he was like Arnold Schönberg, another musical genius who wrote according to his convictions for most of his life without appreciation. Schönberg was

---

[1] Thayer, *op. cit.*, p. 246   [2] Schrade, *op. cit.*, p. 167

overwhelmed with tributes on his 75th birthday, and, somewhat embarrassed by all these hymns of praise, asked, "Is it to be taken for granted if in the face of the whole world's resistance a man does not give up but continues to write down what he produces?" How, he wondered, could Wagner persevere in the face of opposition, how could Beethoven, when the Ninth Symphony was called a jumble, go on writing? "I know only one answer—they had things to say that had to be said."[1]

This duty Beethoven faithfully performed, putting into his production his whole tremendous personality and passionate beliefs. His life as an artist is an example of consistency in ideas and action. From youth on, he held firmly to his belief in freedom, and acted on his convictions through all political developments, changes of rulers, vagaries of public opinion. He made his protest against social injustice and tyranny, in music, and declared his belief in love and in goodness and beauty in his work (as well as in albums, where he liked to inscribe "Das Schöne zu dem Guten", sometimes set as a canon.)[2] For Beethoven, art and social responsibility were inseparable. He would have concurred with George Eliot's musician, Klesmer, who shocked the mid-Victorian drawing-room by declaring, "A creative artist is no more a mere musician than a great statesman is a mere politician. . . . We count ourselves on level benches with legislators. And a man who speaks effectively through music is compelled to something more difficult than parliamentary eloquence. . . ."[3]

Beethoven certainly "spoke effectively", and he has always been understood by listeners of his own persuasion; in our own time, more and more people have come to appreciate him, and since the 1970 bicentenary celebrations it seems that he is at the top of the league, the best known and loved of all composers. And I believe this is not because of the legendary grandeur, heroic proportions and so forth, but because this present generation of listeners feels that Beethoven is one of us, a man of our own time.

It is a far cry from the Schwarzspanierhaus to the UNO Assembly Hall, from the neglected composer scribbling on his scraps of paper and on his window shutters, to the monumental statue and the 1970 exhibition in Vienna. But the conditions and events of his life, as this book has attempted to show, were in many ways similar to those of today, and we may justifiably feel that Beethoven's music which embodies his

---

[1] Schönberg, *Letters*, p. 290   [2] Thayer, *op. cit.*, pp. 874, 949
[3] George Eliot, *Daniel Deronda*, Bk. III, Chap. 22

experiences and reactions has a special relevance for us. The wars which we have lived through and which still torment the world, the social inequality and misery, the wind of revolution blowing across continents, are all part of our own lives, and some of the best composers of our century have reflected this troubled age as Beethoven reflected his, voicing the same longings for peace and human happiness.[1]

The factors which caused Beethoven such misery in the post-1815 years, and which were responsible for the decline of cultural standards, are echoed in our day. Beethoven made his protest against the censorship and the clerical feudalism which "encouraged sensuous music to keep people's minds off politics", by writing the "Ode to Joy", and also by his withdrawal into the stratosphere of the late quartets (who is great enough to make such a protest against obscurantism effectively today?); Habsburg feudalism with its apparatus of spies and censors has gone, but it has been replaced by monopoly capitalism which fights just as hard, if less blatantly, to prevent dangerous ideas from taking root. Whether this system succeeds in stifling culture and imposing the second-rate depends on us, ordinary music-lovers, the general public.

We have the advantage over the nineteenth century of a high standard of musical education and the easy availability of first class works, which make people, the young especially, pretty resistant to pollution; but real music still reaches only a tiny proportion of the public, while the vast majority of potential listeners flounder night and day in a morass of sub-music (what Hindemith called "a non-stop flow of faceless sound".[2])

Classical music is at risk in the general crisis of culture, which is singularly like that of Vienna in the 1820s. The market now, as then, is flooded by trivia which people are seduced into accepting, or by violence and sensation which they cannot resist; only now something new has come on the scene, the deeply pessimistic "black" art. How to shake off the horrors, fears, scepticism and inanities which the daily tide of mass communication washes in on our consciousness? How to restore a climate for appreciating Beethoven's declaration of faith in life, his eternal truths, honesty, optimism and good sense? The problem goes far beyond musical things, because it arises from deep social causes and contradictions. As we have seen, the temporary decline of culture in Beethoven's Austria was due to the economic and social crisis in that country and to the desperate attempts of the feudal ruling class to

---

[1] For example, Shostakovitch, Kodàly, Vaughan Williams
[2] Hindemith, *A Composer's World*, p. 208

protect its interests; today the decline stems from a much sharper crisis, that of capitalist society itself, with its rampant commercialism which penetrates every aspect of life. Twentieth-century technology has given enormous power to the "philistines"—from modern advertising methods to sophisticated weapons of war. The question of how art can survive in the face of the apparently insurmountable evils of our society —mass unemployment, hunger, oppression, genocide—has led musicians to gloomy thoughts. Sir Michael Tippett, speaking about the role of the artist in 1972, mentioned the horrors of the Nazi death camps and asked "What price Beethoven now?"[1] Bruno Walter in a moment of pessimism declared that "it seemed more and more to me as if the conflagration whose smoke darkened . . . the twentieth century also signified a twilight of the gods in the realm of the spirit that had been my homeland". Walter added, however, that "in spite of the world wide crisis of mankind which today endangers our spirit if not life itself" he maintained deep confidence.[2] Hanns Eisler, the German socialist composer, saw capitalist society as alienating the artist: "He is alone, until death alone with his art . . . this solitude is the origin of all the illness which music suffers from today. . . ."[3] (But Eisler too was confident, believing that the forces of sanity could and would organise to save mankind and his cultural heritage.) These three musicians shared misgivings about the present, though they held different views about the cure. They agreed about some of the factors that aggravated the malaise, such as the commercialisation of culture: "The super-abundance of entertaining matter . . . endangers the serious inner life today and spiritual aspirations of those who are exposed to it," wrote Bruno Walter.[4] Schnabel shared his regret about "the enormous influence of radio, cinema and magazine, from which nobody is free", and the composer Hindemith saw another danger: Virtuosity—whose curse is "that it can beget nothing but virtuosity. A civilisation that demands nothing but virtuosity for virtuosity's sake is doomed in the end to produce a nation-wide dementia."[5] Eisler returned from the U.S.A. to Germany in the 1950s, shocked by the power of the American entertainment industry which "levels, standardises and enslaves artists", and appalled by the far-reaching control of the monopolies and agencies with their enormous profits: "For true prophetic art they have substituted false profitable art."[6]

[1] Tippett, on B.B.C. Television, February 1972   [2] Walter, *op. cit.*, p. 203
[3] Eisler, *Reden und Aufsätze*, p. 97   [4] Walter, *op. cit.*, p. 203
[5] Hindemith, *op. cit.*, p. 208   [6] Eisler, *op. cit.*, p. 97

A system which puts profit before use or wellbeing necessarily creates a gap between people and real culture. Art cannot close the gap, as Eisler pointed out. There is only one way out of the dilemma: "Great economic and political revolutions must break the cultural class monopoly and provide social conditions in which people will by right enjoy classical art. Then they will also find a voice of their own, blending simplicity and adventurous curiosity." We have to agree, even if we dislike the idea; like Byron, who "would fain say fie on't/If I had not perceived that revolution/ Alone can save the earth from hell's pollution."[1] (Beethoven perceived this too, as well as Byron and was never afraid to say so.)

It has been shown in Beethoven's own territory, Central Europe, that socialism can help to close the gap. In the former Habsburg dominions, starved of culture throughout the nineteenth century and till the end of World War II when the old order collapsed, there was a flowering of popular culture, a sudden springtime like the one in Italy in 1797 when the citizens of Emilia, Tuscany and Milan set up their republics. The unleashing of vitality, imaginative and joyful art typical of the early years of the Peoples' Democracies was a revelation. Beethoven, who had faintly visualised an ideal society where the artist would be able "to work for the good of the poor" and where his compositions could be distributed through a "Magasin de Musique" run by the people, would have been delighted by the healthy cultural conditions, the music, books, concerts, so cheap and within easy reach of every citizen in Bohemia, Hungary, Poland, and Russia, freed from feudalism.

The future will show how far attempts of Western capitalism succeed in encroaching into the brave new culture and undermining it. One must hope that the popular art in those countries will prove a sturdy enough plant to withstand assault and battery by American commercialism. Perhaps as well as the economic and social changes a great cultural revolution will be needed; there are danger signals which suggest it.

But as Friedrich Hölderlin said, "*Wo aber Gefahr ist, wächst das Rettende auch*" ("where danger threatens, the forces of salvation increase too"). There are multitudes of defenders of the faith, and sooner or later the gap will be closed everywhere.

In the meantime, we have Romain Rolland's prescription of Beethoven as a tonic for depression: "When we become weary of the eternal battle uselessly fought against mediocrity of vice and virtue, it is

[1] Byron, *Don Juan*, Canto 8, v. 51

indescribably good to plunge into that ocean of faith and willpower. His valour is contagious, struggle for him is happiness. . . ."[1]

On a rather less elevated plane, even in battles which are not eternal but those of everyday life and work, Beethoven can help us: on the one hand, by the unlimited human sympathy and involvement in life in all its aspects which is reflected in the music and shared with the listener; and on the other hand, through the immensely stimulating physical and mental experience which he offers: we are caught up by the composer in symphony or sonata and swept along by the dialectic process—statement, conflict, resolution—growing, changing, becoming, till we reach the triumphant goal, breathless, but completely satisfied.

It is hard sometimes, listening to the symphonies, the Grosse Fuge, or the "Hammerklavier" Sonata (to name one's own first choice) to believe that these were actually written by a man who lived and worked and died like anybody else. By chance he was a child of the revolutionary age, and a citizen of the class which responded to the rousing drama of that age; the world's good fortune is that his heart and his genius were in tune with his times, that he could convey their forward-surging spirit in his work, and show posterity their ideals. The great concepts of Joy and Truth and the Brotherhood of Man, always in his mind, are offered to us in his music—and we should take them gratefully, for in the world today these concepts badly need to be protected, reburnished and restored to their place in our lives.

The learned musicologist E. J. Dent wrote in 1927 that "an art of the scope of Beethoven's appears to be conceivable only in an age possessed of a general faith in life".[2] We must hope that a new age of revolution, imbued with similar faith in mankind and dedicated to the overthrow of old tenets and the establishment of real justice and peace on earth, will produce an equally great composer to give it a voice. But Beethoven himself belongs to his own time, and the world will never see his like again. His epitaph might be the words of Swinburne: "Glory to man in the highest!"[3] or perhaps, quite simply, those of Thomas Hardy's Woodlander: "You was a good man and did good things."[4]

[1] Rolland, op. cit., p. 77   [2] E. J. Dent, Music and Letters, 1927
[3] Swinburne, Hymn of Man   [4] Hardy, The Woodlanders, Chap. 48

Select Bibliography

Anon (A Musical Professor), *A Ramble in Germany*, London 1828
Beethoven, L. van, *Briefe. Eine Auswahl*, Henschelverlag, Berlin 1969
—— *Collected Works*
—— *Konversationshefte*, i–iii, ed. Georg Schünemann, Berlin 1941;
   iv, v, ed. VEB Deutscher Verlag fur Musik, Leipzig 1968, 1970
—— *Letters*, ed. and trans. Emily Anderson, London 1961
Berlioz, Hector, *Memoirs*, Panther Books, London 1970
—— *Les Grotesques de la Musique*, Paris 1880
Blake, William, *Milton*
Brentano, Bettina (von Arnim), *Unbekannte Briefe*, Bern 1970
Breuning, Gerhard von, *Aus dem Schwarzspanierhaus*, Vienna 1874
Castelli, I., *Reisenovelle*, Vienna 1835
—— *Aus dem Leben eines Wiener Phaaken*, Vienna 1840
Cooper, Martin, *The Last Decade*, London 1970
Delderfield, R. F., *Imperial Sunset*, London 1969
De Staël, Mme, *De l'Allemagne*, Murray, London 1813
Einstein, Alfred, *Music in the Romantic Era*, London 1947
Eisler, Hanns, *Reden und Aufsätze*, Verlag Philipp, Leipzig 1953
Eliot, George, *Daniel Deronda*, Blackwood, London 1887
Emerson, D. E., *Metternich and the Political Police*, The Hague 1968
Engels, Friedrich, *The Role of Force in History*, London 1968
Grillparzer, Franz, *Prosaschriften*, Vienna 1925
Hazlitt, William, *Complete Works*, ed. P. P. Howe, London 1955
Heine, Heinrich, *Prose and Poetry*, ed. Havelock Ellis, London
Heriot, Angus, *The French in Italy*, London 1957
Hindemith, Paul, *A Composer's World*, Harvard 1952
Hobsbawm, Eric, *The Age of Revolution*, London 1960
Holland, A. K., *The Symphony*, Pelican, London 1960
Holcroft, Thomas, *Life* (cf. Hazlitt, *Complete Works*)
Kann, R. A., *A Study in Austrian Intellectual History*, London 1960
Klein, Rudolf, *Beethovenstätten in Österreich*, Vienna 1969

N

Kneppler, Georg, *Musikgeschichte des 19 Jahrhunderts,* Berlin 1961

Knight, Frida, *University Rebel,* London 1971

Mann, Thomas, *Dr Faustus,* trans., London 1949

Marek, Robert, *Beethoven, Biography of a Genius,* London 1970

Macartney, C. A., *The Hapsburg Empire,* London 1968

Marx, Karl, *Collected Writings*

Maurois, Andre, *A History of France,* London 1964

Mozart, W. A., *The Magic Flute*

Nohl, Ludwig, *Beethoven depicted by his contemporaries,* trans., London
    1880

Orieux, Jean, *Talleyrand,* Paris, 1970

Otto, Jacob-August, *Treatise on the Construction of the Violin,* trans.,
    London 1830

Parry, Sir C. H., *Studies of Great Composers,* London 1887

Pezzl, J., *Skizze von Wien,* Vienna 1780

Reeve, Henry, *Journal of a visit to Vienna and Berlin in the eventful Winter
    of 1805–6, ed. J. Reeve,* London 1885

Robert, André, *L'Idée Nationale Autrichienne,* Paris 1937

Rolland, Romain, *Vie de Beethoven,* Paris 1903

Schindler, Anton, *Beethoven as I knew him,* London 1966

Schnabel, Artur, *My Life and Music,* London 1961

Schrade, Leo, *Beethoven in France,* Yale 1942

Sterba, E. and R., *Beethoven and his Nephew,* New York 1954

Sealsfield, Charles, *Austria,* London 1828

Sharp, W., *Life of Heine,* London 1888

Shaw, G. B., *Music in London,* London 1956

Stendhal, *La Chartreuse de Parme*

—— *Vie de Rossini,* Divan, Paris 1929

—— *Correspondance,* Divan, Paris, 1933

—— *Life of Haydn,* London 1817

Stephens, Morse, *Revolutionary Europe,* London 1924

Sullivan, J. W. N., *Beethoven,* London 1927

Thayer, A. W., *Life of Beethoven,* ed. Elliot Forbes, Princeton, 1967

Tovey, Donald, *Beethoven,* Oxford 1944 (paperback, 1971)

Trevelyan, Janet, *A Short History of the Italian People,* London 1956

Vaughan Williams, R., *Beethoven's Choral Symphony,* London 1953

Walter, Bruno, *Of Music and Music-making,* London 1961

Wangermann, L., *From Joseph II to the Jacobin Trials,* London 1969

Weinstock, H., *Rossini,* O.U.P. 1968

Williams, Merryn, *Revolutions,* London 1971

Yates, D., *Franz Grillparzer, a Critical Biography*, Oxford 1946

Periodicals:
  Music and Letters, 1927
  Der Sammler, Vienna 1810
  Thalia, Vienna 1811–13
  Friedensblätter, Vienna 1813–15
  Modezeitung, Vienna 1810–15
  Salzburgerzeitung, 1817–20

Compositions mentioned in the text

Symphony no. 1 in C major
Septet for Wind and Strings, Op. 20
Piano Sonata, Op. 22
Piano Concerto in C minor, no. 3, Op. 37

801   2 Piano and Violin Sonatas, Op. 23 and 24
Piano Sonatas, Op. 26 and 27, nos. 1 and 2 (the "Moonlight")
Piano Sonata, Op. 28 (the "Pastoral")

1802   Romances for Violin and Orchestra, Op. 40 and Op. 50
Symphony no. 2 in D major, Op. 36
3 Piano Sonatas, Op. 31
Piano Bagatelles, Op. 33
3 Piano and Violin Sonatas, Op. 30

1803   Piano and Violin Sonata, Op. 47 ("Kreutzer")
Song, "Der Wachtelschlag" (The Quail), WoO 129
Six Spiritual Songs (Gellert), Op. 48
Oratorio, Christus am Oelberg, Op. 85
Symphony in E flat, no. 3, Op. 55 (the "Eroica")
Piano Variations on "God Save the King", WoO 78
Piano Variations on "Rule Britannia", WoO 79

1804   Concerto for Piano, Violin and 'Cello, Op. 56
Piano Sonata, Op. 53 (the "Waldstein")
Piano Sonata, Op. 54

1805   Opera, *Fidelio*, Op. 72
Song, "An die Hoffnung", Op. 32
Piano Sonata, Op. 57

1806   3 String Quartets, Op. 59 ("Razoumovsky")
Piano Concerto no. 4 in G major, Op. 58
Fidelio, second version
Symphony no. 4 in B flat, Op. 60
Violin Concerto, Op. 61
Overture, *Leonore* no. 3
32 Variations for Piano, WoO 80

1807   Overture, *Coriolan*, Op. 62
Mass in C, Op. 86

1808   Symphony in C minor, no. 5, Op. 67
'Cello Sonata, Op. 69
Choral Fantasia, Op. 80
Symphony in F major, no. 6 (the "Pastoral"), Op. 68
2 Trios for Piano, Violin and 'Cello, Op. 70
Song, "Die Sehnsucht" (Goethe), WoO 134

1809	String Quartet in E flat major (the "Harp"), Op. 74
	Piano Concerto in E flat, no. 5, Op. 73
	Piano Sonata in E flat ("Das Lebewohl"), Op. 81
	Piano Fantasia, Op. 77
	Piano Sonatas, Op. 78, 79
1810	*Egmont*, Incidental Music and Overture, Op. 84
	3 Songs (Goethe), Op. 83
	String Quartet in F minor, Op. 95
1811	Trio for Piano, Violin and 'Cello, Op. 97
	Ruins of Athens, Incidental Music, Op. 113
	König Stephan, Op. 117
1812	Symphony no. 7 in A major, Op. 92
	Symphony no. 8 in F major, Op. 93
	Sonata for Piano and Violin, Op. 96
	3 Equali for Four Trombones, WoO 30
1813	Song, "An die Hoffnung" (second version), Op. 94
	"Der Bardengeist", WoO 142
	Battle Symphony, *Wellington's Victory*, Op. 91
1814	Cantata, "Der Glorreiche Augenblick", Op. 136
	Vocal quartet, Elegische Gesang, Op. 118
	Fidelio (revised), with new Overture
	Song, "Germania", WoO 94
	Cantata, "Ihr Weisen Gründer glückliche Staaten", WoO 95
	Piano Polonaise, Op. 89
	Piano Sonata, Op. 90
1815	Incidental Music, *Leonore Prohaska*, WoO 96
	Song, "Merkenstein"
	"Meersstille" (Goethe), Op. 112
	Namensfeier Overture, Op. 115
	2 Sonatas for 'Cello and Piano, Op. 102
1816	Piano Sonata, Op. 101
	25 Scottish Songs, Op. 108
	Song, "An die ferne Geliebte", Op. 98
1817	Song, "Resignation", WoO 149
1818	Piano Sonata, Op. 106 ("Hammerklavier")
	12 Scottish Songs WoO 156
	Settings of twenty-three songs of different countries, WoO 158
1819	Piano Sonata, Op. 109
1820	Song "Abendlied", WoO 150

1821   Piano Bagatelles, Op. 119, 7–11
        Piano Sonata, Op. 110
1822   Piano Bagatelles, Op. 119, 1–6
        Weihe des Hauses, Incidental Music, Op. 124
        Song, "Opferlied", fourth version with Orchestra, Op 121b
1823   Mass in D, Op. 123
        33 Variations on a Waltz by Diabelli, Op. 120
        Symphony in D minor, Op. 125 ("Choral Symphony")
        6 Piano Bagatelles, Op. 126
1825   String Quartet in E flat, Op. 127
        String Quartet in A minor, Op. 132
        String Quartet in B flat major, Op. 130
1826   String Quartet in C sharp minor, Op. 131
        New finale to Op. 130
        Arrangement of Grosse Fugue for Piano, Op. 133

The abbreviation WoO means Werke ohne Opuszahl (Works without opus number)

Name Index

Albrechtsberger, J. G., 29
Alexander I, Emperor of Russia, 67, 80, 95, 128, 155
Alvinzi, General, 40
Amenda, Karl, 48, 49
Anschütz, H. (actor), 180
Arnim, A. von, 79, 82, 84
Arnim, Bettina von, *see* Brentano
Averdonk, Severin Anton (poet), 22

Bach, Dr J. B., 120, 127, 165
Bach, Johann Sebastian, 47, 75n, 164
Barbaja, Domenico, 163, 179
Beethoven, Caspar Anton Carl van (brother), 74–5, 103
Beethoven, Johann van (father), 14, 28–9
Beethoven, Johanna van (Caspar's wife), 74, 103, 108, 113, 118, 120–5, 127
Beethoven, Karl van (nephew), 103, 108, 113, 118, 120–34, 135, 137, 139, 141, 147–8, 150, 157, 159, 162, 166, 170–5
Beethoven, Maria Magdalena van (mother), 13–14
Beethoven, Therese van (Johann's wife), 173, 179
Beethoven, Ludwig van:
    biographical: Youth in Bonn, 9, 12–15, 17–22, 24–5; early years in Vienna, 28–32, 34–5; influence of Napoleon's Italian campaign, and the Eroica Symphony, 39–40, 41–3,

BEETHOVEN—*cont.*
    45–56; life in Vienna during Napoleonic wars, 47–88; during Congress of Vienna, 93–7; during post-war depression, 98–119; and during economic recovery, 135–69; last illness and death, 173–9; funeral, 179–81; posthumous assessments, 182–8, 191–2
    Character: 14, 30–1, 94–5, 50–1, 56–9
    Friends: 49, 55–8, 61, 69, 70, 78, 82–4, 92, 111–13, 117–18, 139–40, 141, 165–6
    Guardianship of Karl: 103, 108, 118–19, 120–1, 123–34
    Health: 14, 49, 81, 84, 108, 111–12, 146–7, 157, 172–7
    Housing: 28, 51, 136, 138–40
    Money worries: 19, 28–9, 70–1, 73, 77–8, 96–7, 102–3, 135, 147, 154, 171, 176
    Politics: 17–19, 23, 32, 34, 53–4, 77–8, 82, 89, 94, 100–1, 105–7, 109–10, 113–14, 115–18, 142–5, 148–50, 152–3, 168–9, 178, 189, 191
    Religion: 52–3, 137–8, 155–6, 168, 179–80
    Suffering from war and post-war crisis: 63, 75–7, 102–4, 147
    Works (*see Compositions mentioned in the text,* pp. 196–9):
        up to 1790, 19; *1790–1800,*